Cataloging
of
Audiovisual Materials
and Other
Special Materials

Cataloging
of
Audiovisual Materials
and Other
Special Materials

A Manual Based on AACR 2

by
Nancy B. Olson

Fourth Edition

Edited by
Sheila S. Intner
and
Edward Swanson

MINNESOTA SCHOLARLY PRESS
DeKalb, Illinois
1998

Reprinted with permission of the American Library Association from *Anglo-American Cataloguing Rules*, second edition, 1988 revision, and the *Amendments 1993*.

Printed in the United States of America

ISBN 0-933474-53-9

Library of Congress Cataloging-in-Publication Data

Olson, Nancy B.
    Cataloging of audiovisual materials and other special materials : a manual based on AACR 2 /
by Nancy B. Olson. -- 4th ed. / edited by Sheila S. Intner and Edward Swanson.
        p.   cm.
    Includes index.
    ISBN 0-933474-53-9
    1. Cataloging of nonbook materials--United Stated--Handbooks, manuals, etc. 2. Cataloging of
audio-visual materials--United States--Handbooks, manuals, etc. 3. Descriptive cataloging--United
States--Rules--Handbooks, manuals, etc. 4. Anglo-American cataloguing rules--Handbooks,
manuals, etc. I. Intner, Sheila S. II. Swanson Edward, 1941-   . III. Title.
    Z695.66.043 1998
    205.3'4--dc21   98-5787
                                                                                                    CIP

Published by:
MINNESOTA SCHOLARLY PRESS, INC.
and Media Marketing Group
P.O. Box 611
DeKalb, Illinois 60115

Text composition by Sharon Olson of Apple Blossom Books.

Photography by Jerry Poulson of Poulson Photography Studio, Mankato, Minnesota.

This Book is Dedicated to

PALS
(Project for Automated Library Systems)

and to

Mike Barnett and **Dale Carrison**

who created and developed it

PALS was created at Mankato State University beginning in 1976 when all the state universities and private colleges in Minnesota joined OCLC. By 1980 we had an online catalog. Now, 18 years later, 85 Minnesota libraries are members of PALS, with 4,805,608 bibliographic records, 7,056,461 item records for holdings, and 263,755 registered users (spring 1997). Our North and South Dakota neighbors use the commercial version of PALS; as sold by UNISYS and Ameritech, it has been used worldwide.

The system includes the online catalog ("classic" and Web versions), circulation system, serials system, acquisitions system, interlibrary loan system, MARC editor, and many reference databases. When a user does a search in a reference database (the Expanded Academic Index, for example) and pulls up a citation, that same citation tells the user if we own the periodical, what the call number is, and if that issue is on the shelf. And the cited article may also be available in full text from that same terminal! We never dreamed of these capabilities so long ago when we were first cataloging periodicals.

The system provides statistics on every activity performed by every subsystem, and I used all of them when compiling a five-year program review document for the library a few years ago. It was fascinating to find how much data available and what could be demonstrated through the use of PALS.

PALS has grown to a staff of 17 that continues to develop the system. Over the years they have been responsive to every need expressed by users of the system. It does everything we want, the way we want it done.

> The Minnesota Legislature has decreed that PALS go out of existence,
> to be replaced by some commercial system to
> "develop a statewide on-line information system for libraries"
> to serve all of the state, including K-12 libraries, public libraries,
> state agencies, the state universities, and the University of Minnesota.

PREFACE

Fourth Edition

The title of this work now includes the words "special materials." As I discuss early in this book, terminology has always been a problem for those working with something other than books in a library setting. As I have, over the years, added other materials including maps and computer-related materials and now Internet resources, the term "audiovisual material" no longer seems inclusive enough. So this book is now titled *Cataloging of Audiovisual Materials and Other Special Materials*.

This edition includes 23 new examples: talking books, CD- ROMs (both monographic and serial), interactive multimedia, and Internet resources. All 74 examples carry full MARC coding and tagging for OCLC. For each example the chief source of information is shown through photographs, photocopies, screen displays, and/or other reproductions of the information available to the cataloger. Some photographs of different types of audiovisual material and presented throught the book under the heading "How would you catalog this?" Cataloging of each of these items appears in the *third* edition of this book.

Older types of media are no longer included or are given minimal treatment. You will want to keep your earlier editions of this work for these examples.

Coding and tagging is discussed in a new chapter, along with format integration, fields 246/740 decisions, and the problems of fields 006, 007, and 008. The field 007 chart has been redone.

All examples carry LC subject headings and call numbers. I have also expanded the introductory chapters and the text in all the chapters. I hope this proves helpful.

As I prepare this, I mark my 29th year at Mankato State University: 29 years of cataloging special materials!

Information in this book is current as of January 6, 1998.

Nancy B. Olson, Professor
Library Services and Information Technology
Mankato State University
Mankato, MN 56002

ACKNOWLEDGMENTS

Fourth Edition

I would like to thank Edward Swanson and Sheila Intner for agreeing to edit my book. Editing is a time-consuming task, with little thanks from the one whose work is being criticized. I really do appreciate their suggestions, comments, and corrections.

I also must thank my classes at the University of Pittsburgh, where I teach summer school, for giving me constructive criticism over the years on text and examples. I especially want to thank the 34 students who attended the 1997 summer workshop and worked from a draft of this text. They provided lots of helpful suggestions.

I continue to depend on family members for advice on computers, both hardware and software, and on business matters. Tim is the family computer expert, while his wife, Sharon, does all the stages of book production. I couldn't function without them. The others, Andy, Susan, and Steve, give me advice on many topics, some of them related to business.

EDITORS' FOREWORD TO THE FOURTH EDITION

by

Sheila S. Intner and Edward Swanson

The brave new world of the third millenium is about to dawn as this new edition of *Cataloging of Audiovisual Materials and Other Special Materials* goes to press. As editors, we are pleased to see that the revised text ably addresses the problems associated with the newest types of materials to appear in library cataloging departments—Internet resources and multimedia formats—as well as treating older formats with the most up-to-date versions of cataloging rules and tools. The change in the title proper of this book is external evidence of the ongoing evolution of library and information center collections; the added discussions and examples in the book highlight the greater complexity with which catalogers now must cope.

The layout and visual "look and feel" of *Cataloging of Audiovisual Materials and Other Special Materials* continue to improve over the previous edition, its scope is both broader and deeper, and the coverage is more diverse. Although no attempt is made to be completely comprehensive (such inclusiveness might push the number of pages and price of the volume beyond the means of even the most dedicated teachers, students, and practitioners), the range of examples is sufficiently varied and sophisticated to answer virtually every question arising in formal courses or in-service training sessions teaching the cataloging of nonprint materials. The examples are very clearly presented and described, and are accompanied by excellent images of their bibliographic sources. Perhaps best of all, the examples have been "kitchen-tested" by at least two classes of library school students (at the University of Pittsburgh and Simmons College) as well as by workshop participants and colleagues in the field.

Just twenty years ago the *Anglo-American Cataloguing Rules*, second edition (1978), first provided librarians with one set of rules for describing all media collected by libraries. The notion of integrating all cataloging into a single tool and making it possible for patrons to see the entire range of possibilities for reading, viewing, and/or hearing a work before they selected the one which best met their needs was about to become a reality. In these last two decades, catalogs also have changed in fundamental ways, becoming gateway to the universe of knowledge, not just local finding lists. As our intellectual universe grows, so does the need for high quality access. Because it empowers catalogers to create standard, uniform records for the materials it covers, *Cataloging of Audiovisual Materials and Other Special Materials* helps to enhance access, both locally and beyond the walls of an individual library or information center, adding new opportunities for all searchers, whoever and wherever they are.

Sheila S. Intner
Monterey, Massachusetts

Edward Swanson
Saint Paul, Minnesota

CATALOGING OF AUDIOVISUAL MATERIALS AND OTHER SPECIAL MATERIALS

CONTENTS

INTRODUCTION

"... wherever practicable ... "
"... if no part of the item supplies data that can be used ... "
"... exception to this ... "
"... unless one of the following applies ... "
"... prefer a chief source of information ... "
"... if there is no discernible first part ... "
"... only if this can be done without loss of essential information."
"... appearing prominently ... "
"... record the statements in the order that makes the most sense ... "
"If this criterion is not applicable ... "
"Add an explanatory word or short phrase ... "
"If it is not practicable ... "
"In case of doubt ... "

0.9. These rules recognize the necessity for judgement and interpretation by the cataloguer. Such judgement and interpretation may be based on the requirements of a particular catalogue or upon the use of the items being catalogued. The need for judgement is indicated in these rules by words and phrases such as *if appropriate, important,* and *if necessary.* Such words and phrases indicate recognition of the fact that uniform legislation for all types and sizes of catalogue is neither possible nor desirable, and encourage the application of individual judgement based on specific local knowledge. This statement in no way contradicts the value of standardization. Apply such judgements consistently within a particular context and record the cataloguing agency's policy.

These and similar phrases from the second edition of the *Anglo-American Cataloguing Rules* (AACR 2) illustrate the necessity for judgment and interpretation by the cataloger when using these rules. There is no substitute for common sense, good judgment, and experience in cataloging, especially in the cataloging of audiovisual materials and other special materials.

All types of material can be cataloged using these rules. This book will discuss general principles of cataloging audiovisual material and other special materials, and then the details of cataloging each type.

This book is designed to be used with the *Anglo-American Cataloguing Rules,* second edition, 1988 revision, and the *Amendments 1993*; the relevant rules are referenced, and parts of some basic rules are quoted, but the complete text of the basic rules and all the additional rules themselves must be studied by the cataloger. This book also includes relevant rule interpretations from the Library of Congress.

This is a practical book, not a theoretical one. I explain the way I catalog, and why I do it this way.

Material covered in this book includes cartographic material (*AACR 2* chapter 3), sound recordings (*AACR 2* chapter 6), videorecordings (*AACR 2* chapter 7), graphic material (*AACR 2* chapter 8), computer files (*AACR 2* chapter 9), three-dimensional objects and realia (*AACR 2* chapter 10), microforms (*AACR 2* chapter 11), serials (other than print) (*AACR 2* chapter 12), kits (*AACR 2* 1.10), as well as interactive multimedia (*Guidelines for Bibliographic Description of Interactive Multimedia* (ALA, 1996)) and Internet resources (*Cataloging Internet Resources, a Manual and Practical Guide,* second edition (OCLC, 1997)).

WHY CATALOG AUDIOVISUAL MATERIAL AND OTHER SPECIAL MATERIALS?

"... basic, brute cataloguing becomes ever more important: It is the human
intellectual foundation supporting the increasingly elaborate system of instant electronic access."

from an editorial entitled "Library Futures"
in the Sunday, June 12, 1996, *Washington Post*

Administrators and others sometimes ask why audiovisual materials should be cataloged. The report of the Carnegie Commission on Higher Education called *The Fourth Revolution* said, "... nonprint information, illustration, and instructional software components should be maintained as part of a unified informational-instructional resource that is cataloged and stored in ways that facilitate convenient retrieval as needed by students" (New York: McGraw-Hill, 1979, p. 39).

The 1986 *Standards for College Libraries* recommended: "The library's collections shall comprise all types of recorded information, including print materials in all formats, audiovisual materials, sound recordings, materials used with computers, graphics, and three-dimensional materials" (*College & Research Libraries News*, Mar. 1986, p. 189-200).

The 1990 *Standards for Community, Junior, and Technical College Learning Resources Programs* state: "The learning resources program shall make available an organized collection of materials and diversified forms of information useful in the educational process, including various forms of print and non-print media, computer software, optical storage technologies, and other formats" (*College & Research Libraries News*, Sept. 1990, p. 757-67).

From the 1987 "Guidelines for Audiovisual Services in Academic Libraries": "The goal [of the Guidelines] is to support the development and administration of an increasingly important component of college and university service" (*College & Research Libraries News*, Oct. 1987, p. 533-36). They address planning, budget, personnel, facilities, equipment and supplies, collection development, acquisition, cataloging, collection maintenance, and service of audiovisual materials. The cataloging component states:

1. Make audiovisual materials accessible through the same retrieval mechanisms available for other library materials.
2. Catalog audiovisual materials in accordance with current national standards and practices.
3. Provide full subject access in addition to descriptive cataloging.
4. Classify audiovisual materials like other types of materials but assign location or accession designations as determined by organizational and functional considerations.

In 1970, Warren B. Hicks and Alma M. Tillin stated: "The purpose of the catalog is to enable the user to determine easily all types of materials which might be useful in a given situation" (Warren B. Hicks and Alma M. Tillin. *Developing Multi-Media Libraries*. New York: Bowker, 1970, p. 71). These same authors later wrote, "The comprehensive goal of cataloging is to assist library users and staff in the determination and the location of available resources which will best suit their specific needs and best satisfy their particular purpose" (*Managing Multimedia Libraries*. New York: Bowker, 1977, p. 166).

This is the best reason to catalog audiovisual material: assisting library users.

From another source: "Librarians and media specialists will accept media in all formats and integrate them not only for the benefit of present users but for the even larger number of potential users as well" (Pearce S. Grove, ed. *Nonprint Media in Academic Libraries*. Chicago: American Library Association, 1975, introduction, p. x).

Mary Jane Scherdin discusses curriculum centers, which she defines as facilities including children's literature, textbooks, and curriculum guides for kindergarten through grade twelve, nonprint material and equipment for the campus, and the audiovisual production area. She emphasizes

> Because of the additional time and difficulty in cataloging audiovisual and curricular materials, a strong commitment needs to be made. This support is necessary so these materials have the same accessibility as the traditional book collection ("A Marriage That Works: An Approach to Administrative Structure in Curriculum Centers." *College & Research Libraries News*, Mar. 1984, p. 145).

More justification of the decision to catalog all material is provided by Sandra Jones-Warren.

> A strong case can be made for controlling, storing and distributing media in the same institutional unit as other information sources; i.e., the library. The library, in its role as information gatherer and dispenser, is the location where common sense leads the user when seeking knowledge about a subject. As libraries and librarians have already developed systems for the retrieval and circulation of materials to the user, it is relatively easy to expand and modify these systems to include media. Abbreviated and inconsistent subject entries, with insufficient subject coverage, are too often the result when information control is managed by a non-librarian, untrained in the theories and application of information cataloging. The user is shortchanged by an inadequate and elementary system wherein all relevant resources are not readily identified. The user is also inconvenienced by having to hunt in a variety of locations for information available within the institution. Centralization of all information sources within a library is of immeasurable help to the user. It becomes possible to refer to one catalog of available materials and to locate those materials in a central spot, sometimes even side-by-side on the same shelf ("Cooperating to Provide Information." *Media Management Journal*, Fall 1982, p. 8).

In a 1981 survey of public libraries, Sheila S. Intner found that 83% of them now are providing cataloging for nonprint holdings. She believes her study clearly indicates the trend toward "recognition of the responsibility for providing bibliographic access to nonprint materials directly to the public through vehicles similar, if not identical, to those used for print." She also believes:

> Media cataloging is entering a period of great progress with AACR 2. The immediate benefits will accrue to public library users, who will have increased access to the rich resources now residing in nonprint media collections. Information seekers of all kinds will also benefit from broad dissemination of media information in an integrated mode, made possible by public library adoption of AACR 2 for all holdings ("Equality of Cataloging in the Age of AACR 2." *American Libraries*, February 1983, p. 103).

Online Audiovisual Catalogers prepared the statement that appears on the next page:

<u>Online Audiovisual Catalogers</u>
<u>Rationale for Cataloging Nonprint Collections</u>

The integration of bibliographic records for nonprint resources into library catalogs is fundamental to serving the information needs of library users. Standardized cataloging for all library materials allows access to both print and nonprint resources through common retrieval techniques. The application of internationally accepted cataloging standards to nonprint resources also ensures that characteristics unique to nonprint items are readily apparent in bibliographic records. The growth of distance education and remote use of the catalog make it particularly important that the catalog accurately and comprehensively reflect available materials.

In an increasingly complex and technologically advancing society, nonprint resources offer unique expressions of information and innovative methods of learning and entertainment. While nonprint resources have existed for many centuries (e.g., maps, drawings, etc.), the 20th century has seen an explosion of nonprint formats—from photographs, sound recordings, newsreels, and videorecordings, interactive multimedia, and electronic resources—all of which are an integral part of our historical record. Libraries also may provide access to nonprint materials not physically held, such as electronic journals or web-accessible databases. Complete representation of these unique and significant materials should be present in the library catalog.

Full and standardized bibliographic description of nonprint resources facilitates:

- a heightened awareness of the full range of information resources a library offers its user population;

- a consistent means for both the local and remote user of the catalog to search the entire collection through a single interface;

- identification of material that represents a significant expenditure of library funds;

- international efforts in cooperative cataloging by sharing bibliographic records in the utility databases (e.g., RLIN, OCLC, WLN).

The **Online Audiovisual Catalogers**, Inc. (OLAC), an international organization of nonprint cataloging specialists representing a diverse library consistuency, fully endorses the integration of nonprint holdings and accesible information resources in library catalogs. Furthermore, OLAC strongly encourages all library staff, administrators, trustees, and others who maintain an interest in meeting the complete information needs of their users to support the integration of nonprint holdings in library catalogs and to expend the resources required to fully catalog their nonprint collections.

DECISIONS TO BE MADE BEFORE CATALOGING

There are many decisions to be made by an institution before the first item of audiovisual material is cataloged. Jean Weihs explains why.

> Many catalogers have related a sad tale, which more or less follows the same story line. Their center has acquired a few items, such as a dozen filmstrips or a few rolls of microfilm. In the context of a large book collection, the cataloging of these items seems unimportant and the idea that these are but the forerunners of a large collection of nonbook materials is not considered. These items are cataloged in a nonstandard way with no attempt made to relate them to the general collection. A few more items appear and they are treated in the same manner. Over the next few years the nonbook collection grows and at one point the staff has to start recataloging it all because the materials cannot be retrieved easily by the catalog record which now exists. The moral of this tale is that you should catalog the first nonbook item with the same care you will devote to the ten thousandth and recognize the possibility that your library may become a media center ("Problems and Prospects in Nonbook Cataloging". In *The Nature and Future of the Catalog*. Phoenix, Ariz.: Oryx Press, 1979, p. 272).

Before a library begins to purchase audiovisual material, decisions should be made concerning the processing, storage, and use of the material. All staff who will be involved in the handling of the material should be involved in the decision-making process. Assume the collection is going to grow. Decisions made on the basis of a few items, without taking into consideration the growth of the collection over many years, lead to the kind of problems Weihs relates.

Intner makes an important point in her book *Access to Media* (Neal-Schuman, 1984, p. 15) when she says, "Successfully managing media collections requires that the purpose of the collection and its end uses be clearly identified." Too often a collection has a small beginning and grows without formal direction or purpose.

Cost of audiovisual material

Audiovisual materials are expensive. Average prices for audiovisual material in 1990, based on an unpublished study by David A. Allan (Mankato State University), are $512.04 for a color film, $241.07 for a video, $54.33 for a filmstrip with cassette, and $134.67 for a "kit" that contains a filmstrip, cassette, teacher's manual, worksheets, etc. Film prices varied from $225 for a 10-minute film to $975 for a 60-minute film. Video prices (not including feature films) ranged from $70 to $395 (a markdown from $500). These averages were determined by examining a number of distributor's catalogs, determining a median price for each type and length of film/video for each distributor, then averaging those median prices.

Because of their cost, few libraries can afford to have more than a limited number of audiovisual titles as compared with their holdings of books. The high cost and the relatively small number of items in most collections of audiovisual material justify special treatment through subject access so as to provide the broadest possible access to this material.

Considerations

In making decisions concerning the collection, the librarian organizing the collection of audiovisual material should consider the needs of the users of the collection, the existing practices for the book collection, the budget for material and staff, and the space available.

Throughout this discussion, my general recommendations are to catalog and classify audiovisual material for a library in the same way books are treated in that library.

While the topics that follow are discussed independently, the decisions are interrelated.

Terminology

The terms "audiovisual," "nonprint," and "nonbook" are used in essentially the same way, although they do have different meanings. "Audiovisual" means including both sound and visual components and originally was used strictly for film materials with sound. Its use was broadened gradually to include a wide range of materials that had sound and/ or visual aspects. The term is thought by some to be too school-oriented. "Nonprint" and "nonbook" are both negative terms; they imply what the material is not, rather than what it is. "Media" is used by some to represent audiovisual material, by others to represent the entire range of materials including print. Terminology in this area has always been, and continues to be, a major problem. Sound recordings have been called *audiodiscs, phonodiscs* (and *audiodisks* and *phonodisks*), *audiotapes, phonotapes, audiocassettes, phonocassettes, phonograph records*, and *records*. Patrons are confused by the inconsistency of the terminology. Throughout this book, I use the term "audiovisual material" to refer to material other than books, though I am adding the phrase "and other special materials" to signal the inclusion of computer files and related computer resources. I use the terminology of AACR 2 in referring to the specific types of media.

For definitions of audiovisual material, see *Audiovisual Material Glossary* by Nancy B. Olson (Dublin, Ohio: OCLC Online Computer Library Center, 1988).

QUESTIONS TO BE ASKED

The following sections include questions to be asked before cataloging begins. Each question needs a decision; most decisions should involve all staff who will be working with the collection.

Use

Will the audiovisual material in the collection circulate, or will its use be restricted? Will certain classes of users be allowed to check out audiovisual materials, while other users cannot do so? Will some types of audiovisual materials circulate, while other types are restricted?

Is the collection intended as a demonstration collection, one that must remain intact at all times?

Will the material be available for interlibrary loan? If the material does circulate or go out on interlibrary loan, for what period? What restrictions, if any, apply? Will equipment be available for check out?

If audiovisual material circulates, consider circulating the equipment for viewing or listening.

There will be some damage and loss in the collection whether the material circulates or is used in a supervised or semisupervised setting, or is not used at all (see section on Preservation).

Once the administration and/or public service staff has made decisions about use, decisions can be made on shelving, packaging, and cataloging.

Shelving

Will the collection be housed in open or closed stacks, or will it be split between the two? Will the audiovisual material be intershelved with the books? Will certain types of material be housed in a special collection?

Open stacks encourage use by inviting the patron to browse. Closed stacks theoretically make it possible to control use and loss, but take much more staff time to service. In a library with closed stacks, the patron must approach the material through the catalog or through some other finding tool.

The use of closed stacks, with all filmstrips shelved together, all slides together, etc., has been proposed as a space-saving method of shelving. This may be carried to extremes, with all items removed from packages and filmstrips put into drawers with special filmstrip-sized holes, sound recordings put elsewhere, and teacher's guides filed into drawers. This method requires considerable staff time to retrieve all items for circulation and to put all away upon check-in. If the items are shelved in the packages in which they are received, no additional cost of packaging is incurred. Package sizes, even for one type of media, are not uniform. There will be as much difference in size between filmstrip containers (or between containers for any one type of media) as there is between containers of different types of media. There is no uniformity in packaging nor in the size of material that accompanies the audiovisual component. Wide shelving is available. It will hold most materials.

A library may want to group certain items together into a special collection (e.g., talking books, big books, feature film). This is helpful for users.

Intershelving of books and audiovisual material has been tried in some school and public libraries with great success. Weihs recommends it highly, speaking of easy patron access to all materials. In *Accessible Storage of Nonbook Materials* (Phoenix, Ariz.: Oryx Press, 1984) she also writes about informal studies in which all media were intershelved and says that circulation of books, as well as that of nonbook materials, rose as patrons found related material on the same topic shelved together.

In a large library it may be more practical to house the collection, equipment, and trained audiovisual service and reference staff all in one area.

Packaging

Most audiovisual material comes in containers that can easily be marked and shelved. Packaging of all kinds and sizes is available for those materials needing to be packaged or repackaged.

Some objects are too big to shelve; a block should be put on a shelf in place of the object. The block can be labeled with the name and number of the item and directions for finding the item.

Some libraries have separated out each component of a package, putting all filmstrips together in filmstrip cabinets, sound recordings together in cabinets, slides in slide cabinets, and manuals in vertical files. This method, recommended by some in the late 1960s and early 1970s, is compact shelving carried to the extreme. It certainly makes effective use of space, but is very inconvenient and time-consuming for staff and patrons when the original components of a package have to be reassembled for use and disassembled when returned. The special storage cabinets also are extremely expensive.

Other libraries have repackaged all material in specially designed containers, sometimes printed with the name of the library. These also are expensive. Years ago much audiovisual material was received without packaging or was packaged in flimsy containers. Now most commercially produced material comes in attractive sturdy containers that have useful information printed on them. Throwing away these containers for the sake of uniformity does not make good economic sense. It also causes problems for the cataloger, who frequently needs the container information for descriptive cataloging. The patron should have access to this information. Video containers with an outside clear plastic sleeve are designed so the original flimsy cardboard video container can be cut apart, inserted in the sleeve, and read by the user. We have recently purchased similar containers for use with talking books.

Repackaging should be considered for some material. A set of filmstrips presenting all the concepts covered in a year of fourth grade social studies would be a good candidate for repackaging in a school library. No student or teacher would want the entire set at once. If this set were located in a curriculum center at a university, however, the set might be kept together, since these centers are designed to show those who are learning to teach the kinds of materials available in schools.

Processing

Once all the other decisions have been made, decisions must be made about the physical processing of the material. Will every piece in every container be labeled? What about each card in a deck of cards, each page in a loose-leaf notebook, each wooden bead in a box of 1,000 wooden beads (designed for making "sets")? If each item is labeled, those found on the floor or in the wrong containers can be put where they belong.

A workable guideline is to label everything necessary for use of the item. If loose-leaf pages have a running title that matches the item title, they can be matched up with little difficulty. If five beads of the 1,000 in a set are missing, little harm is done.

A list of package contents can be typed on the book pocket for each package and used by the circulation staff as the material is checked in and out and when inventory is taken. In an online system, book cards, pockets, and date due slips may no longer be used. A list of contents should be somewhere on the item, available to the circulation staff. The circulation check-in system should be programmed to alert the circulation staff when items in the package need to be matched against the list.

Placement of card and pocket, date due slip, ownership information, etc., requires a good deal of common sense. There is no one place on any type of audiovisual material where processing staff can expect to put these things. Labeling each item with the call number also requires a bit of ingenuity at times. These things will be discussed in more detail with the examples in each chapter of this book.

A recent book by Karen Dreissen and Sheila A. Smyth, *A Library Manager's Guide to the Physical Processing of Nonprint Materials* (Greenwood Press, 1995) provides suggestions for processing all types of material.

Cataloging

Weihs says it best: "Catalog no media, see no media, use no media." (*The Nature and Future of the Catalog.* Phoenix, Ariz.: Oryx Press, 1979, p. 285). It makes no sense to spend money on audiovisual material, then not catalog it. Administrators have been heard to say, "But nobody is using it." How can patrons use what they don't know exists?

Before AACR 2, there was no one set of rules for cataloging audiovisual material. Motion pictures, filmstrips and sound recordings could be cataloged using AACR 1, but those rules were designed for large research libraries and were more detailed than necessary for school or public or smaller academic libraries. The Canadian Library Association had developed rules for use in school and small public libraries that applied to all audiovisual materials. In the United States, school librarians developed their own rules, first published by the Division of Audiovisual Instruction of the National Education Association (DAVI); subsequent editions were published by the same group, later known as the Association for Educational Communications and Technology (AECT). State departments of education, school districts, public libraries, church library associations, and individuals published "rules" or "standards" they had developed and/or were using. There was no coordination among any of these groups and no uniformity in the rules developed.

In a survey Carol Truett found that "many school librarians feel no need for the detail found in rules such as the *Anglo-American Catalog[u]ing Code*." She also found that "[school librarians] appear to be more likely to be involved in cataloging [nonprint] materials than print materials, probably due to the fact that commercial processing for nonprint materials is less available than it is for print media ("Is Cataloging a Passé Skill in Today's Technological Society?" *Library Resources & Technical Services*, July/Sept. 1984, p. 272-73).

The following statements provide several important reasons for cataloging audiovisual material, and doing so using a standard set of rules.

> To have a single standard for purposes of cooperation is better than to have several incompatible ones ... the individuals who work as specialists in the newer media—those who feel most comfortable with nonprint—have frequently been unaware of traditional means of bibliographic control because of their different training. Some have even scorned those traditional means as irrelevant, and prefer to reshape the hubcap while reinventing the wheel (Ronald Hagler, "Nonbook Materials." In *The Making of a Code*, ed. Doris Hargrett Clack. Chicago: American Library Association, 1980, p. 74-75).

> A standard bibliographic description based on consistently applied rules and developed from sound principles is the cornerstone to bibliographic networking (JoAnn V. Rogers, *Nonprint Cataloging for Multimedia Collections*. Littleton, Colo.: Libraries Unlimited, 1982, p. 9).

> The purpose of the catalog, as opposed to the shelflist, is to afford ordinary people easy access by multiple access points to the titles in the collections. The purpose of the shelflist, on the other hand, is to provide a record of item-specific information which can be accessed by its location within the collection by trained staff. The call number is, in many libraries, a unique identification mark and thereby an efficient access point as well. The shelflist is intended for specific uses, the catalog for general use (Sheila S. Intner, *Access to Media*. New York: Neal Schuman, 1984, p. 17).

> An online catalog must, if it is to meet needs defined by the user, integrate access to all resource formats in one system (Margaret M. Beckman, "Online Catalogs and Library Users." *Library Journal*, Nov. 1, 1982, p. 2046).

AACR 2 provides general rules for cataloging, as well as specific rules for most types of media. Any item can be cataloged using AACR 2. It is a national and international standard and should be used by everyone cataloging audiovisual material. Changes are made through an international body, the Joint Steering Committee for Revision of AACR (JSC). The rules of AACR 2 are clear and relatively easy to use. A concept new with AACR 2, levels of cataloging, allows the cataloger to put in as much, or as little, detail as is needed for the patrons of a particular library, while still cataloging within the standard.

Classification

AACR 2 covers only descriptive cataloging, that is, the bibliographic description and the choice and form of access points (main and added entries). The kind of classification scheme used and type of subject headings used are not part of this standard, but are decisions to be made at the local level.

For classification, a library may choose to use a classification number system, accession numbers, or some homemade scheme for audiovisual material.

Locally developed schemes should be avoided. Their use depends upon the person who devised the scheme; when that person is no longer available, the scheme deteriorates. Time also is needed to create and revise the scheme; that time could be better spent using an existing scheme.

Accession numbers have sometimes been recommended. Accession numbers take no training to use. Types of media can be kept together when a "media code" is combined with an accession number, for example the code "MP" for motion picture used with the accession number 243.

Media codes were originally established by the Task Force on Computerized Cataloging and Booking of Educational Media, organized in 1966 by DAVI. These codes were used by AECT in their rules for catalogers. Some of these codes, such as "FS" for filmstrip and "MP" for motion picture, were easy for the patron to decipher. As types of media and number of media codes increased, the codes became more confusing for patrons. The lack of standard terminology added to this confusion (examples: "RD" for recorded disc, "RT" for recorded tape vs. the terms audiotape, phonotape, sound recording tape).

There are problems with the use of media codes and/or accession numbers. A patron cannot browse open shelves by subject if the items are shelved by accession number or by media code and accession number. For a small collection, or a small collection handled by one librarian, accession numbers would seem to be satisfactory. But small collections grow and librarians change jobs. As one who has had to recatalog a collection of 10,000 titles that were given media codes and accession numbers rather than classification numbers (and were shelved by broad subject category!), I can attest to the difficulties caused by lack of planning in the establishing of a collection.

The two major classification systems in use in the United States are the Dewey Decimal Classification and the Library of Congress Classification. Classify the audiovisual material by whatever scheme is used for the other materials in the library and shelve by that classification. Patrons then can browse the audiovisual collection in the same way they browse the book collection.

Subject access

Decisions concerning the type of subject heading system to be used are similar to those that must be made concerning the type of classification scheme to be used. A library must choose whether to use a standard subject heading scheme or to make up one. Locally developed schemes take time to develop and depend on the person(s) who developed the scheme.

The *Guidelines on Subject Access to Individual Works of Fiction, Drama, Etc.* published by ALA (1990) gives us suggestions for subject access that is described in more detail in chapter 2 of this book.

The major lists of subject headings in the United States are *Sears List of Subject Headings* and the *Library of Congress Subject Headings*. A library should use the same subject headings for audiovisual material that it uses for books.

The Catalog

What kind of catalog will be prepared? Will there be cards or a list generated by a computer? Will the catalog be online through a bibliographic utility, a local system, or a microcomputer? These are some of the other decisions that must be made before proceeding to process the collection.

Entries for audiovisual material should appear with the entries for books, whether the catalog is a card catalog, an online catalog, or some other form. These entries should look the same, be prepared using the same rules, and contain classification numbers and subject headings established by the same schemes as the entries prepared for books.

Color codes for media cards were once recommended by some. The colors faded. Not enough distinct colors exist for the types of media that can be cataloged. There was no uniformity in card stock from one supplier to the next, nor from one batch of card stock to the next. Computer-produced cards don't come color coded. Computer printouts cannot be color coded. Online catalogs could display audiovisual titles in colors, but it is better to display all types of media uniformly.

We catalog audiovisual material so patrons will have access to them through the catalog by titles, personal authors, corporate bodies, series, and subjects, and, in our online catalogs, by title term, subject term, general term, and by using Boolean logic. We also provide access by actors, producers, publishers, etc., as necessary. Patrons are likely to look in only one catalog/file when searching for material; therefore the catalog records for audiovisual material should be in the same place as catalog records for books. Patrons using an online catalog expect to find everything in that catalog. We must provide that access.

Theft-detection systems

Magnetic theft-detection systems can destroy magnetic materials by erasing or partially erasing some of the magnetically coded information, although some newer systems use weaker magnetic fields that are not supposed to harm magnetic coding. Do not allow sound recording cassettes, videocassettes, magnetic computer cassettes or disks, or any package containing such material to go through such systems. Label these packages with a warning against demagnetization and train all circulation staff to heed the labels.

Selection

There are many useful books and articles available on selection of audiovisual material and other special materials.

A few warnings concerning selection should be included at this point. Watch out for old material that has been packaged in a new container. The box might be attractive and carry a recent copyright date, but the dates on the material inside might be old. For some subject matter this is not important. For material on rapidly changing topics, such as the United States' role in space, or showing what girls and boys can be when they grow up, anything more than a few years old should be evaluated. If there are no dates on the material, one can tell approximate age by the clothing and hair styles shown and by such background details as make and model of automobiles.

Some producers repackage material under different titles. In some cases they simply have glued a strip with the new title over the old title on guides. In other cases they have reprinted guides and created new packaging but have not changed title frames. The original material might well be excellent, but it isn't needed under two titles. If the original title is now part of a series, it still should carry the same original title or have some reference to that title in advertisements and on the package.

Producers also issue the same content in a different format. Old sets of filmstrips and slides have been converted to video. If the content is still valid, this is acceptable practice, but the original dates should be somewhere on the item and in the bibliographic record

Preservation

> "More than 50 percent of the original production elements (negatives, soundtracks, etc.) for all American movies produced before 1951 have been lost due to deterioration and neglect. And, for films of the silent era produced before 1920, the loss rate exceeds 80 percent." (*LC Information Bulletin*, July 1997, p. 246)

I was fortunate to be able to attend an institute in April 1994, sponsored by the Association for Library Collections & Technical Services, "The Magnetic Media Challenge: Preservation of Audio Tape & Videotape in Libraries and Archives." This institute, held on the well-preserved Queen Mary in Long Beach, California, featured speakers from major film studios and archives of sound, film, and video. While it was fascinating to hear about their collections and the efforts they make to preserve those materials, it was depressing to realize how little those of us in the academic or public library world can do to preserve our collections.

Most of us have no control over our heating/ventilating/air conditioning systems. They are shut down evenings, weekends, and vacation times in many institutions, even though studies have shown it is more efficient to run such systems continuously; administrators want to be able to report to taxpayers that the systems are shut down as much as possible to "save tax dollars." Never mind the deterioration this variation causes to the collection (or the morale/comfort of the staff).

For all film-based materials — both film and film coated with magnetic particles — preservation depends upon absolute control of both temperature and humidity. Film shrinks and expands, becomes brittle, and breaks. Film coated with magnetic particles loses those particles as it shrinks and expands; the binder that holds the particles to the film may separate from the film base. When black "dust" coats your hands after handling magnetically coded video tape, sound tape, or computer tape/disks, you are losing the information carried by those magnetic particles, whether they carried images, sound, or computer data. Only absolute control of temperature and humidity — with backup systems in place — can slow down this process. Nothing can prevent it.

We were reminded of the "folk wisdom" of periodically rewinding videos, and of copying tapes onto fresh tape just before the original tape disintegrates. While rewinding may prevent layers of tape from sticking together on the reel/cassette, it puts additional strain on the tape. Fast rewind devices are especially hard on tapes. Remember also that image quality deteriorates with each generation of copy (and this also leads to copyright questions).

If you have special materials that are unique, historically valuable, and very important to your institution/patrons, you might want to investigate storing originals with one of the firms now specializing in this type of storage. For anything else, recognize that the material will deteriorate. Encourage patrons to use it before you lose it.

Weeding

Weeding of a collection should be done before any cataloging begins, and it should be performed periodically. Unfortunately, audiovisual materials and other special materials tend to deteriorate even when kept under controlled conditions. Heat, humidity, and dust are major factors in the deterioration of film and of magnetic materials. Film (motion pictures, film loops, film strips, slides, and transparencies) becomes brittle, and colors may deteriorate to orange or purple, depending upon the type of film used originally. Magnetic media with a film base (videotape, sound recordings on tape, computer tape, and disks) have the film problem of brittleness, coupled with the possibility of the magnetic coating powdering off the film.

Film materials with sprocket holes suffer from wear. Sprocket holes are torn loose, and film surfaces are scratched when used in poorly maintained equipment or by poorly trained operators. Film and filmstrips are torn and content is lost when spliced.

Slide mounts become warped and the corners may swell in humid areas, causing slides to jam in projection equipment.

Sound discs become scratched. Sound discs warp when hot. Dust in the grooves ruins both the playback equipment and the discs.

Periodic inspection during inventory will reveal deterioration. Then one must make the decision to repair, replace, or discard.

Other factors also lead to weeding.

Even though the content of an item may still be current and/or important, when the people seen in a film are wearing outdated clothes and hair styles, and the setting reveals period automobiles, students watching the material will tend to concentrate on the cars and clothes rather than on the content.

The content of the item may no longer be valid or may conflict with current knowledge. It may even give dangerously wrong information. The educational need for the item may be past — the course may no longer be taught; the professor may have retired; the demand for the topic may no longer be high.

The technology may be outmoded. Film loops were an important type of media in the 1960s. We had several self-paced classes using film loops during the 1970s. Eventually we could no longer replace the worn-out film loops, nor could we keep the projectors functioning.

Parts of an item may have been lost, damaged, or stolen. Can they be replaced? Can the rest of the item be used without the missing parts? Is the remaining portion worth keeping? Is equipment available and in working condition?

All these are factors to be considered when evaluating whether or not an item should be added to a collection and when considering the retention of an item in the collection.

New types of media

We can catalog almost anything following rules given in AACR 2 chapter 1.

In past years I have been asked how to catalog holograms, a collection of historical medical instruments, and "parts of people" (a medical library asked this; they wondered about making an added entry for the person from whom the part had been removed!).

One kind of disc I've seen is an "aroma disc," which plays on a special machine. These, however, are used up when played, so they do not present cataloging problems.

One kind of videocassette contains music but no picture. The physical item is a video, but the content is pure music.

Optical discs may contain music, computer files, or any combination of sound, video, pictures, text, maps, and computer files. These discs are available, or have been announced, in 2½, 3, 3½, 4¾, 8, 10, and 12-inch sizes.

Cataloging in the future

The dividing line between types of media is becoming less distinct as new media are developed and as new uses are found for older forms of media.

Joyce made an interesting observation:

> The recent nature of [technological] change has confused the relation between information and the medium in which it is carried. Whether an artifact is a book, microfilm, handwritten or typed document, or newer technological product, it is distinguished from the information it contains. For example, a videodisc can carry both graphic images, text, and music. As one medium develops the capacity to carry different kinds of information, such as the case of machine-readable records, there is increasing emphasis on cataloging the information, not necessarily the medium carrying it (William L. Joyce. "Rare Books, Manuscripts, and Other Special Collections Materials, Integration or Separation?" *College & Research Libraries*, Nov. 1984, p. 444).

Martha Yee has been writing about this confusion between the work and the carrier for some time. She and a number of others spoke at a Joint Steering Committee conference in October 1997, in Toronto as they discussed future directions of cataloging.

Chapter 2

CATALOGING AUDIOVISUAL MATERIALS AND OTHER SPECIAL MATERIALS

"Cataloging should be fun. And challenging. And useful."

Sanford Berman. *The Joy of Cataloging*
(Phoenix, Ariz.: Oryx Press, 1981, p. xi).

This chapter will explain the general rules for cataloging that apply to all types of media. Specific rules for individual types of media will be explained in subsequent chapters.

Cataloging under AACR 2 begins with preparation of the bibliographic description, and then proceeds to the choice of access points. No thought is given to those entries until the description is finished. The process is best explained by Michael Gorman:

> One of the fundamental concepts of AACR 2 is that the cataloging process is viewed as one in which the cataloger establishes a standard description of the physical object (the book, videorecording, map, etc.), using clues derived from that physical object, and then establishes the access points (headings and uniform titles), which not only provide access to the standard description but relate that description to the work of which it is a manifestation. The descriptive process is concerned with the object in hand ... This formula for all international descriptive cataloging was a direct result of the policy decision that was made for AACR 2: all library materials would receive equal and consistent treatment in its descriptive rules ("AACR 2, Main Themes." Doris Hargrett Clack, ed. *The Making of a Code.* Chicago: American Library Association, 1980, p. 42).

Most inconsistencies between chapters in the 1978 edition of AACR 2 have been resolved in the 1988 revision and the 1993 Amendments. With few exceptions, the chapters are now uniform.

Rule interpretations are prepared by the Library of Congress for the guidance of its own catalogers. These useful interpretations are printed in the quarterly *Cataloging Service Bulletin* (*CSB*) for our information. The audiovisual section at the Library of Congress was disbanded in 1991 and no LCRIs specifically for AV materials have been issued since that time.

Materials Needed for Cataloging

• *Anglo-American Cataloguing Rules,* second edition, 1988 revision. (Chicago, Ill.: American Library Association, 1988).

Chapter 1 contains the general rules used for descriptive cataloging of all material; chapters 2-12 are for specific types of material, chapter 13 for analytics, chapter 21 for choice of main and added entries, chapters 22-25 for form of personal name, geographic name, corporate name, and uniform title headings, and chapter 26 for references.

• *Anglo-American Cataloguing Rules,* second edition, 1988 revision. *Amendments 1993* (Chicago, Ill.: American Library Association, 1993).

Rule revisions approved by JSC, 1989-1992.

- *Bibliographic Formats and Standards.* Second edition. (Dublin, Ohio: OCLC, 1996).

  Includes directions and examples for every code, tag, and indicator used in the OCLC MARC format.

- *Cataloging Service Bulletin.* (Washington, D.C.: Library of Congress, Collections Services, 1979-   ).

  This quarterly bulletin is the earliest source of the rule interpretations that are prepared by the Library of Congress. Cumulated rule interpretations are available from the Library of Congress and from Oberlin College.

- *Cataloging Service Bulletin Index.* (Lake Crystal, Minn.: Soldier Creek Press, 1979-   ).

  This is an annual cumulative index to the LC bulletin.

- Online Audiovisual Catalogers. *Newsletter.* (Tucson, Ariz., 1981-   ).

  This quarterly publication of Online Audiovisual Catalogers is available only through membership. While designed for those cataloging online through one of the bibliographic utilities, the *Newsletter* contains as much material on cataloging as on coding and tagging bibliographic records.

  Other books and manuals that apply to specific materials are listed at the beginning each of the following chapters.

DESCRIPTION

According to rule *AACR 2* 0.24, description is based on the *physical form of the item in hand*, not on the original or any previous form in which the work has been published, and not on the content of the item. This is stated as being a "cardinal principle" of description. Information about content is dealt with in notes.

Information for areas 1-4 and 6 is transcribed exactly as found on the item, with some slight variations permitted by certain rules.

Areas of the Bibliographic Record

The bibliographic description is divided into eight areas as follows:

    Area 1. Title and statement of responsibility area
    Area 2. Edition area
    Area 3. Material (or type of publication) specific details area (chapters 3, 5, 9, and 12 only)
    Area 4. Publication, distribution, etc., area
    Area 5. Physical description area
    Area 6. Series area
    Area 7. Notes area
    Area 8. Standard number and terms of availability area

Most areas are subdivided into elements.

In chapters 1-12 of AACR 2 the rule numbers for the chapter begin with the chapter number and a period. Following the period is the area number, followed by an alphanumeric subdivision. Rule numbers containing ".7" are always rules for notes, just as "area 5" or rules containing ".5" always refer to the physical description area regardless of the chapter or type of material involved.

Punctuation of the Bibliographic Record

Areas 2-8 are preceded by a period-space-dash-space (. —) unless the area begins a new paragraph. When typed, this appears as period-space-hyphen-hyphen-space.

> **LCRI 1.0C.** For the ending of either the paragraph that precedes the physical description area or the paragraph that precedes the first note of the note area use a period unless a closing parenthesis or bracket is present. In the latter case, let the parenthesis or bracket be the ending punctuation without period following. As an exception, also of long-standing practice, if the publication distribution, etc., area ends in an "open" date, so that the last mark is a hyphen or some blank space (designated, for monographs, by angle brackets) for an entirely missing date, do not add the period.
>
> Ending punctuation refers to one of the following when it is the very last mark: period, question mark, exclamation point, closing parenthesis or bracket, and double quotation mark.
>
> For punctuation at the endings of notes, see LCRI 1.7A1. (*CSB* 50)
>
> **LCRI 1.7A1.** Start a new paragraph for each note; end each paragraph with a period or other mark of punctuation. If the mark of final punctuation is a closing bracket or parenthesis, however, add a period. (*CSB* 44)

Note that closing brackets or parentheses are followed by a period in a note, but *not* elsewhere. Punctuation also is prescribed within each area to separate elements within that area. Note the punctuation that accompanies the area or element is that *preceding* the area or element.

Levels of Detail in the Description

A new concept is presented in AACR 2, that of levels of detail. This feature enables libraries that want brief records or brief cataloging to follow the standards but include only the minimum information prescribed for first level cataloging as specified in rule 1.0D1. Those libraries wanting all possible information would use the third level as given in rule 1.0D3. Most libraries probably would prepare bibliographic records with some intermediate amount of detail as permitted in rule 1.0D2.

While level one is a minimum, and level two is also given as a minimum, many libraries might want to catalog somewhere between levels one and two or between levels two and three. This is permitted (unless one is part of a cooperative project in which all are required to maintain at least level two cataloging). Levels one and three might be viewed as the two ends of a continuum with permissible descriptive cataloging falling somewhere between those two ends.

Users of audiovisual material have some special needs that must be met by catalogers.

> The same general principles that guide the degree of descriptive cataloging determined for books apply to the cataloging of nonbook materials. However, because of the physical format of these materials and the variety of storage facilities, it may be difficult to examine them. Therefore, the description on the card should be precise and definite, and full enough to inform the searcher that this may be the material he desires. Conversely, the description should not be so complete and lengthy as to be confusing (Warren B. Hicks and Alma M. Tillin. *Developing Multi-Media Libraries.* New York: Bowker, 1970, p. 71).
>
> The nature of most nonbook materials makes immediate access and inspection difficult, so the description provided should be sufficiently complete to identify the work, to distinguish it from all other versions of the same work, and to guide the user in the selection of any equipment which may be necessary to utilize the material (Alma M. Tillin and William J. Quinley. *Standards for Cataloging Nonprint Materials.* Washington, D.C.: Association for Educational Communications and Technology, 1976, p. 19).

In the following examples of the three levels, note the difference in the amount of information included. These bibliographic records are for three similar kits produced by the Minnesota Historical Society. It would be possible to prepare more notes to add to the level three record. These examples are presented without added entries to save space. The main entry in each case would be under title. A later section of this chapter discusses choice of main and added entries. These examples also show cataloging of kits, which is mentioned in AACR 2 only in rule 1.10. The three ways of handling the physical description area for kits are shown in these examples. For each level, the areas required are named first, then the example showing the use of that level is given. There is no standard for the form in which information is presented. If the descriptive cataloging is prepared on cards, there is no AACR 2 requirement as to indentions or lines left blank on the catalog card. Note the capitalization, punctuation, and spacing shown in these examples. This is capitalization, punctuation, and spacing as prescribed in AACR 2.

Examples throughout this text are in Courier type because it shows spacing exactly as it should be.

Level one

> Title proper / first statement of responsibility if different from main entry heading in form or number or if there is no main entry heading. — Edition statement. — Material (or type of publication) specific details (if applicable). — First publisher, etc., date of publication, etc. — Extent of item. — Note(s). — Standard number.

Level one example (using 1.10C2c)

```
     The immigrant experience / produced by the Education
Division, Minnesota Historical Society. -- The Society,
c1979.
     various pieces.
     A Minnesota history resource unit including narrated
filmstrips, posters, and reproductions of original
materials.
```

Level two

> Title proper [general material designation] = parallel title : other title information / first statement of responsibility ; each subsequent statement of responsibility. — Edition statement / first statement of responsibility relating to the edition. — Material (or type of publication) specific details (if applicable). — First place of publication, etc. : first publisher, etc., date of publication, etc. — Extent of item : other physical details ; dimensions. — (Title proper of series / statement of responsibility relating to series, ISSN of series ; numbering within the series. Title of subseries, ISSN of subseries ; numbering within subseries). — Note(s). — Standard number.

Level two example (using 1.10C2a)

```
The Ojibwe [kit] : a history resource unit / produced by
    the Ojibwe Curriculum Committee in cooperation with the
    American Indian Studies Department, University of
    Minnesota, and the Educational Services Division,
    Minnesota Historical Society. -- St. Paul, Minn. : The
    Society, c1973.
        8 filmstrips, 4 sound discs, 18 charts and posters,
    34 identical elementary booklets, 1 secondary booklet, 1
    teacher's guide ; in container 34 x 34 x 34 cm.
        Issued also with 34 identical copies of secondary
```

booklet and 1 copy of elementary booklet.
    Filmstrip titles: Life through the seasons -- Legends
and songs of the people -- To be one of the people --
Adawagan, fur trade : a meeting of the Ojibwe and the
White Man -- The story of a treaty : 1837 -- The battle
at Sugar Point -- The melting pot myth -- The Anishinabe
: 1930-1970.

Level three

For this level, all elements from the rules that are applicable to the item being described are included.

Level three example (using 1.10C2b)

Minnesota politics and government [kit] : a history
    resource unit / produced by the Educational Services
    Division, Minnesota Historical Society. -- St. Paul,
    Minn. : The Society, c1976.
        8 filmstrips : col. ; 35 mm.
        5 sound discs : analog, 33 1/3 rpm ; 12 in.
        1 game (player's manual, cards) ; in portfolio 28 x
14 cm.
        8 reproductions : b&w ; 15 x 28-64 x 46 cm.
        17 cartoons : b&w ; 28 x 22 cm.
        9 biography banners : col. ; 56 x 22 cm.
        4 issue cards : b&w ; 28 x 22 cm.
        1 student guide, intermediate (30 p.) : ill. ; 28 cm.
        35 identical student guides, secondary (64 p.) : ill.
; 28 cm.
        1 teacher's guide (32 p.) ; 28 cm.
        In container 34 x 34 x 34 cm.
        Issued also with 35 identical intermediate student
guides and 1 secondary student guide.
        Filmstrips: The beginnings of a state, 1660-1865 (83
fr.) -- The years of Republican control and the Populist
revolt, 1865-1895 (92 fr.) -- Progressives, patriots,
and ethnic loyalties, 1892-1918 (104 fr.) -- Minnesota's
third-party experiment, 1919-1938 (76 fr.) --
Minnesotans in state and national politics, 1945-1972
(64 fr.) -- The voters, who are they? (93 fr.) -- Making
changes (88 fr.) -- Government response to people's
needs (82 fr.).
        Intermediate student guide title: People serving
people.
        Secondary student guide title: Minnesota, political
maverick.
        Four sound discs narrate filmstrips.
        Title of remaining sound disc: Voices of Minnesota
politicians. Includes voices of Floyd B. Olson, Harold
E. Stassen, Luther Youngdahl, Orville L. Freeman, Elmer
L. Andersen, Walter Judd, Eugenie M. Anderson, Hubert H.
Humphrey, Eugene McCarthy.
        Biography banners: Cushman K. Davis, Magnus Johnson,

```
John Lind, Anna Dickie Olesen, Victor Leon Power, Jane
Grey Swisshelm, Clara Hamson Ueland, Andrew John
Volstead, J. Frank Wheaton.
    Reproductions from Winona times (May 15, 1858),
Minneapolis journal (Sept. 14, 1917), Minneapolis
tribune (Nov. 5, 1930; July 15, 1948; Mar. 20, 1963),
St. Paul pioneer press (Nov. 9, 1938).
```

Unpublished Material

Treat an unpublished audiovisual item of any type in the same way one would a manuscript or unpublished thesis. Include the date as the only item in the publication, distribution, etc., area.

A helpful publication for cataloging all types of unpublished materials is *Cataloging Unpublished Nonprint Materials: A Manual of Suggestions, Comments, and Examples,* by Verna Urbanski, with Bao Chu Chang and Bernard L Karon. (Soldier Creek Press, 1992)

What is it?

The first, and frequently most difficult, decision in the cataloging of audiovisual material is to decide what the item is.

The chapters of AACR 2 are: (those with * are discussed in this manual):

1.* General rules for description
2.   Books, pamphlets, and printed sheets
3.* Cartographic materials
4.   Manuscripts
5.   Music
6.* Sound recordings
7.* Motion pictures and videorecordings
8.* Graphic materials
9.* Computer files
10.* Three-dimensional artefacts and realia
11.* Microforms
12.* Serials
13.* Analysis
21.* Choice of access points
22. Headings for persons
23. Geographic names
24. Headings for corporate bodies
25. Uniform titles
26. References

Chapters 2-11 of part I of AACR 2 cover specific kinds of media. We first must decide what an item **is** to know which chapter to use for cataloging that item. Some things are no problem. A filmstrip is described using chapter 8. A set of slides also is described using chapter 8. A videodisc is cataloged by the rules in chapter 7. A sound recording of a lecture is cataloged by the rules in chapter 6.

But what about activity cards (see example 35); transparencies and teacher's guide and exercise sheets bound together as a book with perforated pages (example 34); a box of materials for a semester unit on social studies (teacher's guide, classroom set of student manuals, test booklets, answer key, progress chart, posters, activity cards, etc.) (example 72); a filmstrip with a sound cassette containing narration for the filmstrip (example 31); a set of four filmstrips with two sound cassettes containing the narration and a third sound cassette with other material (see level 3, example page 17); a microfiche that is all reproductios of art work (example 63)? Is a book with a sound cassette of someone reading the book cataloged as a book with acompanying sound, or as sound recording with accompanying text, or is it two separate items (example 12)?

What do we do with sets of duplicating masters, or spirit masters, or reproduction masters (AACR 2 ch. 8)? What about a set playing cards; a set of flannel-backed shapes for use with a flannel board; a calendar (all AACR 2 ch. 10)?

These are some of the problems. One must study carefully the introductory section of each chapter of AACR 2. This introductory section explains the scope of the chapter and lists the materials to be cataloged using that chapter.

We should look at the item as a whole rather than concentrate on one aspect of it. If one has a replica of a cylinder seal impression, the replica then mounted on plastic, one could be confused by reasoning that an impression of a cylinder seal is a manuscript, a reproduction of a manuscript is a book, etc. When we look at the item as a whole, we see it is a model to exact scale of the cylinder seal impression, and would be cataloged using AACR 2 chapter 10.

When cataloging an item that does not fit neatly into one chapter of AACR 2, decide by elimination which chapter to use. In other words, eliminate all chapters that obviously do not relate to the item and see which chapter is left.

Dominant Medium

When there are two or more kinds of media in the package, one must first decide if one type is dominant. A filmstrip with recorded narration would be cataloged as a filmstrip with accompanying sound. The filmstrip would be considered to be the dominant medium. The addition of a teacher's guide does not change the decision.

This does not mean, however, that every filmstrip-cassette or filmstrip-disc package has the filmstrip as the dominant medium. There are sets in which the filmstrip (or slides) illustrate the discussion of music that is contained on the sound recording. In these cases the sound recording is the dominant medium, and the film material is treated as accompanying material.

There are also sets in which the filmstrip is to be viewed separately and the sound is related, but is not narration, nor is it to be used simultaneously with the filmstrip. In this case, the package that has two or more items of media, none of which is dominant, is treated as a kit.

We cannot make rules such as "a filmstrip with a sound cassette is always cataloged by rules of chapter 8." Each package must be examined individually. In the set *Music 300, An Introduction to Form in Music*, 60 slides "present immediate visual association with the [musical] forms illustrated on the recordings." In this set the sound recording is the dominant medium and the visual material is the accompanying material.

When no one part is dominant, the set may be called a "kit". Kits are cataloged according to rule 1.10 and are defined in rules 1.10A-1.10C. Their cataloging is discussed in a later chapter in this book

Sources of Information

Chief source of information

Each chapter in part I of AACR 2 specifies the chief source of information for the type of material covered by that chapter. We are directed to "prefer information found in that chief source to information found elsewhere." The chief source of information for a book is the title page. We are looking for a "title page equivalent" in identifying the chief source of information for each type of media.

> **LCRI 1.0A.** When more than one title proper appears in the item, choose as the title proper the title that appears in the chief source specified in the particular rule for chief source in the appropriate chapter. (CSB 11)
> **1.0H1a.** In cataloguing an item comprising different works and with no chief source of information pertaining to the whole item, treat the chief sources of information as if they were a single source ….

In this case, if the title varies from piece to piece, find the title containing the fullest information and use that title.

Prescribed sources of information

A table in each chapter of AACR 2 specifies the prescribed sources of information for each area of the bibliographic description.

Area 1
Title and Statement of Responsibility Area
MARC field 245

The title and statement of responsibility area is composed of the following elements:
title proper
general material designation
parallel title(s)
other title information
statement(s) of responsibility.

Title proper (MARC field 245 ‡a ‡n ‡p; field 246)

> **1.1B1.** Transcribe the title proper exactly as to wording, order, and spelling, but not necessarily as to punctuation and capitalization ….
> **1.1B7.** … If no title can be found in any source, devise a brief descriptive title … enclose [it] in square brackets.

A title supplied by the cataloger is always given in square brackets, and a note is made stating that the title is supplied by the cataloger. This is the only time a title is to be enclosed in square brackets.

A rule change (A.4A) from *Amendments 1993* affects the capitalization of a title proper. When a title main entry begins with an article, the word following that article is ***no longer*** capitalized.

Titles always have been a problem with audiovisual material. There may be several forms of a title on an item or even completely different titles on the same item. By first specifying a chief source of information for each type of material, the designers of AACR 2 helped ensure the uniformity of bibliographic records. When we catalog a sound disc, for example, we are told the chief source of information is the disc label(s). We take the title proper from those label(s). If the sound disc has one title on the label, a different title on the front of the sleeve, another title on the spine, and yet another on the back of the sleeve, we no longer are confused. We use the label information for the title proper and make notes of all the other titles. We provide access points for all the variant titles if the differences are significant, and the patron can find the bibliographic record for the sound disc by whatever title happens to be remembered.

There still will be problems when one cataloger has an incomplete package and does not know it is incomplete; the chief source might be missing, leading to differences in the bibliographic description. There also will be problems when a machine is required to view the chief source of information and the cataloger does not have access to such a machine.

Information preceding the title

Another title problem has been encountered with increasing frequency. This is the problem of information appearing before the "real" title. This is found on all types of material.

Examples: Godfrey the Safety Gopher presents the 1983 Minnesota Department of Public Safety Film Library, starring films on ... *(from the cover of their film catalog)*;
Walt Disney Productions present Escape to Witch Mountain *(from the title frames of a motion picture)*;
Xerox Films presents Multiplication Rock *(from the container of a set of filmstrips with sound)*;
Fred Flintstone presents All-Time Favorite Children's Stories and Songs *(from the label of sound disc)*;
Mattel Electronics presents Blackjack & Poker *(from the title frame of a video game)*;

Selznick International, in association with Metro-Goldwyn-Mayer, has the honor
to present its Technicolor production of Margaret Mitchell's story of the Old
South, Gone With The Wind *(from the title frames of a videorecording)*

More examples:

Richard Burton as Winston Churchill in The Gathering Storm *(from the opening
frames of television production)*;
Ed Asner as Lou Grant *(opening of TV series)*;
Mary Martin in The Sound of Music *(sound disc label)*;
Peter Sellers is Inspector Jacques Clouseau in The Return of the Pink Panther
(from title frames of motion picture);
George Minter presents Alastair Sim as Scrooge in Charles Dickens' A
Christmas Carol *(title frames of videorecording)*

More examples:

Neil Simon's California Suite *(title frames of motion picture)*;
Reader's Digest Popular Songs That Will Live Forever *(title page of song book)*;
All The Words to All The Songs in Reader's Digest Popular Songs That Will
Live Forever Songbook *(title page of separately published book of words for
the songs)*.

And more examples:

Alexander H. Cohen // proudly presents // Angela Lansbury // Dear World
(sound disc label, lines marked);
Columbia Pictures and Rastar Pictures present // Barbra Streisand // James Caan
// A Ray Stark Production of a Herbert Ross Film // Funny Lady *(title frames
of motion picture)*;
The Theatre Guild presents Oklahoma! A Musical Play Based on the Play Green
Grow the Lilacs by Lynn Riggs *(score)*.

Relevant rules:

1.1A2. ... Transcribe the data as found, however, if case endings are affected, if the
grammatical construction of the data would be disturbed, or if one element is inseparably
linked to another.

1.1B1. Transcribe the title proper exactly as to wording, order, and spelling ....

1.1B2. If the title proper includes a statement of responsibility or the name of a publisher,
distributor, etc., and the statement or name is an integral part of the title proper (i.e., connected
by a case ending or other grammatical construction), transcribe it as part of the title proper.

1.1E1. Transcribe all other title information appearing in the chief source of information ....

1.1E2. Transcribe other title information in the order indicated by the sequence on, or the
layout of, the chief source of information.

1.1F1. Transcribe statements of responsibility appearing prominently in the item in the form
in which they appear there ....

1.1F3. If a statement of responsibility precedes the title proper in the chief source of
information, transpose it to its required position unless it is an integral part of the title proper.

A special rule interpretation has been written for motion pictures and videorecordings.

LCRI 7.1B1. When credits for performer, author, director, producer, "presenter," etc.,
precede or follow the title in the chief source, in general do not consider them as part of the
title proper, even though the language used integrates the credits with the title. This does not
apply to the following cases:

LCRI 7.1B1 *(cont.)*

1) the credit is *within* the title, rather than preceding or following it;

> CBS special report
> IBM puppet shows

2) the credit is actually a fanciful statement aping a credit;

> Little Roquefort in Good mousekeeping

3) the credit is represented by a possessive immediately preceding the remainder of the title.

> Neil Simon's Seems like old times *

(CSB 13)

* *Amendments 1993* would call for lowercase "s" on "seems."

Ben Tucker, former Chief, Office for Descriptive Cataloging Policy, Library of Congress, commented on this LC rule interpretation as follows: "The rule interpretation is deliberately limited to chapter 7 ... For any materials other than those covered by chapter 7, do not apply our rule interpretation for 7.1B1." (*Music Cataloging Bulletin*, 15 (6), 4)

We transcribe the information exactly as shown on the title page or title page substitute (chief source of information), even if it seems odd. In a national or international cooperative environment, we must be consistent in our cataloging. If the chief source has certain words on it and we transcribe them all, someone else using our record for cataloging or interlibrary loan will know it is the same item. This becomes even more important when foreign languages are involved. If I am trying to match an object in hand to a bibliographic record on OCLC, if the words match exactly, in the same order, I know it is most likely the same item. When words are omitted and/or rearranged, I cannot be sure I have the same item.

The title proper for each of the preceding problems would be as follows, based on LCRI 7.1B1:

```
245 00  Godfrey the Safety Gopher presents the 1983 Minnesota
Department of Public Safety Film Library

245 00  Escape to Witch Mountain ‡h [motion picture]

245 00  Xerox Films presents Multiplication rock ‡h [filmstrip]

245 00  Fred Flintstone presents All-time favorite children's
stories and songs ‡h [sound recording]

245 00  Mattel Electronics presents Blackjack & poker ‡h
[computer file]

245 00  Gone with the wind ‡h [videorecording]

245 04  The gathering storm ‡h [videorecording]

245 00  Lou Grant ‡h [videorecording]

245 00  Mary Martin in The sound of music ‡h [sound recording]
```

```
245 04  The return of the Pink Panther ǂh [videorecording]
```

```
245 00  Charles Dickens' a Christmas carol ǂh [videorecording]
```

```
245 00  Neil Simon's California suite ǂh [motion picture]
```

```
245 00  Reader's digest Popular songs that will live forever ǂh
[music]
```

```
245 00  All the words to all the songs in Reader's digest Popular
songs that will live forever songbook ǂh [text]
```

```
245 00  Dear world ǂh [sound recording]
```

```
245 00  Funny lady ǂh [motion picture]
```

```
245 04  The Theatre Guild presents Oklahoma! ǂh [music]
```

Incomplete titles

Another title problem is one of abbreviated words in titles. Titles often are abbreviated on labels of sound cassettes of speeches from conferences. Because of lengthy titles and small labels, words are abbreviated (sometimes oddly) or omitted. As in all audiovisual cataloging, common sense is needed.

Sound cassette label:

Acid Precipita.: Ecolo/Societal Effects, Pt. 1 American Association for the Advancement of Science 1981 Annual Convention January 3-8, Toronto.

Suggested title proper:

```
245 00  Acid precipita[tion]
```

(Verna Urbanski. "Incomplete Titles on Conference Proceedings." Online Audiovisual Catalogers. *Newsletter.* 2 (Mar. 1982), 8).

Dependent titles

Another kind of title problem is commonly found on videorecordings. This problem occurs when the titles found on individual items are not meaningful by themselves such as:

Introduction,
Operation,
The studio.

The preceding titles depend on the series title for meaning:

```
245 00  Communicating about computers to the educator. ǂn No. 1,
ǂp Introduction ǂh [videorecording]
245 04  The jointer. ǂn Part 4, ǂp Operation ǂh [videorecording]
245 00  Interactive techniques for teleconferencing. ǂn Program 3,
ǂp The studio ǂh [videorecording]
```

If a part title depends on the main title for clarity, the title proper should consist of

```
245 00   Main title. ‡n Part number, ‡p Dependent title ‡h [GMD]
```

If, however, the part title is a complete, understandable, sensible title by itself, it is used as the title proper, and the rest of the information is used as series title and series number.

If one were cataloging an entire set at once, one would look at all the titles and, if any one of them were dependent, would catalog all the set as dependent titles. All titles in the set should be treated the same way. See LCRI 25.6A (*CSB* 11) for further comments on this type of title.

Title added entries should be made for each part title that could be thought of as a title.

General material designation (MARC field 245 ‡h)

In each bibliographic record there are two elements that contain terms identifying the medium of the item being described. The first element is called the general material designation (GMD). Its use is optional, but if it is used, it appears immediately after the title proper in area 1, the title and statement of responsibility area. In *Amendment 1993* the position of the GMD was changed so it always appears after the first title proper.

The second is called the specific material designation (SMD) and appears as part of the extent of item in area 5, the physical description area.

Those preparing AACR 2 could not reach agreement on a single list of terms to be used as general material designations. Therefore there are two lists appearing in rule 1.1C1. One list is to be used by North American agencies, the other list by British agencies. The list we are to use, with corresponding AACR 2 chapters, is as follows:

Chapter 1	kit (rule 1.10)
Chapter 2	text braille
Chapter 3	map globe
Chapter 4	manuscript
Chapter 5	music
Chapter 6	sound recording
Chapter 7	motion picture videorecording
Chapter 8	activity card art original art reproduction chart filmstrip flash card picture slide technical drawing transparency
Chapter 9	computer file interactive multimedia

Chapter 10 art original
art reproduction
diorama
game
microscope slide
model
realia
toy

Ch. 11 microform

The terms *braille, large print,* or *tactile* may be added to the above terms as appropriate.

The GMD *interactive multimedia* may be used in this country by those following the ALA guidelines.

Note that the use of a general material designation is optional. Some of these terms may not be really useful in conveying information to the patron; it might be better to choose to omit them. The specific material designation names the item exactly, and that information is always present in the bibliographic record.

Parallel titles (MARC field 245 ǂb; field 246)

> **1.1D1.** Transcribe parallel titles in the order indicated by their sequence on, or by the layout of, the chief source of information.

Other title information (MARC field 245 ǂb; field 246)

> **1.1E1.** Transcribe all other title information appearing in the chief source of information ....

Because this element is restricted to information appearing on the chief source of information, other title information appearing elsewhere on the item would be mentioned in a note if important. If added entries are wanted, a 246 is used to create a note or not, and generate an added entry or not, as desired (see the chapter on MARC coding and tagging.)

Statement of responsibility (MARC field 245 ǂc)

> **1.1F1.** Transcribe statements of responsibility appearing prominently in the item in the form in which they appear there. If a statement of responsibility is taken from a source other than the chief source of information, enclose it in square brackets.
> **1.1F2.** If no statement of responsibility appears prominently in the item, neither construct one nor extract one from the content of the item ... Do not include in the title and statement of responsibility area statements of responsibility that do not appear prominently in the item. If such a statement is necessary, give it in a note.
> **0.8.** The word *prominently* ... means that a statement to which it applies must be a formal statement found in one of the prescribed sources of information for areas 1 and 2 for the class of material to which the item being catalogued belongs.

The LC rule interpretation for rule 1.1F repeats some of these directives in order to emphasize certain points, e.g., the utility of the note area for recording statements that have to be rejected for the title and statement of responsibility area, or the fact that it will easily happen that the title and statement of responsibility area lacks a statement of responsibility. Ben Tucker, in a letter to the author (10 Mar. 1985), discusses basic issues in bibliographic description and offers some further clarification. "The name of the area designates two elements, the first of which, 'title,' is essential, a *sine qua non* for the record. The second element, 'statement of responsibility,' is like another area, the 'edition area,' in that it is transcribed only when present in the source. For such elements as these, one must emphasize the character of *description* in the record: it describes what is there, not what is not there. When under the rules no formal, prominent statement is found, then the cataloger must not manufacture such a statement, at least for inclusion in the title and statement of responsibility area. When it comes to the note area, where *description* is not the issue, but *information* is, anything is permissible: either picking up non-prominent statements or manufacturing them from information available."

An LCRI for 1.7 (*CSB* 11) tells us that at-head-of-title information can be transposed to the statement of responsibility when appropriate. When the information does not seem appropriate for this area, it goes in a note.

Name in copyright statement

If a person is named only in a copyright statement, a note may be made for that information.

```
500      Copyright by E. Averett.
```

This person may be chosen as main entry, if appropriate under the rules in chapter 21, even though not named in the statement of responsibility.

If the information about the author is found in very small print, whether in the copyright statement, the introduction, or elsewhere, it probably can not be considered to appear prominently, so would be recorded in the note area if at all. Sometimes the name of an author will only appear in a copyright statement. This information may be given in a note, and the name may be chosen as main entry. Be careful, however, to distinguish between a copyright statement that applies only to a single piece of material and one that applies to the entire audiovisual package.

Information that appears on the chief source of information with the statement of responsibility, such as a person's title, faculty rank, or place of employment, is not recorded. This information has traditionally been ignored when it appears on the title page (rule 1.1F7), and is to be ignored when cataloging audiovisual material. The LCRI for 1.1F7 is to be used only when a corporate body for which an access point is needed appears only in conjunction with the author's name on the title page.

Area 2
Edition Area
MARC field 250

1.2B1. Transcribe the edition statement as found on the item ….
1.2B3. In case of doubt about whether a statement is an edition statement, take the presence of such words as *edition, issue, version* (or their equivalents in other languages) as evidence that such a statement is an edition statement, and transcribe it as such.
LCRI 1.2B3. Whenever an item contains a phrase that calls attention to changes from a previous issue of the item, treat that phrase as an edition statement even if it does not otherwise look like one. (*CSB* 27)

The concept of edition is one that catalogers of audiovisual material did not often encounter in the past. Most items were produced or published once and never reprinted, revised, or issued in new editions. Now, however, we are encountering various types of edition statements, especially for computer files and videorecordings.

Computer files are issued for different types of computers and are updated and/or revised repeatedly. We are advised (rule 9.5B2) to consider the words *edition, issue, version, release, level,* and *update* as evidence of an edition.

Motion pictures and videocassette releases of feature films and children's films lead to edition-related problems. The original motion picture might have been reprinted and released later on 16 mm, 8 mm, and super 8 mm film. The video release may be in VHS and Beta, as well as on videodisc. Are these editions or versions? Are they cataloged as new works? And what about the colorized version, or that with closed captioning or described by the Descriptive Video Service, or the "fully-restored version", and the 25th or 50th anniversary editions? And what do we do with remakes of old films, using the same title as the original?

Examples of cataloging of some of these items will be found later in this book, including *A Star is Born, Sound of Music,* and the 50th anniversary edition of the game *Monopoly.*

To carry this to absurd lengths, the General Mills cereal, *Lucky Charms,* came out in 1987 with what was clearly labeled on the front of the box as the "Swirled Whale Edition." Al Sicherman reported this in the *Minneapolis Star and Tribune* with the comment: "Great galloping Gutenberg! Editions of breakfast cereals—where have we gone wrong?" (*Minneapolis Star and Tribune,* Jan. 25, 1987, p. 8 Fx)

Figure 1

⇒ ⇒ ⇒ ⇒

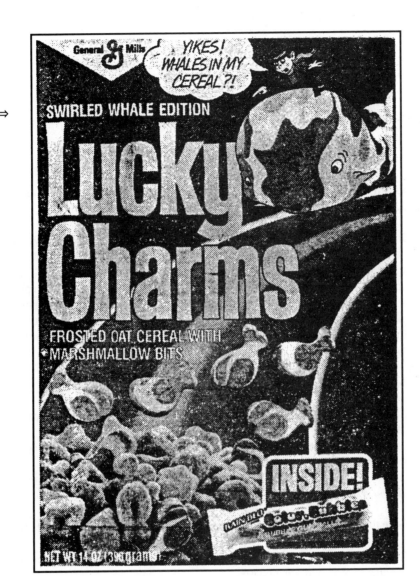

Area 3
Material (or Type of Publication) Specific Details Area

This area is used for the following types of material:

Cartographic materials
Mathematical data area (MARC field 255)

Music (not covered in this book)
Musical presentation statement area (MARC field 254)

Computer Files, Internet Resources
    File characteristics area (MARC field 256)

Serials
    Numeric and/or alphabetic, chronological, or other designation area (MARC field 362)

Area 4
Publication, Distribution, Etc., Area
MARC field 260

A letter from Richard Thaxter, former head, LC Audiovisual Section (1981-1989) included the following information on publication:

> Publication is defined in the copyright law (Title 17, *United States Code*, section 101) as follows:
>
> "Publication" is the distribution of copies or phonorecords of a work to the public by sale or other transfer of ownership, or by rental, lease, or lending. The offering to distribute copies or phonorecords to a group of persons for purposes of further distribution, public performance, or public display, constitutes publication. A public performance or display of a work does not of itself constitute publication (Verna Urbanski. "Publication Defined." Online Audiovisual Catalogers. *Newsletter*, 3 (Sept. 1983), 20).

Place of publication (MARC field 260 ǂa)

> **1.4C1.** Transcribe the place of publication, etc., in the form and the grammatical case in which it appears.
> **1.4C3.** … Supply the name of the country, state, province, etc. … if it does not appear in the source of information but is considered necessary for identification.

Name of publisher, distributor, etc. (MARC field 260 ǂb)

> **1.4D1.** Give the name of the publisher, distributor, etc., following the place(s) to which it relates.
> **1.4D2.** Give the name of a publisher, distributor, etc., in the shortest form in which it can be understood and identified internationally.

Date of publication, distribution, etc. (MARC field 260 ǂc)

> **1.4F1.** … Give the date of the first publication of the edition to which the item belongs.

Multiple dates, a frequent problem, are discussed in the December 1981 Online Audiovisual Catalogers *Newsletter* (p. 6) in which Sara Clarkson shares her letter to LC and the response by Ben Tucker. The following summarizes that discussion.

> Each item in a package of material may carry a different date with the container having yet another date. Use the latest date and make a note with all the dates, or saying the dates vary from "year" to "year." It is important in cases where the individual dates are old and the container date is new to warn patrons they are getting repackaged old material.
> Assume we are cataloging a filmstrip, sound cassette, and teacher's guide. The filmstrip has the date c1977. The sound cassette has no date. The guide has the date c1979. There is no date on the container. We would be cataloging the material under chapter 8 rules; we would be cataloging the package as a filmstrip, with the sound cassette and the guide treated as accompanying material. (Note

we first must decide what we are cataloging, then go to the appropriate chapter to see what the chief source of information would be for this material.) Let us assume all pieces of material in the container carried the same title. In this case, the filmstrip itself is the chief source of information, rather than the container. But our filmstrip carries a copyright date that is obviously earlier than the publication date for the package. (The filmstrip was produced in 1977; sound may have been added later, or the filmstrip and sound may have been done in 1977 with the guide added in 1979, or rewritten in 1979.)

Look again at the rule above. It does not say copyright date, but publication date. So we use [1979] in the date element of the publication, distribution, etc., area, and in a note say the date on the filmstrip is c1977.

This advice is *most* helpful for all types of material. When there are several dates, find the latest date that appears anywhere on the item and use it in brackets as the assumed date of publication.

In a note taken from OCLC record 7262059 (a pre-AACR 2 record, but still appropriate):

```
500     Dates vary: on title frame, c1975; stamped on slide
margin, c1978; guide, c1977; carousel label, c1978;
cassette, side A, c1977; side B, c1979.
```

or

```
500     Dates on items vary from 1975 to 1979.
```

Area 5
Physical Description Area
MARC field 300

Extent of item (MARC field 300 ‡a)

Rule 1.5B1 directs us to record the number of physical units of the item being described and the specific material designation. Multiple copies of material are to be treated as follows:

```
300     12 identical charts
300     10 identical sets of 60 slides
```

1.5B3. Specify the number of components as instructed in the [separate] chapters.
1.5B4. If the material being described has a playing time, give the playing time as follows:

a) If the playing time is stated on the item, give [it] as stated.

```
300     1 sound disc (42 min.)
300     4 sound discs (2 hr., 24 min.)
```

b) If the playing time is ... readily ascertainable, give it.

```
300     1 videocassette (20 min.)
```

c) ... Give an approximate time.

```
300     1 videocassette (ca. 60 min.)
```

d) [Multipart items.]

```
300      4 sound cassettes (12 min. each)
300      3 sound discs (90 min.)
300      6 film loops (ca. 4 min. each)
```

There has been some confusion between the terms cartridge and cassette. Both items have material (film or tape) permanently enclosed in a container. In the cassette the material goes from one reel to another, then back again; in the cartridge the material is a continuous loop on one reel. The containers may hold film, videorecording tape, sound recording tape, or computer tape.

Other physical details (MARC field 300 ǂb)

> **1.5C1.** Give physical data, (other than extent or dimensions), about an item as instructed in the [separate] chapters.

Dimensions (MARC field 300 ǂc)

> **1.5D1.** Give the dimensions of an item as instructed in the [separate] chapters.

Container

> **1.5D2.** *Optionally,* if the item is in a container, name the container and give its dimensions *either* after the dimensions of the item *or* as the only dimensions.

```
300      various pieces ; ǂc in portable shelves 98 x 140 x
90 cm.
300      28 art reproductions : ǂb col. ; ǂc 31 x 52 cm. in
portfolio 28 x 32 cm.
300      6 sound discs : ǂb analog, 33 1/3 rpm, stereo. ; ǂc
12 in. in 2 containers.
300      6 filmstrips : ǂb col. ; ǂc 35 mm. + ǂe 6 sound
cassettes + 1 teacher's guide + 30 identical workbooks in
box 30 x 30 x 28 cm.
```

Accompanying material (MARC field 300 ǂe)

Rule 1.5E1 lists four ways of recording information about accompanying material:

> a) record the details of the accompanying material in a separate entry
> b) record the details of the accompanying material in a multilevel description [this option is not used by the Library of Congress]
> c) record the details of the accompanying material in a note
> d) record the name of accompanying material at the end of the physical description.

When method d is used, the name of the accompanying material is preceded by a space-plus sign-space; multiple items are each preceded by a space-plus sign-space.

> "If the item has any kind of a title on it (teacher's guide, user's manual, program description, student notes, etc.) use that term in the accompanying material statement. If there is no such term or phrase, use a general term (guide, manual, script, etc.) as appropriate." (Ben R. Tucker, letter to author, 21 Feb. 1985)

```
300      + 1 teacher's guide.
```

```
300      + 1 set of teacher's notes.
300      + 1 set of program instructions + 1 user's guide.
300      + 1 booklet.
300      + 3 guides.
```
         (3 different guides)
```
300      + 3 identical guides.
```

Area 6
Series Area
MARC fields 4XX

1.6B1. If an item is issued in a series, transcribe the title proper of the series ...
1.6J1. ... If an item belongs to two or more series and/or ... series and subseries, give separate series statements and enclose each statement in parentheses ...

Area 7
Notes Area
MARC fields 5XX

Notes are optional, according to AACR 2. Notes are needed to justify an access point not mentioned elsewhere in the bibliographic record. A note is required for the source of the title when cataloging computer files. When cataloging a computer file available online, a note giving access information for that file is required.

Notes must be used in the order specified by the general chapter and by the specific chapters. A recent rule change (1.7B) permits us to move the most important note to the first position. CONSER participants, however, are directed to enter notes in order by MARC tag, and some online catalogs rearrange notes into MARC order.

Not all notes are permitted in all chapters. If one is needed, borrow it from chapter 1.

Types of notes:

1.7B1. Nature, scope, or artistic form
1.7B2. Language of the item and/or translation or adaptation
1.7B3. Source of title proper
1.7B4. Variations in title
1.7B5. Parallel titles and other title information
1.7B6. Statements of responsibility
1.7B7. Edition and history
1.7B8. Material (or type of publication) specific details
1.7B9. Publication, distribution, etc.
1.7B10. Physical description
1.7B11. Accompanying materials and supplements
1.7B12. Series
1.7B13. Dissertations
1.7B14. Audience
1.7B15. Reference to published descriptions
1.7B16. Other formats
1.7B17. Summary
1.7B18. Contents
1.7B19. Numbers borne by the item

1.7B20. Copy being described, library's holdings, and restrictions on use
1.7B21. "With" notes
1.7B22. Combined notes related to the original

Punctuation in notes

Each note ends with a question mark, exclamation point, or period, according to LCRI 1.7A1.

If a note has the same information normally found in a bibliographic record (e.g., title proper and statement of responsibility), give the information in the same order as when constructing a bibliographic record. Use the same punctuation, except substitute a period for the period-space-dash-space used to separate areas.

Punctuation within notes seems inconsistent. In response to a letter questioning punctuation, especially the occasional lack of a space to the left of a semicolon, Ben Tucker wrote (23 Feb. 1984):

> Since notes can include both normal punctuation and ISBD punctuation, the primary distinction to be made is between an ISBD mark and a normal mark. This is done by regarding the ISBD punctuation in the areas that precede the notes. Most of the ISBD marks are the same as normal marks, with the addition of a single space fore and aft. Thus,
>
> 1. When a colon is used in a note, it has spaces on either side only when it divides a title from other title information, or separates a place from a publisher:

```
Based on: Nocturnes : a girl's own story.
Reprint. Originally published: New York : Scribner's,
1984.
```

> 2. When a semicolon is used in a note, it has a space on either side only when it separates statements of responsibility, multiple places of publication, and when it separates series from numbers:

```
First published as: The tale of a mouse / Judy Appel ;
drawings by J. Firmin.
```

> 3. The slash is used in a note with a space on either side only when it introduces a statement of responsibility (see previous example).
>
> We have found this policy relatively easy to implement, although I admit that one can see records in which the space has also crept in before the "normal" marks.

Explanation of notes

Each of the notes will be explained in the following section and examples of their use given. Notes from other chapters are included as needed to make a complete listing.

1.7A5. … When appropriate, combine two or more notes to make one note.

```
500     Radio drama, recorded from a broadcast of the
program Lux radio theatre, Nov. 11, 1937, starring Brian
Aherne and Marion Davies.
```

1.7B1, 9.7B1a. Nature, scope, or artistic form (MARC fields 500, 516)

To be used to name or explain the form of the item as necessary.

```
500     Database management program.
500     Radio drama.
```

9.7B1b. System requirements (MARC field 538)

This physical description note for computer files was moved into a new rule number. It is used as a formal note beginning with the words "System requirements:" and including other information (if available) about the type of computer required, how much memory is needed, what other programs are required to use this, and what other hardware is needed.

```
538     System requirements: Macintosh; 4MB RAM; System
7.0.1 or higher; printer.
```

9.7B1c. Mode of access (MARC field 538)

This required note briefly states how one accesses computer files available online.

```
538     Electronic access through the Internet.
```

12.7B1. Frequency (MARC field 310)

Information about the frequency of publication of an item is recorded in MARC field 310. This field follows field 300 in a MARC record. Field 310 does *not* end with a period according to USMARC conventions.

```
310     Quarterly
310     Frequently updated
```

1.7B2. Language of the item and/or translation or adaptation (MARC field 546)

To be used to name the language or languages of the item cataloged if not obvious from other information given.

```
546     Guide in German.
546     Sound accompaniment in French; script in French and
English.
546     Closed-captioned.
546     Described for the visually impaired.
```

1.7B3. Source of title proper (MARC field 500)

To be used if the title proper is taken from other than the chief source of information.

```
500     Title from container.
500     Title supplied by cataloger.
500     Title from title screen.
```

1.7B4. Variations in title (MARC field 246 or 500)

To be used to note any title appearing on the item that differs significantly from the title proper. Field 246 is used when the title applies to the entire item. Field 246 does *not* end with a period according to USMARC conventions.

```
246 1   ‡i Title on cartridge and container: ‡a Trisecting
a straight line with triangles
```
        (*Title proper:* Trisecting a line with triangles)

1.7B5. Parallel titles and other title information (MARC field 246 or 500)

To be used for parallel titles and important other title information not recorded in the title and statement of responsibility area.

```
500      Subtitle on guide: Wildlife management in Northern
Minnesota.
```

1.7B6. Statements of responsibility (MARC fields 500, 508 [creation/production credits], 511 [participants or performers], 536 [funding information], 550 [issuing body]),

To be used to record important information not recorded in the statement of responsibility area.

```
508      Consultant: Carrol J. Schwartz.
500      Software copyright by E. Averett.
511 0    Read by Eileen Heckart, Claudia McNeil, and Mildred
Natwick ; edited by Sharon Donovan.
```

A cataloging decision made at the Library of Congress, published in the *Music Cataloging Bulletin,* June 1989 (p. 4), instructs the use of the same punctuation in performer notes as would be used in the statement of responsibility. The semicolon is set off by a space on each side. This punctuation is followed throughout the other chapters for credits notes.

1.7B7. Edition and history (MARC fields 500, 522 [geographic coverage], 567 [methodology], 580 [relationships with other serials])

To be used for information about earlier editions or the history of the item being cataloged.

```
500      Earlier ed. has title: Step by step.
500      Adapted from the motion picture of the same title.
```

1.7B8. Material specific details (MARC fields 500, 565 [file characteristics], 515 [numbering and chronological designation for serials])

Used only in AACR 2 chapters 3, 5, 9, and 12.

1.7B9. Publication, distribution, etc. (MARC field 500)

To be used for important information not recorded in the publication, distribution, etc., area.

```
500      Not available for distribution in the United
States.
```

1.7B10. Physical description (MARC fields 500, 538)

To be used for any important information not given in area 5, the physical description area.

```
500      HO scale.
500      Gameboards on back of poster.
538      Compact disc.
538      VHS.
```

1.7B11. Accompanying materials and supplements (MARC fields 500, 556 [documentation of a computer file])

To be used for any important information not given in the accompanying material part of area 5.

```
500      Teacher's guide includes bibliography, exercises,
worksheets, glossary, time line.
500      Program notes by Stanley Crouch inserted in
container.
```

1.7B12. Series (MARC field 500)

To be used for any important information not recorded in the series area.

```
500      Originally issued in the series: Vocabulary skills.
```

1.7B13. Dissertations (MARC field 502)

To be used for the standard dissertation note when applicable.

```
502      Thesis (M.A.)--Indiana University, 1968.
```

1.7B14. Audience (MARC field 521)

To be used to record the intended audience of a work. Use this note only if the information is stated on the item. Do not attempt to judge the audience for an item. The first indicator "8" is used when no display constant is needed. The display constant "Audience" is generated when no indicator is provided. Other indicators are used for display constants for reading and interest levels.

```
521      For children 3 to 8 years old.
521 8    MPAA rating: R.
```

1.7B15. Reference to published descriptions (MARC fields 581, 510 [Index], 524 [preferred citation])

To be used to refer to published descriptions of the material.

```
581 8    Described in: Albrecht Dürer : the complete
engravings. Artline, 1987.
```

1.7B16. Other formats (MARC fields 530, 535)

To be used to list other formats in which the work is available. The Library of Congress used to list (when they were cataloging AV) all formats commercially available in this note. (I edit out such information so our patrons will not think we have all these formats.)

```
530      Prints of each negative are available from the
Library of Congress.
530      Also available as slides (b&w or col.) and as
photographic prints.
530      Issued also on videodisc.
```

1.7B17. Summary (MARC field 520)

To be used for a brief objective summary of the content of the item. This may be the most important information we can provide to the user through our cataloging. The summary also provides information that may be used when assigning subject headings and call numbers.

> **LCRI 2.7B17.** Guidelines when creating subject notes:
> 1. Make a concise statement, mentioning only major points of the contents. Phrases, rather than sentences, may be used when clarity and good taste permit.
> 2. Include objective statements only, avoiding any explicit or implicit evaluation of the contents from any point of view. If it is the contents of the work that show a bias, which it is important for the subject note to bring out, word the note carefully so that it is clear the author's bias, not the cataloger's, is the one being related.

LCRI 2.7B17 *(cont.)*

3. Depending on the particular contents of a work note that it is important to bring out such information as

        a. coverage of a time period or of a geographic area;

        b. educational level or slant of the material;

        c. obvious purpose of the contents;

        d. genre of the contents;

        e. any other major information considered important.

(CSB 24)

```
520     Describes and compares television journalism and
press photography using examples of Minneapolis and St.
Paul news items.
```

1.7B18. Contents (MARC fields 505, 500, 504)

To be used for a formal (MARC field 505) or informal (MARC field 500) listing of the contents of the item.

```
505 0   Red shouldered hawk -- Red-tailed hawk -- American
kestrel -- Chuck-will's widow -- Great horned owl.
```

The abbreviations "v.", "pt.", or "no." no longer are capitalized at the beginning of a contents note, according to *Amendments 1993.*

```
505 0   pt. 1. Matching your needs with funding source
interests -- pt. 2. Developing proposal ideas -- pt. 3.
Submitting your proposal.
```

The contents note may contain subfield codes to distinguish authors, titles, and miscellaneous information. This allows searching on titles. It also permits searching on whatever portion of the name is present.

```
505 00  ‡t Father Time/ ‡r W. Marsalis -- ‡t I'll be there
when the time is right/ ‡r H. Hancock -- ‡t RJ/ ‡r R. Carter
...
```

1.7B19. Numbers borne by the item (MARC fields 500, 020, 022, 028, 037)

To be used to list any important number appearing on the item other than those to be recorded in area 8. The note may be quoted. ISBN numbers are recorded in field 020. Record manufacturer numbers are recorded in field 028. Videorecording manufacturer numbers are also recorded in field 028. Other manufacturer numbers may be recorded in field 037.

```
500     "S 1967"
020     096514223X
028 02  ALP 1056-1058 ‡b EMI
028 40  909 ‡b Walt Disney Home Video.
037     No. 789 ‡b Ideal School Supply Co.
```

1.7B20. Copy being described, library's holdings, and restrictions on use (MARC fields 506, 583, 590)

To be used for any notes applicable only to the particular copy of the item being described (MARC field 506). Also used for local library restrictions (MARC field 590) on the material being described, or for information only of use to patrons of the local library.

```
590     Use restricted to Sociology 454 class.
```

1.7B21. "With" notes (MARC field 501)

For two or more works that have been issued together without a collective title, create one bibliographic record, or catalog them separately, connecting them through "with" notes.

```
501     With: Letter game -- Spelling zoo.
501     With: Unsteady sun / J.M. Mitchell.
```

1.7B22. Combined notes relating to the original (MARC field 534)

```
534     ‡p Original version; ‡c London : Routledge Press,
1938.
```

12.7B23. Item described (MARC field 500)

This note is used when the description is based on other than the first issue of a serial, or for a monograph that is changed through updates.

```
500     Description based on: Vol. 91, issue 51 (Nov. 14,
1996).
500     Description based on home page as of October 10,
1996.
```

Area 8
Standard Number and Terms of Availability Area

There are no special standard numbers to correspond to the ISSN or ISBN for any of the types of audiovisual material. Sometimes the material will carry an ISBN (MARC field 020) or an ISSN (MARC field 022).

Inconsistencies in the Rules

There are still some inconsistencies in the cataloging rules from chapter to chapter. Many problems were resolved in the 1988 revision, but some still exist. The more uniform the rules are, the better our cataloging can be.

Stereo.

The term "stereo." is included in area 5 for sound recordings, but is not permitted in area 5 for videorecordings, interactive multimedia, or computer files.

Colored wood

A colored wooden map would be described in AACR 2 chapter 3 as "col. wood" but a colored wooden map cut into a puzzle would be described in chapter 10 as "wood, col." This is not a big problem, but it is another application of the rules that is not uniform.

Summary note

The summary note is not permitted in AACR 2 chapters 3 or 12. We can "borrow" it from chapter 1, but it would be useful to have it allowed in all chapters.

Order of information in credits notes

By tradition, credits in bibliographic records for music follow the pattern

```
Credits: Name(s), function ; name(s), function.
```

For materials other than music, the credits note is as shown below

```
Credits: Function, name(s) ; function, name(s).
```

ACCESS

After descriptive cataloging is finished, access points are chosen and the form of each main and added entry is determined.

Main Entry

There is not necessarily any correlation between statement of responsibility and main entry. One does not automatically use whatever information appears in the statement of responsibility as the main entry, neither is one restricted to the information appearing in the statement of responsibility.

An interesting program, *Chapter 21, AACR 2, and Choice of Access Points for Nonbook Materials, or, How Did We Get From There To Here?*, was held during the 1984 American Library Association conference. This program, sponsored by Online Audiovisual Catalogers, featured Jean Weihs and Michael Gorman as speakers. In his remarks, Gorman noted the concept of main entry is too frequently a time-consuming snag in cataloging. He noted that no practical reason exists to maintain main entry, and stated that the decision not to drop main entry in the development of AACR 2 was purely political and was not decided on a philosophical level; that, as always, the dilemma for cataloging is the conflict between the philosophical concept of authorship versus the practical approach to access.

Personal main entry (MARC field 100)

> **21.1A2.** Enter a work by one or more persons under the heading for the personal author, the principal personal author, or the probable personal author.

> *Personal author.* The person chiefly responsible for the creation of the intellectual or artistic content of a work.

Corporate main entry (MARC field 110)

> **21.1B2.** Enter a work emanating from one or more corporate bodies under the heading for the appropriate corporate body if it falls into one or more of the following categories: [Consider a work to emanate from a corporate body if it is issued by that body *or* has been caused to be issued by that body *or* if it originated with that body.]

> a) those of an administrative nature dealing with the corporate body itself, or its internal policies, procedures, finances, and/or operations, or its officers, staff, and/or membership, or its resources;
> b) some legal, governmental, and religious works of the following types: laws, decrees of the chief executive that have the force of law, administrative regulations, constitutions,

21.1B2 *(cont.)*

court rules, treaties, etc., court decisions, legislative hearings, religious laws, liturgical works;

c) those that record the collective thought of the body (e.g., reports of commissions, committees, etc. ...);

d) those that report the collective activity of a conference, of an expedition, or of an event falling within the definition of a corporate body, provided that the conference, expedition, or event is prominently named in the item being catalogued;

e) those that result from the collective activity of a performing group as a whole where the responsibility of the group goes beyond that of mere performance, execution, etc. ... ;

f) cartographic materials emanating from a corporate body other than a body that is merely responsible for their publication or distribution.

The rules go on to direct us to enter under title if in doubt.

These rules are much more restrictive than past rules. There are few corporate main entries for audiovisual materials or other special materials.

Title main entry (MARC fields 245 or 130)

21.1C1 (as changed in Amendments 1993). Enter a work under its title proper, or, when appropriate, uniform title, if:

1. the personal authorship is unknown or diffuse, and the work does not emanate from a corporate body, or
2. it is a collection of works by different persons or bodies, or
3. it emanates from a corporate body but does not fall into any of the categories given in 21.1B2 and is not of personal authorship, or
4. it is accepted as sacred scripture by a religious group.

The concept of authorship

Martha Yee discusses the question of authorship of audiovisual materials:

Non-textual materials have strong visual and aural components which are frequently non-verbal. Their creation usually involves carrying out multiple functions, and these functions may be carried out by different people and corporate bodies. Thus, the making of a map may involve the gathering of data by one person or group of persons and the encapsulation of the data in map form by another or others; one person or group may be responsible for the geographic aspect of a map, and another for the subject aspect. The making of a slide set may involve the taking of photographs, the compiling of appropriate pictures, the writing of an accompanying text, the writing or performing of accompanying music, etc. Visual materials can involve the maker of a picture, and the subject of a picture, which may itself be the intellectual or artistic work of another or others. Films, for example, are the products of the art of photography, and can be used to display all the other arts, including dance, music, drama, sculpture, etc., or they can display a person presenting his or her intellectual work in any subject area. Sound recordings, motion pictures and videorecordings frequently display the performance by one person or persons of the work of another or others. Traditional cataloging codes dealt predominantly with the monograph, originally a text written by a single person, and still usually a text created by the exercise of a single function, that of writing. Thus traditionally authorship has consisted to a large degree of the creation of or the taking of responsibility for that single function. When one considers the number of functions that are performed in creating nonbook materials, it can be seen that it is no easy matter to integrate rules to deal with these complex forms of authorship into a code originally designed to deal with authorship of monographs (Martha M. Yee. "Integration of Nonbook Materials in AACR 2" *Cataloging & Classification Quarterly*, 3 (Summer 1983) p. 4.

This concept of authorship has been discussed extensively in recent years as it relates to moving image materials. There are those who believe all of Shakespeare's works, for example, should have a main entry for Shakespeare, regardless of form of material or number of other persons or bodies involved in the production or performance of the work. These discussions will continue.

Adaptations

Adaptations have been the focus of many cataloging questions. A sound recording of someone reading a book is not an adaptation, but a dramatized book is an adaptation.

A filmstrip showing each page of a book, accompanied by a sound recording of someone reading the book, may be an adaptation. Weston Woods prepared new illustrations for some works to put them in the proper format for the filmstrip dimensions. They also composed music for the production. These adaptations would be entered under the heading appropriate to the adaptation, not to the original work. An added entry would be needed for the heading for the original work, and for the illustrator in the case of children's picture books, so the user of a catalog would find bibliographic records for the book and bibliographic records for the reading of the book and bibliographic records for the filmstrip of the book all together.

Added Entries
MARC fields 7XX, 246

The following LCRI is related to card format. Online catalogs generate added entries based on tags and/or indicators in several fields.

LCRI 21.29. Give added entries in the following order:

1. Personal name [MARC field 700];
2. Personal name/title [MARC field 700, ǂt];
3. Corporate name [MARC field 710];
4. Corporate name/title [MARC field 710, ǂt];
5. Uniform title [MARC field 730];
6. Title traced as Title-period [MARC field 245 first indicator 1];
7. Title traced as Title-colon, followed by a title [MARC field 246];
8. Series [MARC field 4XX, 8XX].

(*CSB* 12)

For arrangement within any one of these groupings, generally follow the order in which the justifying data appear in the bibliographic description. If such a criterion is not applicable, use judgment.

> **21.29C.** … make an added entry under the heading for a person or a corporate body or under a title if some catalogue users might suppose that the description of an item would be found under that heading or title rather than under the heading or title chosen for the main entry.
> **21.239D.** If, in the context of a given catalogue, an added entry is required under a heading or title other than those prescribed in 21.30, make it.
> **LCRI 21.29D.** In making added entries for audiovisual materials, follow the general rules in 21.29, and apply, in addition to those in 21.30, the following guidelines:
> 1) Make added entries for all openly named persons or corporate bodies who have contributed to the creation of the item, with the following exceptions:
> a) Do not make added entries for persons (producers, directors, writers, etc.) if there is a production company, unit, etc., for which an added entry is made, unless their contributions are determined significant, e.g., the animator of an animated film; the producer/director of a student film, the director of a theatrical film; the filmmaker or developer of a graphic item attributed as author on the data sheet and

LCRI 21.29 D *(cont.)*

or prominently named on the accompanying material ("a film by").

In the absence of a production company, unit, etc., make added entries for those persons who are listed as producers, directors, and writers. Make additional added entries for other persons only if their contributions are determined significant.

b) If a person, filmmaker, developer of a graphic item, etc., is the main entry heading, do not make added entries for other persons who have contributed to the production, unless the production is known to be the joint responsibility of collaboration of the persons or the contributions are determined significant.

2) Make added entry headings for all corporate bodies named in the publication, distribution, etc., area.

3) Make added entries for all featured players, performers, and narrators with the following exceptions:

a) If, for a motion picture or videorecording, the main entry is under the heading for a performing group (in accordance with 21.1B2e), do not make added entries under the headings for persons performing as members of that group. If a person's name, however, appears in conjunction with, preceding or following the name of the group, do not consider him or her to be a member of that group.

b) If there are many players (actors, actresses, etc.), make added entries under the headings for those that are given prominence in the chief source of information. If that cannot be used as a criterion, make added entries under the headings for each if there are no more than three.

4) Similarly, make added entries under the headings for persons in a production who are interviewers or interviewees, delivering lectures, addresses, etc., or discussing their lives, ideas, work, etc., and who are not chosen as the main entry heading.

(*CSB* 45 p. 32-34)

A comment on the preceding LCRI: "These LC policies are mainly a matter of practicality and economics. I would encourage other libraries to make more (or fewer) added entries according to their needs" (Richard Thaxter, letter to author, 10 Mar. 1985). When we are cataloging locally produced works, we might want to make added entries for everyone involved—it is good public relations policy.

An extensive LCRI explains how to construct added entries for works:

LCRI 21.30M Analytical entries

Added Entries for Works

Added entries for works reflect the type of main entry heading of the work being cataloged in the tracing as follows:

Type of main entry	Type of added entry
Personal or corporate name	Name heading/uniform title
Title	Uniform title
Uniform title (e.g., Bible)	Uniform title

The phrase "added entries for works" in these instructions is intended to encompass all the various types of added entries listed above.

Added entries for works are of two types: analytical and simple. They are made on the basis of various rules, some of which prescribe an analytical added entry in explicit terms, others of which do not. Whenever the added entry is made to furnish an access point to the

LCRI 21.30M *(cont.)*

work contained in the item being cataloged, it should be an analytical added entry (e.g., 21.7B1, 21.13B1, 21.19A1). If the added entry serves only to provide an approach to the item being cataloged through a related work, however, and the text of this work is not present in the item being cataloged, then a simple added entry for the work is appropriate (e.g., 21.12B1, 21.28B1, 21.30G1).

The relationship that is expressed between works by means of an added entry, either analytical or simple, is limited to a single access point, namely, that of the main entry. An added entry in the form of the main entry heading for a work provides the sole access to the work; do not trace in addition any added entries for that work's title (when main entry is under a name heading), joint author, editor, compiler, translator, etc.

Analytical Added Entries

Formulate analytical added entries as follows:

Type of analytical added entry	*Components*
Name heading/title	Heading in catalog entry form plus uniform title
Title	Uniform title
Uniform title (e.g., Bible)	Uniform title

In addition, following the uniform title, provide the language (if appropriate). For the Bible and the collective titles "Works" and "Selections," provide the elements appropriate to these uniform titles as called for in the relevant rules and LCRIs: for the Bible, 25.18A; for "Works," LCRI 25.8; for "Selections," LCRI 25.9. Note that all of these specify including in the uniform title the year of publication of the item being cataloged.

In making analytical added entries, note especially the following details:

1. Do not abbreviate the names of languages.
2. For the Bible and the collective uniform titles noted above that include the year of publication, formulate the year according to the guideline stated in LCRI 25.8.
3. Do not enclose uniform titles within brackets.
4. Do not give in the tracing a title found in the item being cataloged that is different from the uniform title.

Simple Added Entries

Formulate simple added entries as follows:

Type of simple added entry	*Components*
Name heading/title	Heading in catalog entry form plus uniform title
Title	Uniform title
Uniform title (e.g., Beowulf)	Uniform title

Note that subject entries for works are formulated in the same manner as simple added entries (*CSB* 63 p. 11-12).

These guidelines call for all headings to be in uniform title format coded in MARC field 700 with subfield ǂt or in MARC field 730. Different forms of titles would be handled by cross-references, or by an authority system. For those of us working in less-than-ideal worlds, we may need to make added entries for the title in other forms, as well as the uniform title form.

Added entries are made for persons and corporate bodies capable of authorship. Puppets and cartoon characters would not qualify for added entry. However rules 21.29D and 21.30H do permit us to make added entries for important access points under certain conditions. Ben R. Tucker told me that subject headings must be used as access points for cartoon characters.

Uniform title

Some motion pictures and/or videorecordings may need uniform title main or added entry when "the title of the work is obscured by the wording of the title proper" or when there are two or more works with the same title in your catalog.

LCRI 25.5B. Conflict resolution

Radio and Television Programs

Add the qualifier "(Radio program)" or "(Television program)" to the title of a radio or television program whenever the program is needed in a secondary entry and the title is the same as a Library of Congress subject heading or the title has been used as the title of another work. (It does not matter if the other work is entered under title or under a name heading.) This same uniform title for the radio or television program must be used in all entries for the particular work. (Existing records in which the radio or television program has been used as a main or added entry must be adjusted.) (*CSB* 66 p. 25)

Motion Pictures

If a motion picture is entered under a title proper that is the same as the title proper of another motion picture (or other work), do not assign a uniform title to either to distinguish them, even if there are multiple editions of either work. However, if a motion picture is needed in a secondary entry and the title of the motion picture is the same as a Library of Congress subject heading or the title is the same as the title of another work, add the qualifier "(Motion picture)" to the title of the motion picture. This same uniform title must be used in all entries for the particular work. (Existing records in which the motion picture is used as a main or secondary entry must be adjusted).

New work

> **Copland, Aaron**, 1900-
>   The red pony ...
>   *(Music for the motion picture of the same title)*

Existing works

> **Steinbeck, John**, 1902-1968
>   The red pony ...
>   *(A book)*

LCRI 25.5B. (cont.)

The Red pony [motion picture] …

Added entry on the new work

I. Red pony (Motion picture)

Revised record for the motion picture

Red pony (Motion picture)
The red pony [motion picture] …

(*CSB* 66 p. 26)

These are *qualifiers* added in parentheses, *not* GMDs.

No GMD in added entries

The Library of Congress does not take the GMD into consideration in filing, so it does not use the GMDs in added entries, including title added entries. The Library also does not use the GMD in uniform titles. If a conflict occurs when filing, a qualifier is added to the entry. That qualifier may use the words of a GMD, but it will be given in parentheses rather than in square brackets.

Form of Access

Form of access is governed by chapters 22-25. Most of us now have access to online authority files and can quickly determine the form of an access point. If the heading we need is not in the authority file, however, we must go to the rules to determine the form we need. These rules guide the cataloger in determining whether, for example, a person's middle initial or birth date may be used in a heading, in what form a corporate body is to be given, and what, if any, qualifiers need to be added to the heading.

Subject Access

Subject access to the contents of an item is provided through subject headings. Access to the form of an item (physical form and/or literary form) may be provided through genre headings. Classification may be used to provide another type of subject access.

Hans Wellisch, at an international symposium held in 1971, said:

> Some catalog studies make it seem as if the subject approach to documents were not very widespread among library users and that most of them look for authors and titles and turn to subject enquiries only when other attempts to locate books fail. But such results tend rather to emphasize the fact that subject retrieval in present day dictionary catalogs is both difficult and frustrating (Hans Wellisch. "Subject Retrieval in the Seventies — Methods, Problems, Prospects." In *Subject Retrieval in the Seventies, New Directions.* Westport, Conn.: Greenwood Press, 1972, p. 4).

David Haykin pointed out some of the problems of subject catalogs and subject cataloging. He said:

> [The subject catalog] suffers from several limitations, some accidental, others inherent in its nature and structure. Whatever rules or principles were applied in choosing or devising headings in the past, it is clear that they were often based on no more than the limited personal experience of the cataloger.

One of the most serious weaknesses of the headings now found in our catalogs is that the terms chosen are not derived from precise knowledge of the approach used by many readers of different backgrounds ... Even if the cataloger were to determine conclusively the mental processes of the reader and to choose the terms, structure, and arrangement of headings which most closely correspond to the reader's approach, he would still have to take account of linguistic problems ... A semantic problem with which catalogers must struggle constantly is that of imperfect synonyms. Scientific terms are, generally speaking, quite precise in their meanings; in other fields of knowledge and in the use of popular terms, which may be preferred to scientific terms in certain instances, meanings are inexact, the same term being used in different senses by different categories of readers or in different regions, just as different terms are applied to the same thing (David Judson Haykin, *Library of Congress Subject Headings*. Washington, D.C.: U.S. G.P.O., 1951, p. 4).

Lois Mai Chan also speaks of the difficulties with subject cataloging:

The frequent criticisms of the subject catalog for being too specific or too general reflect the conflicting demands on the catalog. Modern writers recognize in general two methods of subject representation: summarization and exhaustive (or depth) indexing. The former aims at displaying the overall subject content of bibliographic entities (books, journals, etc.), while the latter attempts to bring out the content of smaller units of information (e.g., chapters in books, articles in journals, etc.) within bibliographic entities. Many users are content to have the subject catalog fulfill the function of summarization, and leave exhaustive or depth indexing to bibliographies and indexes (Lois Mai Chan, *Library of Congress Subject Headings*. Littleton, Colo.: Libraries Unlimited, 1978, p. 19).

Karen Markey Drabenstott states:

A bleak picture has been presented regarding the experiences of traditional subject catalog searchers when matching their vocabulary with that of the catalog (Karen Markey, *Subject Searching in Library Catalogs*. Dublin, Ohio: OCLC, 1984, p. 56).

Haykin also listed the fundamental concepts of subject headings. These are summarized as follows:

1. *The reader as focus.* The reader is the focus in all cataloging principles and practice.
2. *Unity.* A subject catalog must bring together under one heading all the books which deal principally or exclusively with the subject, whatever the terms applied to it by the authors of the books and whatever the varying terms applied to it at different times.
3. *Usage.* The heading chosen must represent common usage or, at any rate, the usage of the class of reader for whom the material on the subject within which the heading falls is intended.
4. *English vs. foreign terms.* Foreign terms should be used only when the concept is foreign to Anglo-American experience and no satisfactory term for it exists, and when the foreign term is precise, whereas the English one is not.
5. *Specificity.* The heading should be as specific as the topic it is intended to cover. As a corollary, the heading should not be broader than the topic; rather than use a broader heading, the cataloger should use two specific headings which will approximately cover it (Haykin, *Library of Congress Subject Headings*, p. 7-11).

Lucienne Maillet explains some of the complications involved in choosing subject headings:

The process of determining subject headings for input into the library's catalog is a complex intellectual operation which is primarily guided by the cataloging policies of the institution. The process involves some subjective judgement which is influenced by the cataloger's background, the individual's understanding of the subject matter, the objectives of the catalog, the needs of the users, and the effectiveness of communication between the author or producer and the cataloger (Lucienne Maillet, *Subject Control of Film and Video*. Chicago, Ill.: American Library Association, 1991, p. 32).

Subject access for each item of special material should be considered carefully. Narrow topics will need narrow subject headings as explained above under point 5, Specificity. General topics will need general subject headings. Titles that cover a range of topics may need many subject headings to bring out all significant aspects of their content.

Every aspect of a topic treated in an item of audiovisual material needs to be considered for subject access, since the item may represent the only audiovisual treatment in the collection on that topic.

When cataloging material to be added to an audiovisual collection that is small in comparison to the library's book collection, consider adding more subject headings to allow access by general term as well as the most specific ones. However, keep in mind the cautions expressed by Sheila S. Intner:

> While it is within the scope of the local library's indexing policies to add descriptors if they are useful, indexers should not lose sight of the standards that govern indexing for all types of library cataloging. The advantages of access to a smaller bibliographic unit that results from doing deeper indexing may have to be balanced against its cost as well as the disadvantages of finding that the special treatments afforded some materials make it difficult to interfile the records into one integrated catalog, or the disappointment of clients upon discovering that the whole film or video is not about the expected topic (Sheila S. Intner and William E. Studwell, *Subject Access to Films and Videos*. Lake Crystal, Minn.: Soldier Creek Press, 1992, p. 2).

The patron wanting information on Indian pottery might not look under the specific heading

```
Martinez, Maria Montoya.
```

but might look under

```
        Pottery.
or      Indians of North America--Pottery.
```

The film *Hands of Maria* should have all of these subject headings.

```
        Martinez, Maria Montoya.
        Pottery.
        Indians of North America--Pottery.
```

Locally devised subject headings

Current topics do present a problem when it comes to selecting subject headings. If I can't find an appropriate subject heading in the Library of Congress authority file (online through OCLC), I go to the Information Access Company General Magazine Database (IAC) file online to see what index term(s) they have used for the concept I want to index. Because I catalog online through OCLC, I can assign a special field code (690) to that term so others seeing the record in our regional catalog will know the subject heading shown is a locally assigned subject heading.

Another problem is presented by very specific topics such as represented in a filmstrip on drawing curves or one on adding two-digit numbers. Sometimes there is a subject heading in *LCSH* for the specific topic. If there is something similar, I can make up a subject heading, patterning it after an existing similar heading. If there is nothing similar, I make up the heading as best I can, again coding it in field 690.

Subject and Genre Headings

Purpose of subject headings

Occasionally there is confusion about the purpose of subject headings. Their traditional purpose is to represent the subject matter of the item, not the form or purpose of the item. A filmstrip on coal mining would have a subject heading reflecting the content,

```
Coal mines and mining.
```

but would not have the subject heading

```
Filmstrips.
```

Form subdivisions

There is some question about the use of subject heading subdivisions for the medium. The subject card for

```
Pottery--Motion pictures.
```

would not be interfiled in a card catalog or an online list with

```
Pottery.
```

but would follow it in a separate sequence. There would also be separate sequences for

```
        Pottery--Slides.
and     Pottery--Filmstrips.
```

If format subdivisions are given to subject headings for audiovisual material, the patron will not find all information on a subject together. Patrons are not likely to look through more than one alphabetic sequence in a catalog. They will, if necessary, look through

```
Pottery.
```

with main entries from A to Z, but are not likely to continue past

```
Pottery--Bibliography.
```

and through all the other subdivisions to find

```
Pottery--Video recordings.
```

In an online catalog with term searching, sequence is not a problem. A special subfield code, "‡v" has been created for form subdivisions and will be implemented by LC and OCLC in the near future.

```
650   0   Pottery ‡v Video recordings.
```

Sometimes it is necessary to use subject headings for form of medium in order to provide otherwise inaccessible information to patrons. An example would be the assigning of the subject headings

```
        Simulation games in education.
or      Management games.
```

as appropriate, to actual games, as well as to materials about these types of games. There is no other way for patrons to find these types of games unless they know game titles. This same reasoning could lead to assigning format headings for all materials, and this has been done by libraries. I am somewhat uncomfortable with this alternate use of subject headings, but Jean Weihs, in a speech at the Institute on NonBook Materials held in Washington, D.C., October 11-14, 1984, said she sees nothing wrong with this practice. This concept of access to *genre* using special headings is now being encouraged by special MARC codes and tags.

Order of subject headings

The order in which LC subject headings are to be listed on the bibliographic record is given in *Subject Cataloging Manual: Subject Headings* (Washington, D.C.: Library of Congress, August 1996, p. H80).

> Assign subject headings in the order of descending significance, i.e. according to the importance of each subject heading for the assignment of the class number:
> a. Tracing 1 should represent the actual class number assigned to the particular work.
> b. In case two headings are required to represent the complete class number, these two headings should be listed as Tracings 1 and 2.
> c. Important headings that narrowly miss representing the class number (such as a special approach to the major topic) should be listed next.
> d. Headings added to designate topics touched on only marginally in the work should be assigned last.

ALA Guidelines

In 1990 ALA published the *Guidelines on Subject Access to Individual Works of Fiction, Drama, Etc.*, prepared by a subcommittee of the Subject Analysis Committee. The Subject Analysis Committee recommends, in these guidelines, "the provision of four kinds of subject access: form/genre access, access for characters or groups of characters, access for setting, and topical access."

Form/genre access provides access to the form of the item — what it *is* rather than what it is *about*.

Topical access is access to the content of the item — what it is about.

Access to setting involves providing geographic subject headings, with time period subdivisions, as appropriate for the location of the content. These settings may be real or imaginary.

Characters in a work may need their own headings.

All these types of access are discussed in the ALA guidelines. When cataloging special materials, these types of access may be especially useful.

Olderr's Fiction Subject Headings, A Supplement and Guide to the LC Thesaurus, by Steven Olderr (ALA, 1991) includes a discussion on the importance of providing subject access to fiction and suggests consideration of topics, genres, geographical settings, chronological settings, characters, and treatment. I suggest you read the introductory matter to his list when considering how to expand subject access for your patrons.

Genre Access

There has been increasing interest in providing genre access to some types of material. *Descriptive Terms for Graphic Materials: Genre and Physical Characteristic Headings,* compiled by Helena Zinkham and Elisabeth Betz Parker (LC, 1986) was developed with the help of many from the archival, museum, and library communities. It was combined with another publication, *Thesaurus for Graphic Materials: Topical Terms for Subject Access*, compiled by Elisabeth Betz Parker (LC, 1987)(and itself based on a 1980 work) to result in *Thesaurus for Graphic Materials. I: Subject Terms. II. Genre and Physical Characteristic Terms*, compiled and edited by the Prints and Photographs Division, Library of Congress (LC, 1995).

Moving Image Materials: Genre Terms, compiled by Martha M. Yee (LC, 1987) provides a standardized list of terms and cross-references for designating moving image material genres and forms.

The ALA Guidelines discussed above include a brief listing of genre headings. *Subject Access to Films and Videos*, by Sheila S. Intner and William E. Studwell, with the assistance of Simone E. Blake and David P. Miller (Soldier Creek Press, 1992) includes 70 pages of such headings selected from the *Library of Congress Subject Headings* and *Moving Image Materials*.

A leader in advocating increased subject access to materials is Sanford Berman from Hennepin County Library in Minnesota. For many years he has written and spoken about problems of subject headings and has suggested alternative headings, changes in terminology, and other improvements. The list of Hennepin County Library headings is available on microfiche.

For most of us, Library of Congress subject headings are what we must use. This list of terms includes many that may be used as genre headings. A complication arises when the same term is used for works about a concept and works that represent the concept itself.

The subject heading "Talking books" can be used for a work about talking books, a bibliography of talking books, or a bibliographic record for a talking book. In the third case, it is used as a genre heading, one that represents the form of the item rather than its content. The MARC field 655 may now be used to represent this use of the term. The other two cases above would use the term coded in field 650. It is then up to system designers to allow users to differentiate between these two concepts, that of *about* and that of *is*.

Many of the examples in the chapters of this book carry genre headings in addition to the standard subject headings. The examples in the video chapter use many genre headings, including

```
650  0   Comedy films.
650  0   Musical films.
650  0   Feature films.
650  0   Video recordings for the hearing impaired.
```

Genre may also be represented through a special subfield, ‡v for genre or form, when LC and OCLC implement this new subfield.

```
651  0   Oregon Trail ‡v Computer simulation.
```

Access to Characters

We may want to provide access to certain characters in a work, particularly those of importance, or those that appear in a series of works. As with all our cataloging, we need to supply access to those aspects of a work under which a patron might search.

For names of characters, we must also consider form of the name.

The Library of Congress has stated that all such entries are to be coded in field 650. Depending on one's local system, this may or may not be a problem. If the patron always uses a term search, Lord Peter Wimsey would be found whether coded as a person or a thing. From the LC authority file:

```
150  0   Wimsey, Peter, Lord (Fictitious character).
```

Another problem:

```
600 10   Keeshan, Robert.
```

with cross reference from

```
Captain Kangaroo
```

I would expect separate records with appropriate cross references for his works as a person and as a television character, though that may happen when a new person assumes the role of the Captain.

There has been some discussion at the national level about access for characters. I would like to see Kermit, the Frog, searchable in the same way persons may be found.

Access to Settings

We may provide access to the place in which a work it set and/or the time period involved. The film *The Sound of Music* is set in Austria just before World War II. Both of these aspects may be brought out by the subject heading:

```
651  0   Austria ‡x History ‡y 1918-1938.
```

Topical Access

Topical access is the standard use of subject headings to represent the content of a work — what it is about. These headings, coded in field 650, include very broad terms as well as specific headings. We are to use the most specific heading that represents the content of the work, or, if no heading quite fits, the two or three headings that together represent that content. In some cases, I also like to use a broader heading if I think a patron might not think of the specific approach. I also might want to use a heading to represent a part of a work, for example, when a film includes a section on a topic I know we have little else on.

For the film *Singin' in the Rain*:

```
650  0  Sound motion pictures ǂx History.
```

CLASSIFICATION

Library of Congress classification

In a discussion of the Library of Congress classification, Phyllis Richmond makes the following comments:

> … making and, to a lesser degree, assigning classification, as with any subject approach to knowledge, can be a highly subjective matter. Here, perhaps, more than in any other area of intellectual endeavor, one man's meat is another's poison. Librarians probably all agree that like materials should be shelved together, but they do not agree on what is like because they approach the subject with different backgrounds and viewpoints. For libraries, the important thing is less that the fields of knowledge should be distinguished precisely in some glorious, universally accepted, ideal, logical classification than that the material put into storage should be found again quickly (Phyllis A. Richmond. "General Advantages and Disadvantages of Using the Library of Congress Classification." In *The Use of the Library of Congress Classification*. Chicago, Ill.: American Library Association, 1968, p. 210).

We should keep her practical approach in mind; the important thing is "that the material put into storage should be found again quickly."

A classification number is chosen to reflect the general subject content of the item. This allows for browsing the shelves as well as for browsing an online shelflist.

LC classification numbers assigned by catalogers at LC are coded in USMARC field 050. Program for Cooperative Cataloging (PCC) members use field 050 with indicators 04 to indicate this LC call number is assigned as part of a core record. PCC members are trained to create core records that are considered to be almost as authoritative as LC records, so they are authorized to use field 050 for the LC class number. The rest of us OCLC participants use field 090 for LC call numbers that we assign.

Work numbers

After the classification number is assigned to a work, something must be added to that classification number to determine the item's position when shelved relative to other items bearing the same class number. A common method is to assign a work number (or book number) based on the main entry using the following directions (from *CSB* 3):

> Library of Congress call numbers consist, in general, of two principal elements: class number and book number, to which are added, as required, symbols designating a particular work.
>
> Library of Congress book numbers are composed of the initial letter of the main entry heading, followed by Arabic numerals representing the succeeding letters on the following basis:

> 1. After initial vowels:

for the second letter:	b	d	l,m	n	p	r	s,t	u-y
use number:	2	3	4	5	6	7	8	9

2. After the initial letter S:

for the second letter:	a	ch	e	h,i	m-p	t	u
use number:	2	3	4	5	6	7-8	9

3. After the initial letters Qu:

for the third letter:	a	e	i	o	r	y
use number:	3	4	5	6	7	9

   for names beginning Qa-Qt use 2-29

4. After other initial consonants

for the second letter:	a	e	i	o	r	u	y
use number:	3	4	5	6	7	8	9

5. When an additional number is preferred

for the third letter:	a-d	e-h	i-l	m	n-q	r-t	u-w	x-z
use number:	2	3	4	5	6	7	8	9

[end of tables]

Since the tables provide only a general framework for the assignment of numbers, the symbol for a particular name or work is constant only within a single class. Each entry must be added to the existing entries in the shelflist in such a way as to preserve alphabetic order in accordance with Library of Congress filing rules.

A problem can arise when working with a series all having the same main entry, or with title main entries that vary only in the last word or words, as in the following examples of a group of films:

The Metal turning lathe. Group 3, Basic operations. Part 1, Facing.
The Metal turning lathe. Group 3, Basic operations. Part 2, Straight outside diameter turning.
The Metal turning lathe. Group 3, Basic operations. Part 3, Straight inside turning or boring.
The Metal turning lathe. Group 3, Basic operations. Part 4, Simple taper turning with the lathe compound.

All these films would have the same classification number. A simple way to distinguish between them would be to construct work numbers as follows: .M4 for the first word in the main entry after "The", Metal; then add the group number and part number, resulting in unique work numbers: .M431 (or .M43 if one follows LC convention not to use numbers ending in "1"), .M432, .M433, .M434, etc. This series of numbers allows us to put the films in order on the shelf by group and part number, rather than arranging them alphabetically by the individual part title, an order that would not be as desirable.

For the following series all of which use the same classification number and which have no numeric designation, we could assign work numbers to produce the following alphabetical arrangement:

   .M43 Metalworking tools, adjustable, open-end, and socket wrenches
   .M44 Metalworking tools, files
   .M45 Metalworking tools, hacksaw
   .M46 Metalworking tools, pliers etc.

This description of LC classification numbers concerns those basic LC call numbers that contain a classification number from one of the LC schedules with the addition of one cutter number. There are many variations on this pattern however. There may be two cutter numbers, with the first representing a more specific aspect of the basic class number, and the second being the work number. There may, in the cases of maps and some music, be three cutter numbers. There may be a date or other information before the last cutter number, in which case both first and last cutter numbers are preceded by a period. One must check the LC schedules carefully when assigning a call number to see if a table must be used or if there are any other special instructions. If the resulting call number is not "standard" in appearance, one must also check the OCLC format document to determine how it is to be subfielded.

Subject cataloging, or subject analysis, includes both subject headings and classification. Neither of these processes is controlled or determined by the *Anglo-American Cataloguing Rules.* A library is free to choose whatever type of subject headings and/or classification it wants to use.

The following Library of Congress guidelines, from *Cataloging Service Bulletin 48,* are LC's own guidelines for subject headings and classification of films. They also include some MARC coding and tagging instructions.

Library of Congress Guidelines for Subject Cataloging of Visual Materials

For convenience, the words film and films are used throughout these guidelines to refer to any type of visual material, including motion pictures, filmstrips, video recordings, and slides.

1. *Target audience.* Films are assigned one of the following MARC codes for target audience:
   a   Age 0-5 (preschool through kindergarten)
   b   Age 6-8 (primary)
   c   Age 9-15 (intermediate through junior high)
   d   Age 16-19 (senior high)
   e   Adult
   f   Special audiences
   g   General

Films coded "a," "b," or "c" are treated as juvenile films. For classification purposes only, fiction films coded "d" are also treated as juvenile. The target audience of films coded "f" must be determined from the title, summary, or intended audience note (521 field). Films coded "e" or "g" are treated as adult films.

2. *Subject headings*
   a. *Topical films.* Since, for all practical purposes, it is impossible to browse a film collection, greater detail in subject cataloging treatment is required for films than is normally provided for books. In addition to the normal rules governing the assignment of subject headings, the below listed special rules are observed when assigning topical subject headings to non-fiction films:

   1. A subject entry is made for all important topics mentioned in the summary statement. If a specific topic is emphasized in order to illustrate a more general concept, subject headings are assigned for both the specific and the general topics. Form subdivisions are assigned only to the extent that such subdivisions are applicable both to print and audiovisual media. The form subdivision **—Pictorial works** is *not* used.

```
520      Describes the highlights of Colombia,
including the production of coffee.
651   0  Colombia ‡x Description and travel.
650   0  Coffee ‡z Colombia.

520      Surveys the industries of India, with special
emphasis on the steel industry.
651   0  India ‡x Industries.
650   0  Steel industry and trade ‡z India.
```

LC Guidelines for Subject Cataloging *(cont.)*

```
520      Documents the intellectual expansion in
medieval Germany, as illustrated by the Nuremberg
chronicle.
600 10   Schedel, Hartmann, ǂd 1440-1514. ǂt Liber
chronicarum.
651  0   Germany ǂx Intellectual life ǂx History.
```

2. When a topic is discussed in conjunction with a particular place, a subject entry is made, insofar as possible, under both the topic and place.

```
520      Describes the oases of the Sahara.
650  0   Oases ǂz Sahara.
651  0   Sahara ǂx Description and travel.
```

```
520      Interviews with medical personnel and
participants in a drug abuse treatment program in New
York City
650  0   Drug abuse ǂz New York (N.Y.).
651  0   New York (N.Y.) ǂx Social conditions.
```

3. When a film treats a particular person as illustrative of a profession or activity, a heading is assigned for both the person and the field of endeavor. Such films are not, as a general rule, treated as biographies.

```
520      A day in the life of prizefighter Muhammad
Ali as he trains for a championship bout.
600 10   Ali, Muhammad, ǂd 1942-
650  0   Boxing.
```

```
520      How modern dance exponent Martha Graham
functions as an artist and choreographer
600 10   Graham, Martha.
650  0   Modern dance.
650  0   Choreography.
```

4. *Commercials.* A heading is assigned for the generic name of the product being advertised. A heading is also assigned for the particular advertising medium, if it is identified.

```
520      Television commercial for Bayer aspirin.
650  0   Aspirin.
650  0   Television advertising.
```

b. *Fiction films.* The following headings are assigned, as appropriate, to individual fiction films:

1. Topical headings with the subdivision —**Drama** (or, in the case of juvenile fiction films, the subdivision —**Juvenile films**). Headings of this type are assigned to the same extent that such headings are assigned to individual dramas in book form (cf. *Subject Cataloging Manual: Subject Headings,* H 1780, p. 2, sec. 4).
2. Form headings that express either genre (e.g., **Comedy films, Western films**) or technique (e.g., **Silent films, Experimental films**).
3. The form heading **Feature films** or **Short films. Feature films** is assigned to fiction

LC Guidelines for Subject Cataloging *(cont.)*

films with a running time of 60 minutes or more. **Short films** is assigned to those with a running time of less than 60 minutes.

Note that headings (1) and/or (2) are assigned only as appropriate for the particular film being cataloged, but that heading (3) is required for *all* fiction films. When more than one of these headings are assigned to a particular film, they are assigned in the order listed above.

c. *Films for the hearing impaired.* Either **Films for the hearing impaired** or **Video recordings for the hearing impaired** is assigned to all films produced with captions or sign language for viewing by the hearing impaired.

3. *LC classification number*

a. *Specificity of class numbers.* Films are assigned the most specific class numbers available in the LC classification schedules, including Cutter numbers for topics, places, or persons, if they are printed in the schedule. Cutter numbers are not included for places or individuals if the caption in the schedule reads, for example, "By region or country, A-Z," or "Individual, A-Z" and printed Cutters are not present. Shelflisting subarrangements are not provided. New topical class numbers are not established for films. If a number for the specific topic of the film has not been established, the next broader class number is assigned.

b. *Adult belles lettres.* To critical films about an individual literary author, the appropriate literary author number is assigned from the relevant subclass of the P schedule. Literary author numbers are also assigned to films of an author reading his or her work. If a specific Cutter number has not yet been established for the author, a class number is assigned with an incomplete Cutter, e.g., [PR6052.B].

Adult fiction films. The following guidelines are observed in classifying individual adult fiction films (i.e., those coded "e" or "g," as well as those that are coded "f" and that are determined to have an adult targeted audience):

1. All individual adult fiction films, except for comedy, experimental, and animated films, are classed in PN1997, provided that their primary purpose is entertainment. Films that are dramatizations of literary works are classed in literary author numbers only if their intention is clearly to teach about or criticize the author or the author's style or to provide opportunity for discussion, rather than simply to entertain. Certain series, such as *The Novel* or *The Short Story*, fall into this category.

2. Comedy films are classed in PN1995.9.C55; experimental films in PN1995.9.E96. These numbers are assigned to a film only when it is explicitly described as a comedy or experimental film in the 520 field.

3. Adult animated fiction films are classed in PN1997.5.

c. *Foreign language teaching films.* Films intended for use in teaching foreign languages are classed in the P schedules with the language being taught, rather than in the class for the special topic of the film. As a corollary, the heading **[...] language—Films for [...] speakers** is assigned as the first heading, and any special topics are brought out by assigning additional headings.

4. *Juvenile films.* Films are assigned a MARC code for targeted audience as described above. Films with the codes "a," "b," or "c" are treated as juvenile films. Films coded "f" are also treated as juvenile if it is clear from the title, summary, or intended audience note (521 field) that the film is juvenile in nature. For classification purposes only, fiction films coded "d" are treated as juvenile.

LC Guidelines for Subject Cataloging *(cont.)*

Films coded "e" or "g" are not treated as juvenile. The guidelines below are observed when treating a film as juvenile.

a. *Subject headings.* The free-floating form subdivision **—Juvenile films** is used after all topical subject headings assigned. Children's literature catalogers assign bracketed juvenile headings as required

b. *Classification.* Topical juvenile films are classed with the appropriate topic in classes A-Z, using the number for juvenile works if one is provided under the topic. All juvenile fiction films (i.e., those coded "a," "b," "c," or "d"), whether animated or live action, are classed in PZ5-90.

c. *Special categories of juvenile films*

1. *Folk tales.* When possible, a subject entry is made under the name of an individual hero or figure around whom a series of tales or legends have been told, e.g., **Bunyan, Paul (Legendary character)—Juvenile films.** An entry is also made for the form, even in the case of individual tales, e.g., **Tales—United States—Juvenile films** and **Folklore—United States—Juvenile films**, and for the category, i.e., **Children's films.**

2. *Juvenile reading films.* A subject entry is made to bring out the topic, if the film is topical, and to bring out the form. The heading **Reading (Primary, [Elementary etc.])—Juvenile films** is generally used to bring out the form. The heading **Readers** or **Primers** is *not* used. Such films are classed in the numbers for readers in the subclasses of the P schedule.

```
520     A reading readiness film for primary grades
on the subject of rain.
650  0  Rain and rainfall ǂx Juvenile films.
650  0  Reading readiness ǂx Juvenile films.
650  0  Reading (Primary) ǂx Juvenile films.
050     PE1127.
```

[end of LC guidelines]

Video examples in this book have been assigned subject headings, including genre headings, as outlined in the above guidelines. For LC classification, I have used the breakdown at PN1995.9 rather than the more general PN1997 in which films are alphabetized by title. The above policy was that used at LC for their cataloging of films from data sheets, none of which go into their collections. A general classification number serves as guidance for eventual users of LC catalog copy. In actual use, the subject/genre breakdown at PN1995.9 has worked well at the library for which I catalog. An online browse through the shelflist shows films of the same type classed together.

All examples in this book include LC subject headings, and LC classification numbers are given with each example.

"IN" ANALYTICS AND OTHER METHODS OF ANALYSIS

One of the many problems in cataloging audiovisual materials is deciding what to do when a boxful of material might be cataloged as a unit, but one or more parts of it seem important enough to be cataloged separately.

Chapter 13 of AACR 2 includes rules for cataloging such material. It describes analytics of monographic series and multipart monographs, treatment in the note area of such material, analytical added entries, "In" analytics, and multilevel description. The Library of Congress is not using multilevel description; however, we are free to use any of the methods described in this chapter.

In chapter 4 of this book, one example shows the cataloging of a map in a book as an "In" analytic.

If we have a large package of material we wish to catalog as a kit, and that package contains a motion picture that was designed as part of the kit but could be used separately, we can catalog the kit as a whole, and, in addition, make a separate bibliographic record for the motion picture as an "In" analytic.

Sets of material

Frequently we receive boxes of material containing several titles that could be cataloged individually or could be cataloged as a unit. Either treatment is correct. These items can be treated as one unit, or the individual titles can be cataloged separately as a monographic series. The decision on treatment is a matter of cataloger's judgment and library policy. See the example of presidential speeches in chapter 5 of this book.

If the separate titles would have similar, or identical, summaries and would all have the same subject headings and the same added entries, the whole package should be cataloged as a unit, with added entries made for each title. If, however, each title should have its own distinctly different summary, and each would have different subject headings, each should be cataloged with its own bibliographic record.

A set that could be cataloged as a whole with a contents note taking the place of a summary, is a set of filmstrips, part of a series on elementary mathematics, called *Addition and Subtraction of Fractional Numbers With Any Denominator*. Individual titles are:

> Review and Extension,
> Union of Two Sets and Addition of Two Numbers,
> Separation of Sets and Subtraction of Numbers,
> Fractional Numbers and Some Basic Properties,
> Addition and Subtraction of Fractional Numbers with the Same Denominator.

A set of filmstrips that clearly needs individual cataloging is the set titled *Continental Europe in Revolution (1789-1890)*. In this set, the individual summaries would provide information important to the user, and each title would have different subject headings. Individual titles are:

> Prelude to the French Revolution (1789),
> The French Revolution (1789-1795),
> Napoleon and the Empire (1795-1815),
> The Metternich Era (1815-1848),
> The Revolution in Ideas (1840-1860),
> The Unification of Italy (1848-1870),
> The Rise of Germany (1860-1890).

These filmstrips would have very different summaries and many different subject headings. They should be treated as a monographic series. It is not necessary to repackage items when cataloging them separately. The set comes in a sturdy box and can be left in the box. The series area on the bibliographic record for each separate title will carry the information about the title of the set, and the series added entry will direct the user to the set, as will the individual bibliographic records. The titles can be cataloged individually, but the set can remain packaged as a unit, or one can choose to repackage these individually.

The arithmetic example would get the same classification number whether the titles would be cataloged individually or as a set. The European history item would not. If one wanted these items each to be shelved with the appropriate number for the country and time period, one could choose to repackage them individually as they were cataloged. They could be classified individually at that time.

SOME ADVICE

Here I'd like to offer some advice to catalogers. The rules and their changes may be bewildering, and you may have difficulty in deciding what is *right*. While we want our cataloging to be done correctly, the more important word of those two (*done* and *correctly*) is, I believe, "done." We catalog materials to provide a service to our users, to describe the material so they know enough about it to decide if it is what they might want to use, and to provide access by enough words, terms, phrases, and names so the user can find it. But we must complete the cataloging before that description or access or the item itself is available to the user.

Don't worry about your cataloging. Do it step by step, beginning with the information on the item designated as the chief source of information. Decide on the title proper. Then decide on the GMD. Then decide if there is other title information. And so on. Concentrate on one little decision at a time, and, if one presents a problem, skip over it and go on to the next. Look up rules and rule interpretations as needed. Make a decision, then go on to the next. Once a decision is made, don't go back to it. Get the cataloging *done*.

Another secret. The fewer bits of information there are on an item to be cataloged, the easier the cataloging is. You might have to supply a few bits of information to complete the cataloging, but you don't have to deal with multiple forms of title, excess publishers and distributors, or other confusing words strewn over a container. Try it.

CARD FORMAT

Card format as shown below is used in some examples. There is no standard format for layout of catalog cards; those using cards may choose whatever format they wish.

```
Main entry (personal, corporate, conference, or uniform
title)
    Title proper [GMD] : other title information / statement
of responsibility. -- Edition information. -- Place of
publication : Name of publisher, distributor, etc., Date of
publication.
    Extent of item : color or other information ; size. --
(Series ; series number)

    Notes ..............................and continuation
of notes.
    Each note begins a separate paragraph.

    1. Subject heading.  I. Added entry.
```

```
Title main entry with title proper [GMD] : other title
    information / statement of responsibility. -- Edition
    information. -- Place of publication : Name of publisher,
    distributor, etc., Date of publication.
        Extent of item : color or other information ; size. --
    (Series ; series number)

        Notes .........................................and
continuation of notes.
        Each note beings a separate paragraph.

        1. Subject heading.  I. Added entry.
```

The Library of Congress ceased printing cards in May 1997. They had printed cards for their use, and ours, beginning in 1901. Because some libraries still have card catalogs, and many libraries have card shelflists, several examples in this book show the bibliographic record in card format as well as in MARC format.

PROCESSING

Processing special materials requires ingenuity and common sense. Because physical packaging and presentation varies so much from item to item even within the same format of material it is not possible to set up rigid instructions for handling these materials. The Dreissen-Smyth book mentioned in chapter 1 provides guidance for processing.

I have developed (and continue to refine) a set of 14 different processing slips for the kinds of material I catalog. I have attempted to include all the common decisions I must make on each type of material. Some of these slips are shown in the following illustration.

Processing slips

These are photoreduced examples of some of the processing slips I use every day. Each is essentially a checklist of procedures that are too extensive and varied to remember.

BIG BOOKS   XMNB   ERC
                                 Big
    Keep all paperwork, labels, Books
etc., with item till done
    Acquisitions is to tape
barcode to book, not apply it

OCLC/BIB ID_____Date updated_____
Number of labels to be made____

BARCODING Circle one **LIR**   **CAI**
    Location   ERC
    Circ class   06
    Shelflist   XMNB
    Note (contents in order of importance)

PROCESSING in big plastic hanging bag
    Title label as highlighted on printout
with call number label on upper left
corner of bag -- date due slip taped to
inside, upper left, of bag
    Laminate book covers -- heavy plastic
with Kapco easy hold reinforcements
at top, bottom of spine; then barcode
    On book: call number label, contents
label, not-in-book drop label
__Make pocket for guide, booklets

    Special directions:

FINAL CHECK -- SEND TO ERC   10/96

SOUND RECORDINGS, MUSIC

MNMT ____   **MNMP** CCD   **MNMT** CD
                       ____   ____

CATALOGING
    a.e. for each composer, title, etc.

OCLC/BIB ID_____Date updated_____

BARCODING   Circle one   **LIR**   **CAI**

              Records   CCD   CD

    Location   MUS   MUS   MUS
    Circ class 23   09   09
    Shelflist MNMT   MNMP   MNMT
    Note (contents in order of importance)

PROCESSING
    No labels on CDs; write with sharpie
pen on inner ring
    No date due slip
    Make ___ call number labels for
container (use slim label for spine),
booklet(s)

FINAL CHECK -- SEND TO MUSIC   10/96

NEW ERC COMPUTER SOFTWARE

XMNJ if accompanies K-12 text
XMNI if designed to be used by K-12
MNMX if for general use; circulates
    Keep item, labels, paperwork together
    throughout this process

CATALOGING
Search OCLC, print any record found,
    report duplicates to OCLC
Edit copy, esp. 245/246/740, 300, 538,
    notes, 650s
Check/edit or create call number
If serial, fill out serial worksheet
If item to be shelved as parts, call
    number slip on each; name of part as
    last line of call number
OCLC
Edit copy as marked, 949 all barcodes
OCLC/BIB ID_____ Date updated_____
Make ___ labels (1 for each separate
    item, disk, backup, container)

    XMNJ   **XMNI**   **MNMX**
    ERC   ERC   ERC
    K-12   K-12   Computer
    Texts   Software   Software

If serial, check out to Acquisitions and
    send all to Kris with serial worksheet;
    barcode before_____

BARCODING Circle one   **LIR**   **CAI**
    Location   ERC   ERC   ERC
    Circ class   25   08   29
    Shelflist   XMNJ   XMNI   MNMX
    Holdings *name of part as on label
    Note (contents in order of importance)
PROCESSING after barcoding in Cat/ACQ
Copy K-12 magnetic disks and put call
    no. label on original, store in ERC
Circulating magnetic disk: call number
    label, title label if needed
CD-ROM: no labels on discs; new case?
If no container, use brown binder
If flimsy container with useful info.,
    use white 3-ring binder with outside
    sleeves; cut up box, insert in sleeves
Remove sheet inside back of CD-ROM case
    if useful, glue inside binder cover
Labels on container: Contents, type-of-
    computer, warning/virus/desensitize,
    (CD-ROM: warning label only), call
    number, govpub prop. stamp, date due
    slip, title label as highlighted on
    printout
Tattletape if CD-ROM
FINAL CHECK -- Send to ERC
    ERC disk   8/97

Chapter 3

THE MARC FORMAT AND CATALOGING OF SPECIAL MATERIALS

MARC (Machine-Readable Cataloging) is a communication format developed to carry bibliographic information. The version of MARC used in this country is called USMARC. The bibliographic information carried by the USMARC record is described according to the Anglo-American Cataloguing Rules. The rules control the content of the bibliographic record while the USMARC format controls the codes and tags that identify parts of that content.

The USMARC format is maintained and developed by the Library of Congress working with MARBI, an American Library Association committee made up of representatives from several ALA units. This group responds to changes in the cataloging rules as well as to requests for changes to the format based on needs of various user groups. Changes are considered twice a year at MARBI meetings during ALA conferences. Revisions to existing MARC elements and newly-adopted elements are published by the Library of Congress and implemented by OCLC and other utilities and local systems.

The version of USMARC used in this book is the version used by members of OCLC. The OCLC document explaining the use of OCLC-MARC is *Bibliographic Formats and Standards*, second edition (OCLC, 1996). This massive document explains and illustrates the use of every field and code and tag for every type of material. I will not repeat any of that material in this book; the user is referred to the document itself. In addition to this basic document, there are also lists of codes for languages, country of publication, geographic areas, and source and relator codes.

Every example in this book is illustrated by a complete OCLC-MARC record, using all the applicable codes and tags.

Each area of a bibliographic record is contained in a separate field in the USMARC format. A bibliographic record contains all the fields for a cataloged item. Fields may be fixed or variable. **Fixed fields** are composed of separate pieces of coded information about the item, with each of the fixed fields always a standard pre-determined length. **Variable fields** vary in length and contain an area of the bibliographic record or coded information about the bibliographic record or about some part of it.

Each variable field is identified by a **tag**, a three-digit code. This may be followed by 1 or 2 **indicators**. Variable fields may be divided into smaller units called **subfields**. Subfields are preceded by subfield codes. Each subfield code is preceded by the symbol " ǂ" called a **delimiter**.

Variable fields are grouped broadly as follows:

1XX   Main entry headings

2XX   Title and Statement of Responsibility Area
        Edition Area
        Material (Or Type of Publication)
        Specific Details Area
        Publication, Distribution, Etc., Area

3XX   Physical Description Area
        and related information

4XX   Series Area

5XX   Notes Area

    6XX   Subject Headings

    7XX   Added Entries
           Linking Entries

    8XX   Series Added Entries
           Electronic Location and Access

    9XX   Local-use fields

    0XX   Bibliographic control numbers
           Classification numbers
           Miscellaneous variable and fixed fields

Some codes, tags, fields, etc., are mandatory, while others are optional, or mandatory if applicable.

Format Integration

The original MARC format, developed at the Library of Congress during 1966-1968, applied only to books. A serials format was developed soon after this and was used as the basis for the CONSER project. LC also developed formats for films, music, and maps during the mid-1970s. The film format was gradually expanded for other types of two-dimensional projected material (filmstrips, later slides and transparencies, and video), then two-dimensional non-projected audiovisual materials (posters, charts, etc.) and again for three-dimensional materials. During 1976-1977, OCLC began use of some of these other formats, and eventually offered catalogers the choice of eight different MARC formats:

    Archives and Manuscript Control
    Audiovisual Media
    Books
    Computer Files
    Maps
    Scores
    Serials
    Sound Recordings

As some of us cataloged materials using most or all of these formats, we saw inconsistencies in treatment of similar information across the formats. Certain information would be coded a certain way in one format, but a different way in other formats. And a print serial was no problem, but a serial in any other type of material — whether a serial map, serial video, serial filmstrip, serial motion picture, etc. — could be coded as a map, video, filmstrip, motion picture, etc., or as a serial, but the bibliographic information didn't fit neatly either way. So the Library of Congress and MARBI began talk of integrating all the formats into one uniform "integrated format."

The process of developing an integrated format began in the late 1980s and was developed and implemented in several phases. The first (and easiest) changes were implemented at OCLC in September 1991, with additional changes in July 1994. The remaining changes were implemented by OCLC in two phases, in January 1995 and March 1996. Many of the changes were simple, such as declaring certain values obsolete, or reconciling differing practices concerning indicators. Others, at least for audiovisual catalogers, were major changes in our cataloging practice. The change that most affected audiovisual catalogers was the adoption of field 246 for varying form of the title being cataloged while retaining field 740 for titles pertaining to a part of the whole item. The other major change for us was the creation of field 006 for an item that belonged to more than one type — for example, a serial computer file. A minor change was made to coding for dates.

Format integration allows the use of all MARC codes, tags, etc., for cataloging of any title.

Dates

Some changes have been made to the codes for type of date and for the coding of dates.

A probable date is now coded as "s" instead of "q" in the fixed field "DtSt:" with "u" for the missing digit(s) in the date instead of a range of dates in the fixed field "Dates:"

```
DtSt: s
Dates: 198u,
260 ǂc [198-?].
```

For an item with both publication date and copyright date, we now use code "t" instead of "c" in "DtSt:"

Access to Title Through Fields 246 and/or 740

Throughout the history of the MARC format, audiovisual catalogers coded title added entries as field 740 while serial catalogers provided access to varying forms of title with field 246. Some MARBI discussions during the format integration process became quite heated as catalogers argued for one type of access or the other. Finally a compromise solution was accepted in which both fields are available for use.

Field 246 is used for varying forms of the title of the **entire** work. An added entry for the title of a **part** of the work (something from the contents note, title of an accompanying guide, etc.) is coded in field 740.

MARC Field 246 Varying Form of Title

First indicator (these control card printing and may control online catalog display)

0 Note, no title added entry
1 Note with title added entry
2 No note, no title added entry
3 No note, but title added entry

Second indicator (designed for serials; some print constants not relevant to certain types of material)

blank None of the other indicators fit, no display constant used, may begin with subfield "i" for display text

```
245 00   Trudy's time & place house
246 3    Trudy's time and place house

245 00   Hollywood Hounds story pack
246 1    ǂi Title on disk label: ǂa Story pack for Storybook
weaver deluxe, featuring Hollywood Hounds
```

0 Portion of field 245, no display constant

```
245 00   Trudy's time & place house
246 30   Time & place house
246 30   Time and place house

245 00   SimCity 2000 ǂh [computer file] : ǂb the ultimate city
simulator
246 30   Ultimate city simulator

245 04   The story of fashion. ǂn Program 1, ǂp Remembrance of
things past ǂh [videorecording]
246 30   Remembrance of things past
```

1   Parallel title,
no display constant

2   Distinctive title,
Constant: Distinctive title:

3   Other title,
Constant: Other title:

4   Cover title,
Constant: Cover title:

5   Added title page title,
Constant: Added title page title:

6   Caption title,
Constant: Caption title:

7   Running title,
Constant: Running title:

8   Spine title,
Constant: Spine title:

MARC Field 740 Added Entry—Uncontrolled Related/Analytical Title

Field 740 is used for an added entry for a part of the total package: titles found in contents note, titles from field 245 for a collection without a collective title, titles of items found in a package, titles of guides or manuals, etc.

The first indicator is the standard filing indicator (0-9), the second indicator is blank if the added entry is not for an analytic, "2" if for an analytic entry.

```
245 00   Science sleuths. ‡n Volume 2 ‡h [computer file]
505 0    Mystery of the biogene picnic — Mystery of the traffic
accident.
740 02   Mystery of the biogene picnic.
740 02   Mystery of the traffic accident.
```

Fixed Fields 006, 007, and 008

MARC field 006 is new with format integration, and is explained below. MARC field 008 includes values that, in OCLC, are contained in the "fixed fields" that display in the top several rows of the bibliographic record. MARC field 007 (described later) contains additional physical characteristics for the material being cataloged; characteristics that could not be included in field 008. A field 007 for computer files was added during format integration.

MARC Field 006 Fixed-Length Data Elements—Additional Material Characteristics

While, under format integration, one may use any MARC code/tag/field for any bibliographic record being created, one must still choose one value for "Type:" (Type of record). This code is based on the physical form of the material being cataloged, though there is discussion about changing this to reflect content rather than physical form.

An additional type code is available through use of field 006.

If the item is also a serial, field 006 for serial characteristics is added. If the item might be thought of as some type other than that chosen (for example, a book with a computer disk that might be thought of as a computer disk with a book) an 006 for that other type is also used.

This allows online catalogs to be searched by, or searches qualified for, more than one type code per bibliographic record.

Eight different type codes are allowed through use of field 006: Books, serials, visual materials, mixed materials, maps, scores, sound recordings, and computer files. Given the correct prompt, the OCLC system responds by displaying an alternate "fixed-field" that is filled in and sent. The system then displays in the bibliographic record a line for field 006, in brackets, with values spaced appropriately.

MARC Field 007 Physical Description Fixed Field

There seems to be some confusion among catalogers about fields 006, 007, and 008.

Field 008 appears to OCLC users as the "fixed field" with each type of record having its own set of values displayed on the workform.

Field 006 is explained above as the fixed fields for an alternative type of record.

Field 007 contains additional coded information about the physical description of the material being cataloged. A certain amount of information about the item is coded in field 008 (the fixed field); additional information is coded in field 007.

There may be multiple 007 fields in a MARC record for a bibliographic record of an title with several physical parts. A filmstrip with accompanying sound needs only one field 007, as the coding of the accompanying sound is handled in that 007. But a package containing a captioned filmstrip and a separate sound recording of a lecture, designed not to accompany the filmstrip but to supplement it, would need field 007 for the filmstrip and a separate field 007 for the sound recording.

Nine 007 fields are available in OCLC: motion pictures, videorecordings, projected graphics, nonprojected graphics, sound recordings, maps, globes, computer files, and microforms.

A chart accompanying this book lists the current 007 fields and their subfield codes. The most common values are highlighted for each 007.

MARC Fields 020, 024, 028, 037 for Numbers

MARC field 020 is used to record an ISBN. This is recorded in the same way for all types of materials. No hyphens are used.

    020   0965145603

Binding information or qualifications related to the ISBN may be added in subfield ǂa in parentheses following the number. You may include the price in subfield ǂc if you have that information.

MARC field 024 is used when a barcode is printed on an item by the manufacturer. There is an error in the OCLC documentation that will be corrected; the field contains all the numbers that appear under the barcode. There may be 10, 11, or 12 numbers. The first indicator "1" is used for a barcode or UPC (Universal Product Code). No hyphens are used in recording this number.

    024 1   605961104158

The OCLC documentation explains what each part of the UPC represents.

MARC field 028 was originally used for the record manufacturer's number, or issue number. This is the number that appears prominently on the label, the container (usually front, back, and spine), and on the insert.

The 028 was expanded to include other types of record numbers, plate numbers appearing on scores, and manufacturer's numbers for videorecordings.

The first indicator is for the type of number. The second indicator is designed to control printing and added entries.

The record number uses first indicator "0" with a second indicator of "2" to indicate a note is wanted, but an added entry is not needed. The number is recorded just as it appears including spacing, capitalization, and punctuation. There may be a series of numbers appearing on a set of records. The OCLC documentation explains how to handle each type of numbering one might encounter. Subfield ǂb contains the label name, just as it appears in field 260.

    028 02   MD+GL 3211--MD+GL 3212 ǂb Musikproduktion Dabringhaus und
    Grimm

Field 028 for videorecordings uses a first indicator "4" with a second indicator of "0" to say no note or added entry is needed. The number to be recorded is the manufacturer's number that may be on the spine or lower back of the container and/or label of the videocassette or videodisc. Subfield ǂb contains the name of the distributor as stated in field 260.

    028 40   909 ǂb Walt Disney Home Video

MARC field 037 may be used to record a manufacturer's number for material other than sound recordings or videorecordings. It has no indicators. Subfield ǂb is for the name of the distributor. Other subfields contain information on terms of availability, form of issue, additional format characteristics, and notes. I would use this field only if I had a prominent number on the item that did not fit anywhere else. We have quoted numbers in our bibliographic records that we could not record anywhere else, but included them in quoted notes because they looked important. This is the field in which they may now be recorded.

    037   No. 789 ǂb Ideal School Supply Co.

NOTES

There are 50 fields in 5XX available for notes. There are 23 rules in AACR 2 for notes. In chapter 2 of this book are listed the 23 rule numbers with some explanation of the use of each rule and the MARC field(s) used for the rule. As pointed out in that chapter, notes are to be used in the bibliographic record in the order of the rules, though some local systems rearrange them, and CONSER participants are directed to enter notes in order by MARC field rather than by rule number

Ed Glazier (RLG), in an Autocat message dated 15 July 1997, summarizes the history of rules for notes and reminds us that notes may also be generated from other fields in USMARC, including the 246, 307, 310, 321, 351, 362, 76x-78x, and fixed fields such as frequency and regularity.

Here I will list the 5XX note fields together with the applicable rule numbers. Some note fields have been made obsolete so do not appear on this list.

For detailed explanations and examples of each note, see the OCLC documentation. Remember, even if a note is only found in one chapter in *AACR2*, the MARC field can be used in any bibliographic record.

MARC 5xx Notes

    310   Frequency Note (AACR 2 12.7B1)
    500   General Note (any note that doesn't fit elsewhere)
    501   "With" Note (1.7B21)
    502   Dissertation Note (.7B13)
    504   Bibliography, Etc. Note (.7B18)
    505   Formatted Contents Note (.7B18)
    506   Restrictions on Access Note (.7B20)
    507   Scale Note for Graphic Material (pre-AACR 2 3.3)
    508   Creation/Production Credits Note (1.7B6)
    510   Citation/References Note (.7B15)
    511   Participant or Performer Note (.7B6)
    513   Type of Report and Period Covered Note (.7B7)
    514   Data Quality Note (.7B7)
    515   Numbering Peculiarities Note (12.7B8)
    516   Type of Computer File or Data Note (9.7B1a)
    518   Date/Time and Place of an Event Note (1.7B7)
    520   Summary, Etc. Note (.7B17)
    521   Target Audience Note (.7B14)
    522   Geographic Coverage Note (.7B7)
    524   Preferred Citation of Described Materials Note (.7B15)

525   Supplement Note (.7B11)
530   Additional Physical Form Available Note (.7B16)
533   Reproduction Note (AACR 2 Chapter 11, LCRI in CSB 58)
534   Original Version Note (.7B22)
535   Location of Originals/Duplicates Note (.7B16)
536   Funding Information Note (.7B6)
538   System Details Note (9.7B1b, B1c, 1.7B10)
539   Fixed-Length Data Elements of Reproduction Note (.7B9)
540   Terms Governing Use and Reproduction Note (.7B20)
541   Immediate Source of Acquisition Note (.7B7)
544   Location of Associated Archival Materials Note (.7B11)
545   Biographical or Historical Note (.7B7)
546   Language Note (.7B2)
547   Former Title Complexity Note (.7B4)
550   Issuing Body Note (.7B6)
551   Entity and Attribute Information Note (.7B10)
555   Cumulative Index/Finding Aids Note (12.7B17)
556   Information About Documentation Note (.7B11)
561   Provenance Note (.7B7)
562   Copy and Version Identification Note (12.7B20)
565   Case File Characteristics Note (.7B8)
567   Methodology Note (.7B7)
580   Linking Entry Complexity Note (.7B7)
581   Publications About Described Materials Note (.7B15)
583   Action Note (.7B20)
584   Accumulation and Frequency of Use Note (.7B10)
585   Exhibitions Note (.7B15)
586   Awards Note (.7B15)
590   Local Note (.7B20)
599   Differentiable Local Note (.7B20)

EDIT AN EXISTING RECORD OR CREATE A NEW RECORD?

One often finds a record that looks, at first glance, like it fits the item in hand. On closer examination it may not quite fit. One must then decide whether to use the record, editing it as needed, or to create a new record. OCLC has set up some guidelines for this decision that are listed in chapter 4 of *Bibliographic Formats and Standards*.

The first directive is:

If in doubt, use an existing record.

If you need something done to a record to reflect local or nonstandard practice, edit an existing record. If no record exists in the database, create a record that is standard, then edit it to reflect your local needs and update or produce for your online catalog.

> **Edit** an existing record to:
>   reflect new cataloging rules,
>   reflect different cataloger's judgement, (record is for a kit; you think it isn't, but have the
>   same items),
>   include additional information,
>   correct errors,
>   add a classification number,
>   reflect presence or absence or change in accompanying material, or
>   reflect local practices or cataloging adaptations,

Create a **new** record if:
> the physical form is different, (film vs. video; VHS vs. videodisc, CD-ROM vs. paper, etc.),
> it is a different edition, (regular video vs. 25th anniversary video; student edition vs. teacher edition; Midwest edition vs. Eastern edition)
> manufacturer's number is different,
> language is different, (Spanish vs. English; with and without closed captioning, etc.),
> time is significantly different, when the difference reflects something added or edited,
> publisher is different, (but not when several publishers/distributors named and one in the bibliographic record matches item in hand), or
> accompanying material is in a different format. (3 1/2 computer disk vs. 4 3/4 in. computer optical disc.)

Multipart items may be cataloged as individual items or as a whole item; bibliographic records for both may coexist in the OCLC database.

LOCAL SYSTEMS
AND ADAPTING YOUR CATALOGING TO THEIR NEEDS

Before you do any cataloging online or through your utility, you must know, in great detail, exactly how your local system works. You may have to adapt your cataloging to fit the idiosyncracies of your local system. You need to know exactly which fields your local system searches and how the system searches. What fields does it do term searches on? Are searches based on entire words, or on truncated terms, or both? If you have good term searching, you may not need to supply every important term through a subject heading.

Does your system limit you to one barcode (holding) per bibliographic record and/or one bibliographic record to one barcode? Or can it handle multiple holdings attached to one bibliographic record, as needed for individually barcoded slides attached to one bib record, and, of course, serial holdings? And can it handle multiple bibliographic records attached to one barcode, as needed for a box of individually cataloged filmstrips with one barcode on the box? Can it handle analytic entries as needed for the CD-ROM serial *Ethnic Newswatch* that contains (as of summer 1997) about 180 separate serials, each with an analytical bibliographic record?

Does the patron-display show clearly the location of the item, so the patron can go from the online record to the item itself? Or do you need to supply additional information so the patron knows that a particular item is not in the CD-ROM cabinet but loaded on a certain workstation?

Are there certain collections in your library that need more detail in their cataloging? Do you have a local history collection that needs special treatment including detailed notes, local subject headings, and geographic codes and time period codes?

While the cataloging rules are international standards, and the USMARC format is becoming an international standard, subject access and classification are local decisions. Online catalog displays are governed by the vendor rather than by any standards. Online catalog capabilities are also controlled by the vendor. We catalog according to certain standards, but the display of the bibliographic record we create, and the indexing and search capabilities of the total USMARC record, are controlled by the vendor. We have codes and tags for many aspects of an item, but not all vendors make use of everything we create and input through our cataloging.

When patrons or staff members want access to certain types of information, catalogers should be able to work with systems people and vendors to point out where the information is coded in the bibliographic record, and how bits of coded information might be combined to meet the needs of the patrons.

OCLC USER GROUPS

Catalogers of special materials have advocates in the OCLC user groups that have been established. These groups may have national and/or regional meetings with workshops and may have newsletters and/or other publications of use to catalogers of those special materials. A complete directory of OCLC user groups and advisory committees may be found on the World Wide Web at http://www.oclc.org/oclc/man/adcomm/toc.htm.

The following user groups and their contact names and addresses are valid as of summer 1997.

Online Audiovisual Catalogers (OLAC)
Sue Neumeister
Head, Bibliographic Control
Central Technical Services
Lockwood Library
University at Buffalo
Buffalo, NY 14260-2200
neumeist@ubvm.cc.buffalo.edu

Music OCLC Users Group (MOUG)
Karen Little
University of Louisville
School of Music — Music Library
Louisville KY 40292
http://www.music.indiana.edu/tech_s/moug/index.htm

Health Science OCLC User Group (HSOCLCUG)
Carole Francq Gall
Indiana University School of Medicine
Ruth Lilly Medical Library
975 W. Walnut St.
Indianapolis IN 46202-5121
http://www.unc.edu/~btysingr/hsoclcug/hsoclcug.htm

INTERNET ACCESS AND LISTS

Internet access is becoming increasingly important for catalogers. The previous section included Internet addresses for each of the OCLC user groups. An increasing amount of important information is available through (sometimes only through) the Internet. Recent examples:

Draft Document of the Task Force on the Cataloging of Works Intended for Performance for Discussion by CC:DA and the Cataloging Community. Martha Yee, chair
http://darkwing.uoregon.edu/~mrwatson/ccdapage/perftfrp.html

Joint Steering Committee for Revision of Anglo-American Cataloguing Rules. International Conference on the Principles and Future Development of AACR
http://www.nlc-bnc.ca/jsc/index.htm

OCLC user groups and advisory committees directory
http://www.oclc.org/oclc/man/adcomm/toc.htm

Online lists for catalogers are very useful. When I began cataloging audiovisual material, I didn't even know anyone else who worked with this kind of material. I'd never met or talked with anyone cataloging these materials, and there were no rules to go by for most of them. By going to American Library Association meetings and meeting Library of Congress people and visiting the Library of Congress, I developed contacts whom I could ask about cataloging problems. But this took years (and money) and wasn't very efficient. When Minnesota libraries joined OCLC in 1976, there were state-wide training sessions on cataloging as well as coding and tagging in the MARC format for OCLC. For many catalogers, this was their first opportunity ever to go to a professional meeting and "to get out of the back room" as one of them told me. These meetings provided an opportunity for each of us to meet colleagues and find others with the same concerns and problems. This was one of the unanticipated benefits of automation and joining OCLC — the contacts that were made, as well as the training that resulted in a statewide network of catalogers, all using the same rules and the same approach to cataloging.

Now we have access to the Internet; some of us have faster and better access than others, but that is always the way with technology and equipment. The online discussion lists that are available to catalogers allow us to ask colleagues from all over the world about problems of cataloging, processing, preservation, classifying, weeding, software, hardware, and anything else that we need information on. I monitor several such lists, and have benefited from this access.

Some of the lists I use:

Autocat
  listserv@listserv.acsu.buffalo.edu
  several thousand catalogers worldwide

MLA-L
  listserv@listserv.indiana.edu
  Music Library Association list

emedia
  majordomo@majordomo.elon.edu
  primarily concerns about electronic media

InterCat
  INTERCAT@OCLC.ORG
  cataloging Internet resources

List or Listserv?

There is some confusion about terminology when discussing lists. Autocat is a discussion list, or an online discussion list or electronic list, or just a list. The program used for administering the list is a listserv. A listserv may run dozens or thousands of lists depending upon the capacity of the host site. I think of the listserv as "serving the list."

Chapter 4

CARTOGRAPHIC MATERIALS

AACR 2 Chapter 3

This chapter covers cartographic materials of all kinds. For items that have cartographic content, but whose physical form would be covered by another chapter (for example, map puzzles), rules for both relevant chapters are used together. For more detailed information, users are referred to: *Cartographic Materials: A Manual of Interpretation for AACR 2,* prepared by the Anglo-American Cataloguing Committee for Cartographic Material, Hugo L. P. Stibbe, general editor (Chicago, Ill. : American Library Association, 1982) (new edition being prepared). This AACCM manual is out of date in some respects, but still contains much helpful information. Another publication that may be helpful is *Map Cataloging Manual,* prepared by Geography and Map Division, Library of Congress (Washington, D.C.: Cataloging Distribution Service, Library of Congress, 1991).

Special Rules for Cataloging Cartographic Materials

In this section the special rules for cataloging cartographic materials will be discussed. Fotr rules and/or areas not discussed here, see chapter 2 of this book. Parts of some of the rules are given; the user is referred to AACR 2 for the complete text and examples.

Chief Source of Information

The chief source of information is the cartographic item itself. If there are multiple parts, all the parts are considered as one.

Title and Statement of Responsibility Area
MARC field 245

Rule 3.1E2 directs us to supply, in brackets, a word or phrase indicating the geographic area covered by the map if the title proper and other title information do not indicate this geographic area.

```
245 04   The National Road ǂh [GMD] : ǂb [Ohio]
```

The GMD is not used at the Library of Congress for maps.

Mathematical Data Area
MARC field 255

Area 3 is used in this chapter for statement of scale, statement of projection, and statement of coordinates and equinox.

Statement of scale (MARC field 255 ǂa)

The scale is given as a representative fraction expressed as a ratio. Other expressions may be added.

```
255       Scale 1:1,550,000
255       Scale 1:71,000. 1 cm. = ca. 0.7 km. 1 in. = ca. 1.1 mi.
```

If the scale found on the item is not given in this form, calculate it from the information given.

Example of calculations

On the item: `1 inch = 58.4 miles.`

We need to find the number of inches in 58.4 miles. There are 63,360 inches in 1 mile (5,280 ft. x 12 in./ft.;. 63,360 in./mi. x 58.4 mi. = 3,700,224 inches. Round to 3,700,000.

```
255       Scale [ca. 1:3,700,000]
```

The fraction is given in brackets because it is calculated; it did not appear on the chief source in this form.

Statement of projection (MARC field 255 ǂb)

The projection statement, and phrases associated with it, are given following the scale statement.

```
255       ... ; ǂb Lambert conformal conic proj., standard parallels
47°55´ and 59°35´
255       ... ; ǂb transverse Mercator proj.
255       ... ; ǂb Albers conical equal-area proj., standard
parallels 29°30´ and 45°30´
```

Statement of coordinates (MARC field 255 ǂc)

Coordinates are given in degrees, minutes, and seconds. Longitude (up and down) is given first, then latitude (width). The four coordinates are given in order: westernmost extent of area — easternmost extent of area/northernmost extent of area — southernmost extent of area. The minute and second marks are not the same as quote marks, but are special marks in the MARC format.

```
255       ... ; ǂc (W 97°--W 89°/N 49°30´--N 46°)
255       ... ; ǂc (W 145°--W 102°/N 67°--N 46°)
255       ... ; ǂc (W 140°00´00´´--W 138°30´00´´/N 45°00´00´´--N
42°30´00´´)
```

Physical Description Area
MARC field 300

Extent of item (MARC field 300 ǂa)

Terms that may be used as specific material designations include:

> atlas
> diagram
> globe
> map
> map section
> profile
> relief model
> remote-sensing image
> view

Terms may be borrowed from other chapters if needed.

```
1 puzzle
```

One map may be printed in parts (segments) designed to fit together. Several maps may be printed on one sheet. Rule 3.5 gives very detailed directions on extent of maps.

```
300      1 map on 3 sheets
300      3 maps on 1 sheet
```

Other physical details (MARC field 300 ‡b)

Details specified here include:

> number of maps in an atlas
> color
> material (if other than paper)
> mounting

Dimensions (MARC field 300 ‡c)

The size of a map is given as height, then width, in centimeters, rounded up to the next whole centimeter (68.4 cm. is rounded up to 69 cm.).

If the map has a border, the border is *not* included in the dimensions. If there is a *neat line* (a narrow line enclosing and touching the actual map) measurements are made within the neat line.

```
300      1 map : ‡b col. ; ‡c 69 x 103 cm.
```

If a part of the map extends through the neat line into the border, that extension is included in the measurement. If there is no border, the entire map is measured, and the words "on sheet" are used.

```
300      1 map : ‡b col. ; ‡c on sheet 58 x 89 cm.
```

AACR 2 gives direction for handling the many complications of describing and measuring maps. The AACCM manual illustrates some of these possibilities with diagrams. Measuring folded maps also is explained.

Notes Area
MARC fields 5XX

Notes permitted in this chapter are:

> 3.7B1.   Nature and scope of the item
> 3.7B2.   Language
> 3.7B3.   Source of title proper
> 3.7B4.   Variations in title
> 3.7B5.   Parallel titles and other title information
> 3.7B6.   Statements of responsibility
> 3.7B7.   Edition and history
> 3.7B8.   Mathematical and other cartographic data
> 3.7B9.   Publication, distribution, etc.
> 3.7B10. Physical description
> 3.7B11. Accompanying material
> 3.7B12. Series

3.7B13. Dissertation
3.7B14. Audience
3.7B16. Other formats
3.7B18. Contents
3.7B19. Numbers
3.7B20. Copy being described, library's holdings, and restrictions on use
3.7B21. "With" notes

Explanation of notes

Each of the notes will be explained in the following section and examples of their use given.

3.7B1. Nature and scope of the item (MARC field 500)

To be used to make notes on the nature or scope of a cartographic item, unless that information is obvious from the rest of the bibliographic description. Also used to note unusual features of the item.
There is no summary note used in this chapter, though you may borrow from the rules in chapter 1 if needed.

```
500     Locates covered bridges existing in Ohio in 1972.
500     "Contour interval 10 feet."
500     Relief shown by contours, hachures, and spot heights.
```

3.7B2. Language (MARC field 546)

To be used to name the language or languages of the item if not obvious from the description.

```
546     Text in English and French.
```

3.7B3. Source of title proper (MARC field 500)

To be used if the title proper is taken from other than the chief source of information.

```
500     Title supplied by cataloger.
```

3.7B4. Variations in title (MARC fields 500, 246)

To be used to note any title appearing on the item that differs significantly from the title proper. Field 246 is used if the title applies to the entire work.

```
246 30  ‡i Panel title: ‡a New York, New Jersey, Pennsylvania
        (Title proper: The Northeast)
```

3.7B5. Parallel titles and other title information (MARC field 500)

To be used for parallel titles and important other title information not recorded in area 1.

```
500     Panel title: I [love] NY.  The word "love" is represented
by a heart.
```

3.7B6. Statements of responsibility (MARC field 500)

To be used to record information not given in area 1.

```
500     "Produced for and funded by the United States Department
of Education, Office of Special Education and Rehabilitative Ser-
vice."
```

3.7B7. Edition and history (MARC fields 500, 525)

To be used for information about earlier editions or about the history of the item.

```
525      Supplement to The National Geographic magazine, v. 153,
no. 1 (Jan. 1978).
```

3.7B8. Mathematical and other cartographic data (MARC field 500)

To be used for important information not already given in area 3.

```
500      Scale of most counties ca. 1:210,000.
```

3.7B9. Publication, distribution, etc. (MARC field 500)

To be used for important information not recorded in area 4.

```
500      Base map by Jeppesen & Co., 1964.
```

3.7B10. Physical description (MARC field 500)

To be used for important information not recorded in area 5, especially if the details may affect the use of the item.

```
500      Raised outlines for buildings, raised dotted lines for
streets, street names and building symbols in braille and large
print.
```

3.7B11. Accompanying material (MARC field 500)

To be used for details not given in area 5 concerning the accompanying material.

```
500      Sheet of additions, deletions, and corrections dated
"1972, revised 1984."
```

3.7B12. Series (MARC field 500)

To be used for additional series information.

```
500      Some maps also part of series: Maps of Asia.
```

3.7B13. Dissertations (MARC field 502)

To be used for the standard dissertation note when needed.

```
521      Thesis (Ph. D.)--University of Wisconsin, 1990.
```

3.7B14. Audience (MARC field 521)

To be used to state the intended audience of an item, *if* the information is stated on the item. A blank first indicator will generate the display constant "Audience:"

```
521      Students in grades K-3.
```

3.7B16. Other formats (MARC field 530)

To be used to name other formats the item has been published in.

```
530      Also issued in microfiche and on CD-ROM.
```

3.7B18. Contents (MARC fields 505, 500)

To be used to describe contents of a collection. To be used to list contents of an item, including insets, ancillary maps, illustrations, and/or information on the verso of an item. Inset maps are separate maps positioned within the neat line of a larger map. Ancillary maps are separate maps outside the neat line of the main map.
Field 505 with first indicator "0" generates the display constant "Contents:"
Field 505 with first indicator "8" does not generate a display constant.

```
500      On verso: Glittering cities, lonely wild lands.
505 8    Includes inset maps: W. Washington County -- N. Perry
County -- Cent. Preble County.
```

3.7B19. Numbers (MARC field 500)

To be used to record important numbers on the item other than ISBN or ISSN, or numbers that could go in field 037.

```
500      "[Roll] 226--[frame] 14 44916 HAP 85."
```

3.7B20. Copy being described, library's holdings, and restrictions on use (MARC field 590)

To be used for local information.

```
590      Library copy lacks accompanying brochure.
```

3.7B21. "With" notes (MARC field 501)

To be used for "with" notes.

```
501      With: Lands of the dinosaur.
```

I'm not an experienced map cataloger, although for the past several years I have cataloged the items for which we could not find copy on OCLC. When working in an unfamiliar format, or with unfamiliar materials, it always helps to begin with items that have good OCLC copy, then progress to those that have copy needing minor editing, then to those needing major editing, and finally to those that need original input. Thus we learn from others who are cataloging this material, even though we might never meet any of them. I would suggest you begin with National Geographic maps, searching OCLC to find copy. By comparing the good copy you will find to the maps, you will learn map terminology and what to include in a map description. In the examples that follow, I have attempted to use all the rules as well as the suggestions from the AACCM manual listed at the beginning of this chapter.

Map classification numbers have more parts to them than other classification numbers in the LC system. Map classification numbers may have three cutter numbers, the third, given after the situation date, being for the main entry. Both the first cutter number and the cutter number after the date begin with a period.

Example 1. Geologic map of the vicinity of the outlet …

From the bottom of the map

GEOLOGIC MAP OF THE VICINITY OF THE OUTLET OF GLACIAL LAKE AGASSIZ, NORTH DAKOTA, SOUTH DAKOTA, AND MINNESOTA

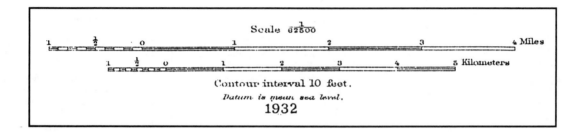

A. Hoen & Co. Lith. Baltimore, Md. Geology by Frank Leverett
in part after Warren Upham

Scale $\frac{1}{62500}$

Contour interval 10 feet.
Datum is mean sea level.
1932

From the upper left hand corner of the map

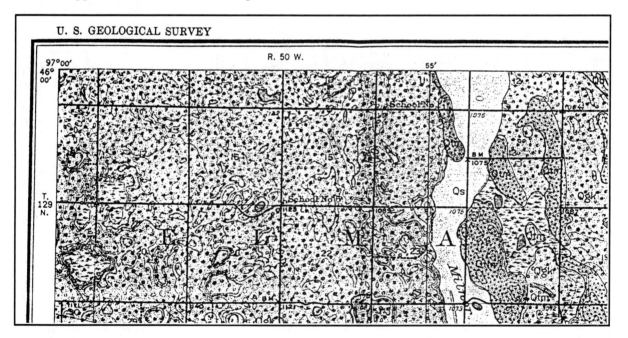

U. S. GEOLOGICAL SURVEY

Example 1: Geologic map of the vicinity of the outlet …

From the upper right hand corner of the map

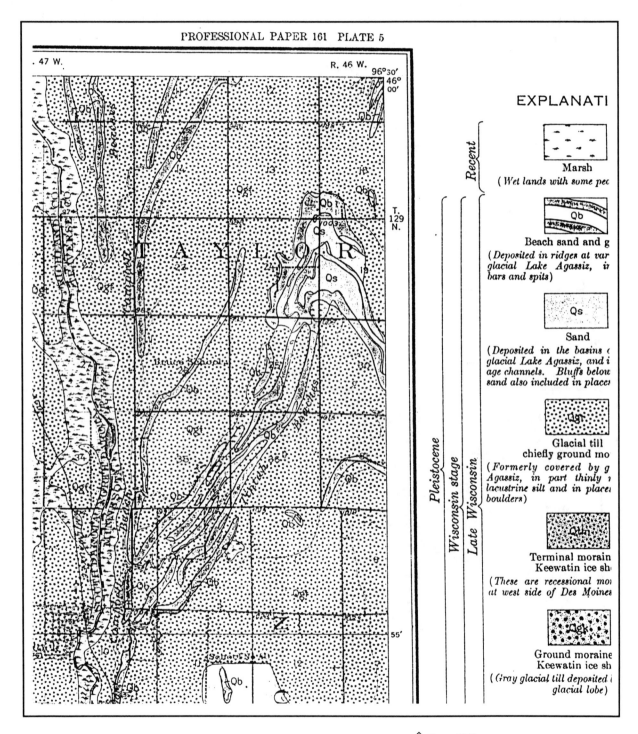

⇑ **"neat" line**

Example 1. Geologic map of the vicinity of the outlet ...

```
Type: e     ELvl: I     Srce: d     Relf: ad    Ctrl:       Lang: eng
BLvl: m     SpFm:       GPub: f     Prme:       MRec:       Ctry: mdu
CrTp: a     Indx: 1     Proj:       DtSt: s     Dates: 1932,
Desc: a
 1 040        XXX ‡c XXX
 2 007        a ‡b j ‡d c ‡e a ‡f n ‡g z ‡h n
 3 034 1      a ‡b 62500 ‡d W0970000 ‡e W0963000 ‡f N0460000 ‡g N0453000
 4 043        n-us-mn ‡a n-us-sd ‡a n us-nd
 5 052        4140
 6 090        G4141.C5 1932 ‡b .G4
 7 049        XXXX
 8 110 2      Geological Survey (U.S.).
 9 245 10     Geologic map of the vicinity of the outlet of glacial Lake Agassiz,
North Dakota, South Dakota, and Minnesota ‡h [map] / ‡c U.S. Geological Survey
; geology by Frank Leverett in part after Warren Upham.
10 255        Scale 1:62,500. ‡c (W 97°00'--W 96°30'/N 46°00'--N 45°30').
11 260        Baltimore, Md. : ‡b A. Hoen, ‡c 1932.
12 300        1 map : ‡b col. ; ‡c 89 x 63 cm.
13 500        Relief shown by contour lines, hachures; contour interval 10 ft.
14 500        Issued as plate 5 in: Quaternary geology of Minnesota and parts of
adjacent states / by Frank Leverett. Washington : U.S. G.P.O., 1932.
(Geological Survey (U.S.) Geological Survey professional paper ; no. 161)
15 500        Includes index, explanation.
16 650 0      Geology ‡z Minnesota ‡x Maps.
17 650 0      Glacial lakes ‡x Maps.
18 651 0      Agassiz, Lake ‡x Maps.
19 700 1      Leverett, Frank, ‡d 1859-1943.
20 700 1      Upham, Warren, ‡d 1850-1934.
```

Comments

This map had been in our collection for a long time, but had never been cataloged. It had lots of information on it, and had latitude and longitude clearly marked in each corner. The scale is given on the map as a fraction, so it did not have to be calculated.

Cataloging: The Library of Congress does not use the GMD for map cataloging.

Rules for notes are 3.7B1, 3.7B18.

Classification: Map call numbers may have two or three cutter numbers with a date before the last cutter number. First and last cutter numbers are, in this case, each preceded by a period.

Access: The subject subdivision "Maps" is actually a form subdivision, so it would be coded ‡v when that code is available for use.

MARC coding/tagging: One must be careful to use the correct characters for the degree, minute, and second marks. The OCLC documentation tells what keystrokes to use for these.

Processing: We put the barcode and call number label on the back of the lower right corner. All our maps are laid flat in drawers in map cabinets.

Example 2. Mankato Area Satellite Image

Map of Mankato, Minnesota

Example 2. Mankato Area Satellite Image

```
Type: e   ELvl: I   Srce: d   Relf:      Ctrl:      Lang: eng
BLvl: m   SpFm:     GPub: f   Prme:      MRec:      Ctry: sdu
CrTp: a   Indx: 0   Proj:     DtSt: s    Dates: 1986,
Desc: a
 1 040      XXX ǂc XXX
 2 007      a ǂb r ǂd a ǂe a ǂf z ǂg d ǂh a
 3 034 1    a ǂb 85000
 4 043      n-us-mn
 5 052      4144 ǂb M3
 6 090      G4144.M3A3 1986 ǂb .E3
 7 049      XXXX
 8 110 2    Earth Resources Observation Systems.
 9 245 10   [Mankato, Minnesota, area satellite image] ǂh [map].
10 255      Scale [ca. 1:85,000].
11 260      [Sioux Falls, S.D. ; ǂb U.S. Geological Survey, EROS Data
Center, ǂc 1986].
12 300      1 remote-sensing image : ǂc 23 x 23 cm.
13 500      Title supplied by cataloger.
14 500      Sheet dated 8-8-86.
15 500      "[Roll] 228-[frame] 14 449416 HAP 85."
16 651  0   Mankato (Minn.) ǂx Photographs from space.
```

Comments

General: This photo has no information on it except a line of numbers and letters. The shipping container gave me some information.

Cataloging: The main entry is as found in the online authority file in OCLC.

When one makes up a title for a map, be sure to include the name of the geographic area shown in the map and what kind of a map it is.

Rules for notes are 3.7B3, 3.7B9, 3.7B19.

Access: In the classification number G4144 stands for Minnesota cities with M3 for Mankato. A3 is for an aerial photo while 1986 is the situation date, the date corresponding to the image recorded on the map. The final cutter is for the main entry.

Processing: This is a photograph, so it should be kept dry.

Example 3. Ohio Covered Bridges

Map of Ohio covered bridges

Example 3. Ohio Covered Bridges

```
Type: e   ELvl: I   Srce: d   Relf:      Ctrl:       Lang: eng
BLvl: m   SpFm:     GPub: s   Prme:      MRec:       Ctry: ohu
CrTp: a   Indx: 0   Proj:     DtSt: s    Dates: 1972,
Desc: a
 1 040      XXX ǂc XXX
 2 007      a ǂb j ǂd c ǂe a ǂf n ǂg z ǂh n
 3 034 0    a
 4 090      G5081.P24 1972 ǂb .O4 1972
 5 049      XXXX
 6 245 00   Ohio covered bridges ǂh [map].
 7 255      Scale not given.
 8 260      Columbus, Ohio : ǂb Ohio Historical Society, ǂc 1972.
 9 300      1 map : ǂb col. ; ǂc 42 x 54 cm. on sheet 43 x 55 cm. + ǂe 1 sheet
of additions, deletions & corrections.
10 500      Shows location of covered bridges existing in 1972.
11 500      Published "with the cooperation and assistance of the Ohio
Covered Bridge Committee."
12 500      Additions, deletions & corrections dated "1972, revised 1984."
13 505 8    Includes inset maps: W. Washington County -- N. Perry County --
Cent. Perry County.
14 500      Text, sketches of truss designs and list of covered bridges on
verso.
15 650  0   Covered bridges ǂz Ohio ǂx Maps.
16 710 2    Ohio Historical Society.
17 710 2    Ohio Covered Bridge Committee.
```

Comments

General: This map came with a sheet of additions, deletions, and corrections that showed how many covered bridges no longer existed twelve years after the map had been made. It also told which ones had been moved to safe locations.

Cataloging: I treated the sheet of information as accompanying material. The title of the sheet used an ampersand, so that is what I transcribed.

Rules for notes are 3.7B1, 3.7B9, 3.7B11, 3.7B18, 3.7B18. There is no neat line on this map, so these smaller maps could probably be called either inset maps or ancillary maps.

MARC coding/tagging: If anything is stated about scale in the bibliographic record, something must be coded in field 034. This minimal coding shows the scale, though not given, is linear.

The contents note has an indicator "8" so it will not generate a display constant.

Example 4. The National Road

Reprinted booklet uses original title page

THE
NATIONAL
ROAD

in song and story

Compiled by
Workers of the Writers' Program
of the Work Projects Administration
in the State of Ohio

—————————

Published by
The Ohio Historical Society
Columbus, Ohio 43211

Copyright, 1940

Example 4. The National Road

Map of The National Road

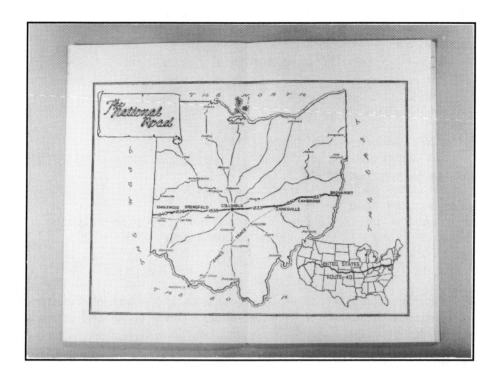

```
The National Road [map] : [Ohio]. -- Scale
    indeterminable.
        1 map ; 17 x 24 cm.

        Inset: Map of United States Route 40.
        In Writers' Program (U.S.). Ohio. The National Road
    in song and story. -- Columbus Ohio : Ohio
    Historical Society, [198-].

        1. Cumberland Road--Maps.
```

Example 4. The National Road

```
Type: e    ELvl: I    Srce: d    Relf:        Ctrl:        Lang: eng
BLvl: m    SpFm:      GPub:      Prme:        MRec:        Ctry: ohu
CrTp: a    Indx: 0    Proj:      DtSt: s      Dates: 198u
Desc: a
 1 040       XXX ǂc XXX
 2 007       a ǂb j ǂd a ǂe a ǂf n ǂg z ǂh n
 3 034 0     a
 4 043       n-usc--
 5 090       HE356.C8 ǂb W7
 6 049       XXXX
 7 245 04    The National Road ǂh [map] : ǂb [Ohio].
 8 255       Scale indeterminable.
 9 300       1 map ; ǂc 17 x 24 cm.
10 500       Inset: Map of United States Route 40.
11 651  0    Cumberland Road ǂx Maps.
12 773 0     ǂ7 uuam ǂt National Road in song and story. ǂd Columbus, Ohio :
Ohio Historical Society, [198-]. ǂw (OCoLC)nnnnnnn
```

Comments

   General: This is an example of an "In" analytic. The map is the centerfold of a pamphlet about the National Road. The pamphlet is a reprint of a 1940 document; no reprint information is given. This "In" analytic technique can be used with all types of material.

   Cataloging: Because no geographic information is given in the title, it is supplied in brackets as other title information as directed in rule 3.1E2.

   Access: The call number shown is that of the document in which the map is contained. If the map were removed and cataloged as a separate map, it would have a map call number.

   MARC coding/tagging: Field 773 generates a note beginning "In".

Example 5. Capitol Hill and the Mall

From the top right hand corner of the map

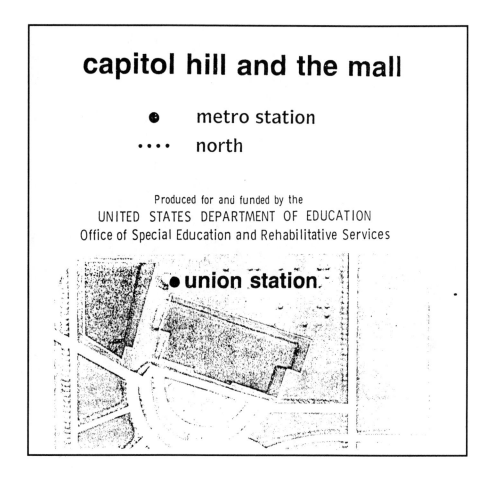

From the bottom left hand corner of the map

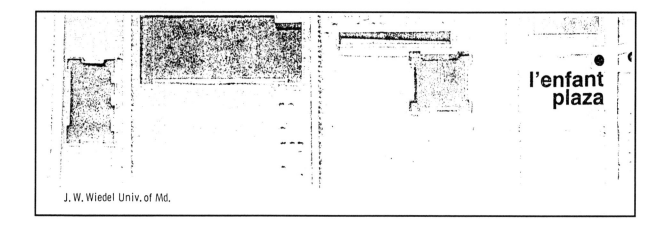

Example 5. Capitol Hill and the Mall

Map of Capitol Hill and the Mall

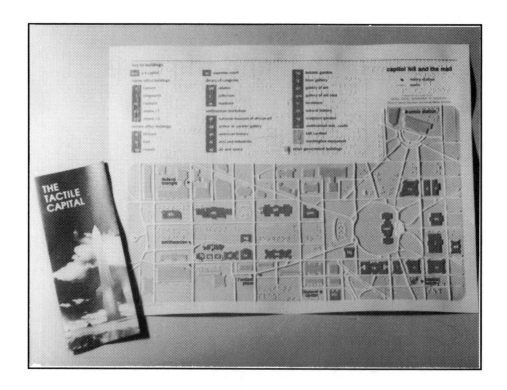

Example 5. Capitol Hill and the Mall

```
Type: e   ELvl:      Srce:      Relf:      Ctrl:       Lang: eng
BLvl: m   SpFm: m    GPub: f    Prme:      MRec:       Ctry: mdu
CrTp: a   Indx: 1    Proj:      DtSt: s    Dates: 1988,
Desc: a
 1 010       89-690307/MAPS
 2 040       DLC ǂc DLC ǂd OCL ǂd MNM
 3 007       a ǂb j ǂd c ǂe e ǂf n ǂg z ǂh n
 4 034 0     a
 5 043       n-us-dc
 6 050 0     G3852.C32A7 1988 ǂb .W5
 7 052       3852 ǂb C32 ǂb M3
 8 049       XXXX
 9 100 1     Wiedel, Joseph W.
10 245 10    Capitol Hill and the Mall ǂh [map] / ǂc J.W. Wiedel ;
produced for and funded by the United States Department of Education,
Office of Special Education and Rehabilitative Services.
11 255       Scale not given.
12 260       [Ellicott City, Md. : ǂb Schuyler Fonaroff Associates, ǂc
1988].
13 300       1 map : ǂb col., plastic ; ǂc 26 x 45 cm., on sheet 36 x 49
cm. + ǂe 1 brochure.
14 500       Tactile map for the blind.
15 500       Covers the Mall west of the Washington Monument.
16 500       Names in braille and lower-case type.
17 500       Streets and government buildings in raised relief.
18 500       Includes indexed legend.
19 500       Brochure, "The tactile capital," describes exhibit,
photographs, maps, and model of the Tactile Capital project for the
blind, visually impaired, and others with disabilities.
20 651 0     Capitol Hill (Washington, D.C.) ǂx Maps for the blind.
21 651 0     Mall, The (Washington, D.C.) ǂx Maps for the blind.
22 650 0     Public buildings ǂz Washington (D.C.) ǂx Maps.
23 710 1     United States. ǂb Office of Special Education and
Rehabilitative Services.
24 740 02    Tactile capital.
```

Comments

General: This item is a plastic map with raised lines and braille and print names of streets and buildings. This MARC record is taken from OCLC. I have modified it to include information from and about the brochure.

Cataloging: Information about the publisher was given in the accompanying brochure.

Rules for notes are 3.7B1, 3.7B1, 3.7B10, 3.7B10, 3,7B10, 3.7B11.

Access: I included a title added entry for the brochure in field 740 rather than field 246 because it is an accompanying item rather than a varying form of the title of the whole item.

In line 21, "Mall, The ..." is as found in the LC authority file.

Example 6. New Mexico in 3-D

Map of New Mexico in 3-D

Facsimile of information at the bottom of the map

© 1964 Jeppesen & Co., Denver, Colo., U.S.A.

All Rights Reserved

Revised 5-68

NEW MEXICO IN 3-D

Printed 1975
Vertical Scale 1/16" = Approx. 1000'
Horizontal Scale 1" = Approx. 25 Miles

Produced by Kistler Graphics, Inc.
Denver, Colorado U.S.A.

Example 6. New Mexico in 3-D

```
Type: e    ELvl: I    Srce: d    Relf: z    Ctrl:      Lang: eng
BLvl: m    SpFm:      GPub:      Prme:      MRec:      Ctry: cou
CrTp: a    Indx: 0    Proj:      DtSt: s    Dates: 1975,
Desc:
 1 010
 2 040      XXX ǂc XXX
 3 007      a ǂb q ǂd c ǂe e ǂf n ǂg z ǂh n
 4 034 1    a ǂb 1584000 ǂc 192000
 5 043      n-us-nm
 6 052      4321
 7 090      G4321.C18 1975 ǂb .K4
 8 049      XXXX
 9 110 2    Kistler Graphics, inc.
10 245 10   New Mexico in 3-D ǂh [map] / ǂc produced by Kistler Graphics.
11 255      Scale [ca. 1:1,584,000]. 1 in. to ca. 25 miles. Vertical scale [ca.
1:192,000].
12 260      Denver, Colo. : ǂb Kistler, ǂc 1975.
13 300      1 relief model : ǂb col., plastic ; ǂc 42 x 38 cm.
14 500      Relief shown by raised areas, spot heights.
15 500      Base map by Jeppesen & Co., 1964; rev. 5-68.
16 651  0   New Mexico ǂx Relief models.
17 710 2    Jeppesen and Company.
```

Comments

General: This plastic relief map has one scale for linear distance and a different scale for distance above sea level.

Cataloging: Rules for notes are 3.7B1, 3.7B7. MARC coding/tagging: All the scale information goes into one subfield in field 255.

In the fixed fields, relief is coded "z" for "other"; there is no code for raised models.

Processing: This model is designed to hang on a wall. It can be put in a drawer, but nothing heavy should be placed on top of it.

Example 7. Minnesota Outdoor Atlas

Minnesota outdoor atlas

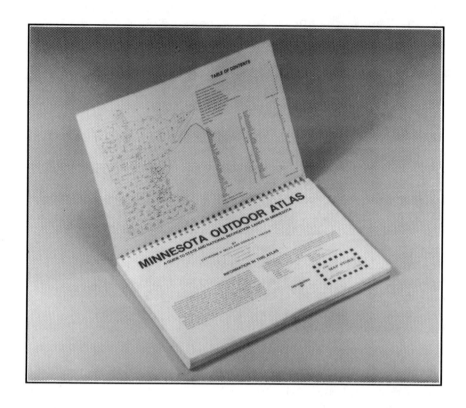

Example 7. Minnesota Outdoor Atlas

```
Type: e    ELvl: I    Srce: d    Relf:       Ctrl:       Lang: eng
BLvl: m    SpFm:      GPub: 0    Prme:       MRec:       Ctry: mnu
CrTp:      Indx:      Proj:      DtSt: s    Dates; 1979,
Desc: a
 1 010
 2 040       XXX ‡c XXX
 3 020       0932880002
 4 034 0     a
 5 043       n-us-mn
 6 090       G1426.E63 ‡b M4 1979
 7 049       XXXX
 8 100 1     Miles, Catherine H.
 9 245 10    Minnesota outdoor atlas : ‡b a guide to state and national
recreation lands in Minnesota / ‡c by Catherine H. Miles and Donald P. Yaeger
; two-color photographs by D. Yaeger.
10 255       Scales vary.
11 260       [Minnesota : ‡b s.n.] ; ‡a West St. Paul, Minn. : ‡b Distributed by
The Map Store, ‡c c1979.
12 300       1 atlas (232 p.) : ‡b ill. (some col.), col. maps ; ‡c 44 cm.
13 500       Scale of most counties [ca. 1:210,000].
14 650  0    Outdoor recreation ‡z Minnesota ‡x Maps.
15 650  0    Public lands ‡z Minnesota ‡x Maps.
16 700 1     Yaeger, Donald P.
```

Comments

General: We do not know anything about the publisher of this atlas, but there is a phrase beginning "Distributed by ..."

Cataloging: Each map in this atlas has its scale given, but there are several different scales used.

There is no GMD for an atlas.

MARC coding/tagging: Atlases used to be coded on the books workform; now they are done on the maps workform.

Notice the coding in field 260 where we have information about the distributor but not the publisher. When the name of a state or country is all the information we have, it can not be abbreviated.

Example 8.   Replogle Stereo Relief Globe

Globe   **Legend on globe**

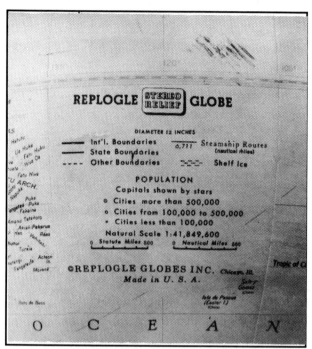

Example 8.   Replogle Stereo Relief Globe

```
Type: e    ELvl: I    Srce: d    Relf: z    Ctrl:      Lang: eng
BLvl: m    SpFm:      GPub:      Prme:      MRec:      Ctry: ilu
CrTp: d    Indx: 0    Proj:      DtSt: s    Dates: 197u,
Desc: a
 1 010
 2 040        XXX ‡c XXX
 3 007        d ‡b c ‡d c ‡e u ‡f u
 4 034 1      a ‡b 41849600 ‡d W1800000 ‡e E1800000 ‡f N0900000 ‡g S0900000
 5 052        3170
 6 090        G3171.C18 1970 ‡b .R4
 7 049        XXXX
 8 110 2      Replogle Globes.
 9 245 10     Replogle stereo relief globe ‡h [globe].
10 246 30     Replogle globe
11 255        Scale 1:41,849,600 ‡c (W 180°--E 180°/N 90°--S 90°).
12 260        Chicago, Ill. : ‡b Replogle Globes, ‡c [197-].
13 300        1 globe : ‡b col. paper and cardboard, on metal and wood stand ; ‡c
31 cm. in diam.
14 500        Raised relief globe.
15 650  0     Globes.
16 650  0     Relief models.
```

Comments

Cataloging: This globe has the words "stereo relief" in a box, one over the other, between the words "Replogle" and "Globe". I decided to use the order shown in the title proper and made a title added entry for the words outside the box.

There was no date anywhere on the item. There was a copyright symbol, but no date with it.

MARC coding/tagging: Globes are cataloged on the maps workform.

Processing: One could place a barcode on a leg, and a call number label on the wooden base or near the legend on the globe itself, but this item would be difficult to tattletape. On the equator, perhaps?

Example 9. Global Pursuit

Game box and pieces

Example 9. Global Pursuit

```
Type: r    ELvl: I    Srce: d    Audn: g    Ctrl:       Lang: eng
BLvl: m    TMat: g    GPub:      AccM:      MRec:       Ctry: dcu
Desc: a    Time: nnn  Tech: n    DtSt: s    Dates: 1987,
```

1	040	XXX ‡c XXX
2	007	a ‡b j ‡d c ‡e a ‡f u ‡g u ‡h n
3	006	[e df a 0]
4	034 1	a ‡b 67200000
5	090	GV1485 ‡b .G4 1987
6	049	XXXX
7	245 00	Global pursuit ‡h [game] / ‡c National Geographic.
8	246 3	National Geographic global pursuit
9	260	Washington, D.C. : ‡b National Geographic Society, ‡c c1987.
10	300	1 game (6 decks trivia cards, 4 sets map cards, wall map, twelve-sided die, colored plastic tokens, and manual) ; ‡c in box 26 x 42 x 8 cm.
11	500	"A fun-filled geography game for the whole family."
12	500	Map card artist, Susan Sanford.
13	500	Map: The world / produced by the Cartographic Division, National Geographic Society. Scale 1:67,200,000 ; Van der Grinten proj. Washington, D.C. : The Society, c1987. 1 map : col., plastic ; 46 x 61 cm. "Prepared specially for national Geographic's Global pursuit game." Insets: Language groups -- Religions (both Eckert equal-area proj.) -- Antarctica -- Arctic Ocean.
14	500	Map cards are five-sided; each set forms a complete dodecahedron; includes political map, physical map, map of natural resources, and map of explorations.
15	520	Player must answer questions and correctly assemble map pieces to earn points. For 2-6 players or teams.
16	650 0	Geographical recreations.
17	650 0	World maps.
18	650 0	Educational games.
19	700 1	Sanford, Susan.
20	710 2	National Geographic Society (U.S.)

Comments

General: This game is a favorite in my family, and one we do circulate in my library. One must answer questions about explorations, physical geography, economic geography, and political geography, then correctly assemble five-sided map cards into a flat map (and with four sets of these five-sided cards, one can assemble a continuous flat map with four of each continent, ocean, etc.). It's tricky, and challenging, and fun. It can also be embarrassing when you realize you don't know where the map piece in your hand fits into the world.

Cataloging: I have cataloged this as a game using rules for games from AACR 2 chapter 10, with the map notes based on AACR 2 chapter 3. The Library of Congress has cataloged it on the maps workform, emphasizing the world map.

Rules for notes are, in order, 10.7B1, 10.7B6, 3.7B11, 3.7B11, 10.7B17.

Access: The added entry for National Geographic Society includes the qualifier "(U.S.)" without any code preceding the qualifier. This can cause searching problems in some catalogs as a user is not likely to know this qualifier has been added. A term or keyword search will, of course, find National Geographic Society material, whether a qualifier is present or not.

MARC coding/tagging: This needs field 006 for maps, so it can be searched as a map as well as a game.

Processing: This is one of those games where every single part needs a call number label or some kind of identification, as all pieces are needed for playing.

Example 10. Minneapolis/St. Paul Scene

Game board, pieces and box

From the side of the box

City Scene Games

Each Scene Game is a unique interpretation of a specific city, highlighting streets, major businesses, and local personalities. Have fun and at the sme time become educated while playing the Games about prominent American cities.

JOHN N. HANSEN CO. INC. 369 Adrian, Millbrae, CA 94030 (415) 697-7353
2861 La Cresta Ave., Anaheim, CA 92806 (714) 630-7000

From the instruction sheet

1 Playing Board
48 Scene Cards (including 1 blank)
24 Ownership Cards
4 Debtor Cards
4 Power Group Badges
16 Connection Cards
6 Tokens
2 Dice
1 Cardboard Card with Individual
   Markers
5 Denominations/Money

THE OBJECT
The object of the game is to accumulate wealth. A player buys Ownership Cards representing various properties and businesses. A player may develop his acquisitions once he has made a deal with some of the Power Groups that control business in Minneapolis/St. Paul. The game ends when all the players are bankrupt except one, or at a predetermined time, or when a ball game is starting on TV.

Example 10. Minneapolis/St. Paul Scene

```
Type: r   ELvl: I   Srce: d   Audn: g   Ctrl:       Lang: eng
BLvl: m   TMat: g   GPub:     AccM:     MRec:       Ctry: cau
Desc: a   Time: nnn Tech: n   DtSt: s   Dates: 1981,
 1 040       XXX ǂc XXX
 2 043       n-us-mn
 3 090       GV1469.M4 ǂb M4 1981
 4 049       XXXX
 5 245 00    Minneapolis/St. Paul scene ǂh [game].
 6 246 3     Minneapolis/Saint Paul scene
 7 246 3     Minneapolis, St. Paul scene
 8 260       Milbrae, CA : ǂb John N. Hansen Co., ǂc 1981.
 9 300       1 game (various pieces) : ǂb col. ; ǂc in box 51 x 26 x 4 cm.
10 440 0     City scene games
11 500       Contains 1 playing board, 48 scene cards (including 2 blanks),
24 ownership cards, 4 debtor cards, 4 power group badges, 16 connection cards,
6 tokens, 2 dice, 1 cardboard card with individual markers, and 5
denominations/money.
12 520       A game for two to six players in which the players try to
accumulate wealth through buying and developing property, gaining power, and
acquiring connections. All properties represent actual places and companies
from Minneapolis and St. Paul, Minnesota. Game board includes photo from space
of the Twin Cities area.
13 650  0    Board games.
14 651  0    Minneapolis (Minn.) ǂx Photographs from space.
15 651  0    Saint Paul (Minn.) ǂx Photographs from space.
16 710  2    John N. Hansen Company, Inc.
```

Comments

General: This is a game, but it is based on a geographic area and has a playing board featuring a map that is a reproduction of an actual space photo of a city.

Cataloging: The title has a slash in it, one of the prescribed marks of punctuation. The title must be recorded as shown with no space on either side of the slash, or the slash may be changed to a comma followed by a space. One needs to know how one's online catalog treats a slash — as a separator or as a connector. If the slash joins the words on either side of it, the title becomes difficult to search and an added entry for the title without the slash would be needed.

Access: The authorized form of St. Paul, Minnesota, is "Saint Paul (Minn.)"

How would you catalog this?

This is a set of a glass coffeepot with two glass cups. Each item is engraved with lines of latitude and longitude and shapes of the continents; each has a "map" on it. On the coffee pot the latitude lines are marked for 2, 4, and 6 cups. Impressed into the bottom of the glass are the words "Taste your way, Nescafé".

Chapter 5

SOUND RECORDINGS

AACR 2 Chapter 6

This chapter shows cataloging of sound recordings. Most examples are non-musical. For cataloging music, catalogers are referred to: *Describing Music Materials,* by Richard P. Smiraglia. 3rd ed. (Lake Crystal, Minn.: Soldier Creek Press, 1997).

Special Rules for Cataloging Sound Recordings

In this section the special rules for cataloging sound recordings will be discussed. For rules and/or areas not discussed here, see chapter 2 of this book. Parts of some of the rules are given; the user is referred to AACR 2 for the complete text and examples. All of the Library of Congress rule interpretations for the material in general, and for non-music items, are included.

Chief Source of Information

The chief source of information for the common types of sound recordings is the information on the label or labels; two labels (sides one and two) are treated as a single chief source.

Rule 6.01B1 allows the use of the container as chief source if it gives a collective title and the labels do not.

Title and Statement of Responsibility Area
MARC field 245

LCRI 6.1B1. If the *chief source* shows the name of an author or the name of a performer before the titles of the individual works and there is doubt whether the publisher, etc., intended the name to be a collective title proper or a statement of responsibility, treat the name as the title proper. *Exception:* If the works listed are musical compositions and the name is that of the composer of the works, treat the name as a statement of responsibility in cases of doubt.

If the chief source being followed is the label of a sound recording and the decision is to treat the name as a title proper but one name appears on the label of one side and another name on the second side, transcribe the two names as individual titles (separated by a period-space). (*CSB 44*)

6.1F1. Transcribe statements of responsibility relating to writers of spoken words, composers of performed music, and collectors of field material for sound recordings ... If the participation ... goes beyond that of performance, execution, or interpretation of a work (as is commonly the case with popular, rock and jazz music), give such a statement as a statement of responsibility. If, however, the participation is confined to performance, execution, or interpretation (as commonly the case with "serious" or classical music and recorded speech), give the statement in the note area.

LCRI 6.1F1. The rule allows performers who do more than perform to be named in the statement of responsibility. Accept only the most obvious cases as qualifying for the statement of responsibility. (*CSB 11*)

Amendments 1993. Producers "having artistic and/or intellectual responsibility" may now be named in the statement of responsibility for sound recordings.

Publication, Distribution, etc., Area
MARC field 260

The May 1982 issue of *Music Cataloging Bulletin* included the question, "What will be the authority for place of publication for sound recordings if none is given on the label or container?" The answer from the Library of Congress was that LC will use only what appears on the item. If no city is given and there is a country, this will be used. "S.l." can be used if a probable country cannot be given.

A date may be preceded by the letter "p." The symbol ℗ indicates the copyright date of recorded sound. The date is transcribed preceded by the letter "p" instead of "c."

```
260        ... ; ‡c p1989.
```

If several dates appear on an item, the latest may be used to infer date of publication. An inferred date is bracketed.

Physical Description Area
MARC field 300

Extent of item (MARC field 300 ‡a)

Rule 6.5B1 lists the terms that may be used as specific material designations:

> sound cartridge
> sound cassette
> sound disc
> sound tape reel
> sound track film

If none of these terms is appropriate, we are to give the specific name of the item.

Playing time (MARC field 300 ‡a)

New rules in chapter 1 provide four possibilities for recording playing time. If the playing time is stated on the item, we are to give the playing time as stated. It is not to be rounded up or down. If the playing time is not stated, but is readily ascertainable, we are to give it. As an option, if no playing time is stated or readily ascertainable, we may give an approximate time, using "ca."

```
(ca. 5 min.)
```

When one is cataloging a multipart item, the playing time is treated as above, with the addition of the word "each", or a total time may be given.

```
(15 min. each)
(ca. 15 min. each)
```

LCRI 6.5B2. When the total playing time of a sound recording is not stated on the item but the durations of its parts (sides, individual works, etc.) are, if desired add the stated durations together and record the total, rounding off to the next minute if the total exceeds 5 minutes.

Precede a statement of duration by "ca." only if the statement is given on the item in terms of an approximation. Do not add "ca." to a duration arrived at by adding partial durations or by rounding off seconds.

If no durations are stated on the item or if the durations of some but not all the parts of a work are stated, do not give a statement of duration. Do not approximate durations from the number of sides of a disc, type of cassette, etc. (*CSB 33*)

Other physical details (MARC field 300 ǂb)

Each sound recording must be identified as "analog" or "digital." (*CSB 28*)

Playing speed is not given if standard for the item. (*CSB 28*) It is not given for sound cassettes and compact discs. Playing speed is given for sound discs and for tape reels.

Groove characteristics are specified only if not standard for the type of disc.

Number of tracks is not given if standard for the item.

The terms "mono.", "stereo.", and "quad." are used only when the information is on the item. (*CSB 33*)

Dimensions (MARC field 300 ǂc)

Dimensions of cartridges and cassettes are to be given only if they are other than the standard dimensions.

Notes Area
MARC fields 5XX

Notes permitted in this chapter are:

6.7B1.   Nature or artistic form and medium of performance
6.7B2.   Language
6.7B3.   Source of title proper
6.7B4.   Variations in title
6.7B5.   Parallel titles and other title information
6.7B6.   Statements of responsibility
6.7B7.   Edition and history
6.7B9.   Publication, distribution, etc.
6.7B10. Physical description
6.7B11. Accompanying material
6.7B12. Series
6.7B13. Dissertations
6.7B14. Audience
6.7B16. Other formats
6.7B17. Summary
6.7B18. Contents
6.7B19. Publisher's numbers
6.7B20. Copy being described, library's holdings, and restrictions on use
6.7B21. "With" notes

Explanation of notes

Each of the notes will be explained in the following section and examples of their use given.
Two or more notes may be combined into one.

```
500      Radio programs from Dec. 29, 1946, and July 27, 1947, that
"journey into the realm of the strange and the terrifying."
```

6.7B1. Nature or artistic form and medium of performance (MARC field 500)

To be used to name or explain the form of the item as necessary.

```
500      Radio program.
```

6.7B2. Language (MARC field 546)

To be used to name the language or languages of the spoken or sung content of the item cataloged if not obvious from other information given.

```
546      Narration in Spanish, guide in Spanish and English.
```

6.7B3. Source of title proper (MARC field 500)

To be used if the title proper is taken from other than the chief source of information.

```
500      Title from container.
500      Title supplied by cataloger.
```

6.7B4. Variations in title (MARC fields 246, 500)

To be used to note any title appearing on the item that differs significantly from the title proper. Field 246 is used if the title applies to the entire item.

```
246 1    ‡i Title on container: ‡a Folklore in the church
```
         (*Title proper*: Church folklore)

6.7B5. Parallel titles and other title information (MARC field 500)

To be used for parallel titles and important other title information not recorded in the title and statement of responsibility area.

```
500      Subtitle on guide: An elder wise man describes his life &
poetry.
```
         (*Title proper*: Robert Frost & his world)

6.7B6. Statements of responsibility (MARC fields 508, 511)

To be used to record important information not recorded in the statement of responsibility area. Performers are input in MARC field 511; production credits in MARC field 508.

> **LCRI 6.7B6** In giving the names of players in nonmusic sound recordings, caption the note Cast. Add the roles or parts of players if deemed appropriate, in parentheses after the name (cf. 7.7B6). (*CSB 13*)

```
511 0    Storyteller, Ringo Starr.
508      Compilation produced by Samuel Brylawski and Cooper C.
Graham of the Library of Congress, Motion Picture, Broadcasting,
and Recorded Sound Division.
```

6.7B7. Edition and history (MARC field 518)

To be used for information about earlier editions or to record the history of the item being cataloged.

518   Recorded in Los Angeles, Jan. 8, 1972.

6.7B9. Publication, distribution, etc. (MARC field 500)

To be used for important information not recorded in the publication, distribution, etc., area.

500   Imprint on label: Learning Plans, Inc., Tucson, Arizona.

6.7B10. Physical description (MARC fields 500, 538)

To be used for any important information not given in area 5, the physical description area.

> **LCRI 6.7B10.** Give a note on the presence of container(s) only when the number of containers is not clear from the rest of the description. (*MCB* Mar. 1981)

500   In two volumes.
538   Compact disc.

There is no space before the semicolon according to MCD 6.7B10 (*MCB* Jan. 1992)

500   Durations: 16 min., 7 sec.; 12 min., 32 sec.

6.7B11. Accompanying material (MARC field 500)

To be used for any important information not given in the accompanying material part of area 5.

500   Notes by Sharon Donovan on container.

6.7B12. Series (MARC field 500)

To be used for any important information not recorded in the series area.

500   Also issued as part of series: Man and molecule.

6.7B13. Dissertations (MARC field 502)

To be used for the standard dissertation note when applicable.

502   Thesis (M.A.)--University of Minnesota, 1964

6.7B14. Audience (MARC field 521)

To be used to record the intended audience of a work. Use this note only if the information is stated on the item. Do not attempt to judge the audience for an item. A blank first indicator generates the display constant "Audience."

521   Kindergarten to grade 3.

6.7B16. Other formats available (MARC field 530)

To be used to list other formats in which the work is available. The Library of Congress lists all formats commercially available in this note.

```
530      Issued also on cassette.
```

6.7B17. Summary (MARC field 520)

To be used for a brief objective summary of the content of the item.

```
520      Interviews with Jewish immigrants and with immigrants
from China, Ireland, Italy, Mexico, Poland, Cuba, Germany,
Greece, Hungary, Japan, Finland, Norway, Denmark, and Sweden who
arrived in America between 1902 and 1968.
```

6.7B18. Contents (MARC fields 505, 500)

To be used for a formal (MARC field 505) or informal (MARC field 500) listing of the contents of the item.

```
505 0   General introduction (2 min.) -- Street gang (9 min., 43
sec.) -- Antiwar demonstration (5 min., 16 sec.) -- Viet Nam
veterans (5 min., 46 sec.) -- Frank Garcia (5 min., 30 sec.) --
Rachel Ortiz (14 min., 30 sec.)
```

6.7B19. Publishers' numbers (MARC field 028)

To be used to list any important number appearing on the item other than those to be recorded in area 8, or MARC field 020. This information is recorded in field 028 rather than in a 5XX note field.

> **LCRI 6.7B19.** The label name and number note will be the first note on the bibliographic record. (*CSB 14*)

Cataloging Service Bulletin 14 gives details of transcription of spaces, punctuation marks, etc., of this number.

> "The label name is to be the same as the information given in the publication, distribution, etc., area" (Glenn Patton, OCLC, letter to the author, 27 Dec. 1984).

```
028 02  CK 37574 ǂb CBS
```

6.7B20. Copy being described, library's holdings, and restrictions on use (MARC fields 500, 506, 590)

To be used for any notes applicable only to the particular copy of the item being described (MARC field 500 or field 506 if there are restrictions). Also used for local library restrictions (MARC field 590) on the material being described, or for information of use only to patrons of the local library.

```
590      Use restricted to those enrolled in Law Enforcement 534.
```

6.7B21. "With" notes (MARC field 501)

To be used for "with" notes.

```
501      With: The fusion torch / B.J. Eastlund
```

Cataloging Conference Proceedings

Conference proceedings on sound cassettes or videocassettes can be especially difficult to catalog. In addition to the abbreviated titles often found on the labels (mentioned in chapter 2), there may be problems in determining the names of the speakers, titles of the speeches, and information about the conference itself. Too often the speaker is introduced with "The following speaker needs no introduction." Or "Tom will now tell us about his latest research findings."

When I have a group of conference proceedings to be cataloged, and I cannot find any bibliographic records in OCLC for the titles as given on the labels, I contact the faculty member who ordered or donated the tapes. That person might have a conference program with all the information I need. If not, the faculty member probably will be able to tell me the name of the association that was meeting, or something about the conference. If it is an annual conference of an association or a meeting sponsored by an association, the association's newsletter probably has the information I need.

As I listen to the tapes, I search for any clue as to the actual title and subject matter of each speech, the name of the person speaking or reading a paper (sometimes not the intended speaker), the date of the presentation, site of the meeting, etc. By listening to all the introductions, closings, and speeches themselves, I can sometimes get all the information needed for cataloging. Some speaker might accidentally mention the name of the city or something about the national news of the day that enables me to determine the date. Or a speaker might thank his "esteemed colleague Joe Jones, who has collaborated with me on this research for ten years now." A search of OCLC on the colleague's name could pull up a research paper written by him and our speaker "Tom" on the topic being presented at the conference.

Problems of cataloging these materials are discussed in *Bibliographic Control of Conference Proceedings, Papers, and Conference Materials*, edited by Olivia M. A. Madison and Sara Shatford Layne. (Chicago: ACRL, 1996).

Main Entry for Sound Recordings

There are special, and lengthy, rules and rule interpretations for the main entry of sound recordings. Rule 21.23D splits recordings into those "in which the participation of the performer(s) goes beyond that of performance, execution, or interpretation" and those in which it does not.

Excerpts from some of these rules and rule interpretations:

> **21.23A1.** Enter a sound recording of one work under the heading appropriate to that work....

> **21.23B1.** Enter a sound recording of two or more works all by the same person(s) or body (bodies) under the heading appropriate to those works....

> **21.23C.** Rule change (*CSB 25*) If a sound recording containing works by different persons or bodies has a collective title, enter it under the heading for the person or body represented as principal performer.
>
> If there are two or three persons or bodies represented as principal performers, enter under the heading for the first named....
>
> If there are four or more persons or bodies represented as principal performers, or if there is no principal performer, enter under title.

> **21.23D.** Rule change (*CSB 25*) for a sound recording of popular, rock, or jazz music that contains works by different persons or bodies with no collective title, directs us to enter under principal performer.
>
> If there are two or three principal performers of the popular, rock, or jazz music, we enter under the heading for the first named performer.
>
> If there are four or more performers, and no principal performer, we enter under the heading for the first work.
>
> For classical or "serious" music, enter works with no collective title under the heading appropriate to the first work.

Preservation

Sound recordings have been made of various types of materials over the years, and users assume they will be available forever. They will not.

Vinyl scratched easily and was easily broken. Some users still prefer vinyl, despite its problems. Magnetic tape contains tiny particles of magnetic material imbedded in a binder and coated onto a strip of plastic material. Heat and humidity cause the binder to deteriorate and the magnetic particles that carry the sound information are loosened and fall off. The plastic strip becomes brittle with age and breaks. Tapes that have deteriorated cannot be restored by any means.

Compact discs were welcomed as a means of permanent storage. However, it has been found that some chemicals, including those present in inks and label glues, can migrate through the plastic coating and cause deterioration of the stored information, whether sound, images, or computer data. Because the discs spin at such a high speed when in use, any type of label that is applied to the disc surface can cause a variation in the speed and distortion in the sound. While sound or image distortion might not be noticeable, loss of data from a computer file could happen without the user being aware of this.

A recent report of corrosion of compact discs was caused by a lacquer used for coating CDs between 1988 and 1993 at one factory. This is seen as a coppery- bronze discoloration, usually on the edge of the label side of the disc, that begins at the outer edge and, over time, migrates toward the center. It is said to cause sound distortion that sounds like rhythmic LP surface noise. For more information, check <http://www.hyperion-records.co.uk/bronzed.html>

How would you catalog this sound recording?

Side 1 ALP 1056
(2XEA.355)

An Introduction by
His Grace The Lord Archbishop of Canterbury (Dr. Fisher)
THE CORONATION SERVICE OF
HER MAJESTY QUEEN ELIZABETH II
WESTMINSTER ABBEY—2nd June, 1953
The Entrance into the Church—The Recognition
The Oath—The Presenting of the Holy Bible
Commentators: John Snagge and Howard Marshall

MCPS LTD.
MADE IN   GT. BRITAIN

MONO

Around the edge of the label: EMI RECORDS LTD.   ALL RIGHTS OF THE PRODUCER AND OF THE OWNER OF THE RECORDED WORK
RESERVED OR AUTHORISED COPYING PERFORMANCE AND BROADCASTING OF THIS RECORD PROHIBITED

The attractive graphic from the record label is shown together with the wording that appears on the label. Be careful
— this is a liturgical work.

Example 11. Children's Living French

Container, booklets, cassettes

Facsimile of box edge

CASSETTE EDITION

CHILDREN'S

Living FRENCH

THE COMPLETE
LIVING LANGUAGE COURSE®

0-517-56329-0

Example 11. Children's Living French

```
Type: i   ELvl: I    Srce: d   Audn: c   Ctrl:         Lang: eng
BLvl: m   Form:      Comp:     AccM:     MRec:         Ctry: nyu
Desc: a   FMus: n    LTxt: j   DtSt: s   Dates: 1986,
 1 040      XXX ǂc XXX
 2 007      s ǂb s ǂd l ǂe u ǂf n ǂg j ǂh l ǂi c
 3 020      0517563290
 4 028 02   563290 ǂb Living Language
 5 041 0    engfre
 6 090      PC2121 ǂb .C4 1986
 7 049      XXXX
 8 245 00   Children's living French ǂh [sound recording] : ǂb the complete
living language course.
 9 246 1    ǂi Title on cassettes: ǂa Children's living French lessons
10 250      Cassette ed., 1986 updated ed.
11 260      New York, N.Y. : ǂb Crown Publishers, ǂc c1986.
12 300      2 sound cassettes (120 min.) : ǂb analog + ǂe 2 books.
13 500      Title from container.
14 500      Accompanied by manuals: Children's living French illustrated lesson
book / by Suzanne Jacob ; illustrations by Claudine Nankivel (128 p. : ill. ;
26 cm.) -- Children's living French picture dictionary : French-English,
English-French / by Suzanne Jacob ; illustrations by Bea Curtis (64 p. : ill.
; 26 cm.)
15 520      Forty lessons for children ages 5-12.
16 650  0   French language ǂx Self-instruction.
17 700 12   Jacob, Suzanne. ǂt Children's living French illustrated lesson
book.
18 700 12   Jacob, Suzanne. ǂt Children's living French picture dictionary.
19 700 1    Nankivel, Claudine.
20 700 1    Curtis, Bea.
```

Comments

Cataloging: The title is taken from the container as it represents the whole item better than the various titles on any of the parts. The title on the cassettes is Children's Living French Lessons.

There were two statements giving edition information. I put them into one edition statement.

Information for two notes (6.7B14, 6.7B17) is combined into the last note in this bibliographic record.
Rules for notes are 6.7B3, 6.7B11, 6.7B17.

Access: I used added entries for the two illustrations. I tend to make added entries for most people named when doing original cataloging in OCLC, but don't edit existing records to add that type of information unless it seems quite important.

MARC coding/tagging: Language coding needs to reflect the presence of English on all the materials with both English and French in the contents of the books. I used field 041 for this. Field 028 includes subfield ǂb with a label name that does not match that in field 260. The only publisher name appearing on the cassettes was recorded in field 028.

Processing: As always with magnetic materials such as these cassette tapes, be sure the package is marked so it does not get sensitized or desensitized in any magnet-based security system.

Example 12. A Cow on the Line

Book and cassette

Example 12. A Cow on the Line

```
Type: i   ELvl: I   Srce: d   Audn: j   Ctrl:        Lang: eng
BLvl: m   Form:     Comp: nn  AccM:     MRec:        Ctry: nyu
Desc: a   FMus: n   LTxt: f   DtSt: s   Dates: 1992
 1 010
 2 040       XXX ǂc XXX
 3 007       s ǂb s ǂd l ǂe u ǂf n ǂg j ǂh l ǂi c
 4 020       0679834761 (combination)
 5 020       0679819770 (book)
 6 020       0679834753 (cassette)
 7 090       PZ7 ǂb .C6 1992
 8 049       XXXX
 9 245 02    A cow on the line ǂh [sound recording].
10 260       New York, NY : ǂb Random House, ǂc [1992].
11 300       1 sound cassette : ǂb analog + ǂe 1 book ([31] p. : col. ill. ;
21 cm.).
12 440 0     Thomas the Tank Engine and friends
13 500       Book: A cow on the line and other Thomas the Tank Engine stories /
based on the Railway series by W. Awdry ; photographs by David Mitton and
Terry Permane. New York : Random House, c1992.
14 511 0     Storyteller, Ringo Starr.
15 500       Cassette dated c1986, p1989.
16 520       Sir Topham Hatt's railroad engines discover that respect for the
rules and for each other pays off in the end.
17 505 0     Double trouble -- A cow on the line -- Old iron -- Percy takes the
plunge.
18 650  0    Talking books for children.
19 650  0    Railroads ǂx Trains ǂx Fiction.
20 650  0    Conduct of life.
21 700 1     Starr, Ringo.
22 700 1     Mitton, David.
23 700 1     Permane, Terry.
24 700 1     Awdry, W. ǂt Railway series.
25 730 02    Cow on the line and other Thomas the Tank Engine stories.
26 740 02    Double trouble.
27 740 02    Old iron.
28 740 02    Percy takes the plunge.
```

Comments

General: These items are available separately and together so carry individual ISBNs and one for the package. They could be cataloged as a book with cassette, as a cassette with book, or as a kit. I chose to do this as a cassette with accompanying book. There are four stories in the book and on the cassette.

Cataloging: The packaging includes lots of confusing information. I used the latest date I could find on the item for the date of publication.

Rules for notes: 6.7B6, 6.7B9, 6.7B11, 6.7B17, 6.7B18.

Access: Title added entries are provided for each of the stories on the tape. I didn't provide an added entry for "Cow on the line" as that access is already provided through the 245.

MARC coding/tagging: Be careful to code non-music things as Type "i" rather than "j".

Processing: The package for this was designed for display in a store. The item would need repackaging into a sturdy container for circulation.

Example 13. A Tale of Two Cities

Facsimile of spine of box

BRILLIANCE CORPORATION'S
Classic Collection

A Tale of
Two Cities

————

CHARLES
DICKENS

UNABRIDGED
COMPLETE BOOK
IN AUDIO

5

CASSETTES

15

HOURS OF LISTENING

[UPC symbol]

Example 13. A Tale of Two Cities

```
Type: i   ELvl: I   Srce: d   Audn: g   Ctrl:       Lang: eng
BLvl: m   Form:     Comp: nn  AccM:     MRec:       Ctry: miu
Desc: a   FMus: n   LTxt:     DtSt: s   Dates: 1993,
 1 040      XXX ǂc XXX
 2 007      s ǂb s ǂd l ǂe u ǂf n ǂg j ǂh l ǂi c
 3 020      1561005010 : ǂc ǂ19.95
 4 090      PR4571 ǂb .A32 1993
 5 049      XXXX
 6 100 1    Dickens, Charles, ǂd 1812-1870.
 7 245 12   A tale of two cities ǂh [sound recording] / ǂc Charles Dickens.
 8 260      Grand Haven, Mich. : ǂb Brilliance Corp., ǂc p1993.
 9 300      5 sound cassettes (900 min.) : ǂb analog, stereo.
10 440 0    Brilliance Corporation's classic collection
11 511 0    Read by Buck Schirner.
12 500      Unabridged.
13 520      The classic tale of the young Englishman who gives up his life
during the French Revolution to save the husband of the woman he loves.
14 651   0  France ǂx History ǂy Revolution, 1789-1799 ǂx Fiction.
15 700 1    Schirner, Buck.
```

Comments

General: This is one of the talking books that are so popular with our patrons. They are checked out for those long commutes to and from night classes, we are told. It is important to let patrons know whether these are abridged or unabridged. This one is clearly labeled, though some are not.

Cataloging: Rules for notes: 6.7B6, 6.7B10, 6.7B17.

Processing: Do not put any kind of label on a cassette or disc that is inserted into a machine. Those labels can peel off and stick inside the machine. Write minimal information on the original label with a "Sharpie" pen.

This item would need to be repackaged for circulation.

Example 14. Men are from Mars

Front cover of box

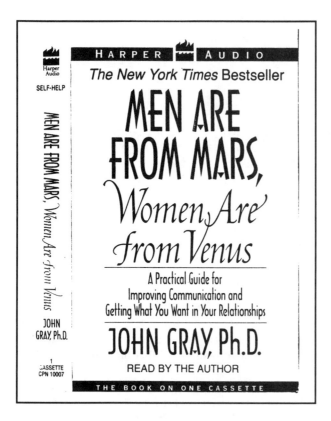

Back cover of box

"A valuable, much-needed book. A contribution to the understanding of the communication styles of men and women."
—Harville Hendrix, Ph.D., author of *Getting the Love You Want**

Once upon a time Martians and Venusians met, fell in love, and had happy relationships together because they respected and accepted their differences. Then they came to Earth and amnesia set in: they forgot they were from different planets.

Using this metaphor to illustrate the commonly occurring conflicts between men and women, Dr. John Gray explains how these differences can come between the sexes and prohibit mutually fulfilling, loving relationships. Based on years of successful counseling of couples and individuals, he gives advice on how to counteract these differences in communication styles, emotional needs, and modes of behavior to promote a greater understanding between individual partners.

MEN ARE FROM MARS, WOMEN ARE FROM VENUS is an invaluable tool for developing deeper and more satisfying relationships.

John Gray, Ph.D., is the author of the national bestseller *Men Are From Mars, Women Are From Venus* as well as *What You Feel, You Can Heal* and *Men, Women and Relationships*. He has been conducting seminars in major cities for twenty years and has a private therapy practice for couples. He lives in Mill Valley, California, with his wife, Bonnie, and their three children.

Recorded on June 15, 1993 in San Francisco, CA.
Running time: Approximately 90 minutes
Abridged with music.

℗ & © 1993 HarperCollins Publishers, Inc.
All rights reserved.

Harper Audio
A Division of HarperCollins Publishers
10 East 53rd Street
New York, NY 10022

[ ] DOLBY B NR

Dolby and the double-D symbol are trademarks of Dolby Laboratories Licensing Corporation.

Made in the USA.

* From a review of the book.

THIS ABRIDGMENT HAS BEEN APPROVED BY THE AUTHOR

$12.00 US/$15.95 CANADA

ISBN: 1-55994-878-7

Example 14. Men are from Mars

```
Type: i   ELvl: I   Srce: d   Audn: f   Ctrl:      Lang: eng
BLvl: m   Form:     Comp:     AccM:     MRec:      Ctry: nyu
Desc: a   FMus: n   LTxt:     DtSt: s   Dates: 1993,
 1 040      XXX ǂc XXX
 2 007      s ǂb s ǂd l ǂe u ǂf n ǂg j ǂh l ǂi c
 3 020      1559948787
 4 028 01   CPN 10007 ǂb Harper Audio
 5 090      HQ734 ǂb .G7 1993
 6 049      XXXX
 7 100 1    Gray, John, ǂd 1951-
 8 245 10   Men are from Mars, women are from Venus ǂh [sound recording] / ǂc
John Gray ; produced and directed by Rick Harris and Suzanne Wilder Carr.
 9 246 30   Men are from Mars
10 246 30   Women are from Venus
11 260      New York, NY : ǂb Harper Audio, ǂc p1993.
12 300      1 sound cassette (ca. 90 min.) : ǂb analog, Dolby processed.
13 440 0    Harper audio. ǂp Self-help
14 500      Abridged by Claire Keller ; music by the Music Bakery.
15 511 3    Read by the author from the book published in 1992.
16 518      Recorded on June 15, 1993, in San Francisco, CA.
17 500      "This abridgment has been approved by the author"--Container.
18 520      Based on years of successful counseling of couples and
individuals, the author gives advice on how to counteract these differences
in communication styles, emotional needs, and modes of behavior to promote a
greater understanding between individual partners.
19 650  0   Marriage.
20 650  0   Communication in marriage.
21 650  0   Interpersonal relations.
22 700 1    Keller, Claire.
```

Comments

Cataloging: There are lots of credits on the package. I chose to use some in the statement of responsibility, others in notes, and ignore the rest.

You will notice the information that this is abridged is given in very tiny print. On the package notice the phrase on the bottom "The book on one cassette." That would seem to imply this contains the complete book.

I could have combined three or four of the notes about the abridgment into one note.

Rules for notes: 6.7B1, 6.7B6, 6.7B7, 6.7B7, 6.7B7, 6.7B17

Processing: This item would need to be repackaged. It is so small it would easily be lost on the shelf. We put these in pambinders or in boxes.

Example 15. The Library of Congress Presents Historic Presidential Speeches, 1908-1993

Facsimile disc label

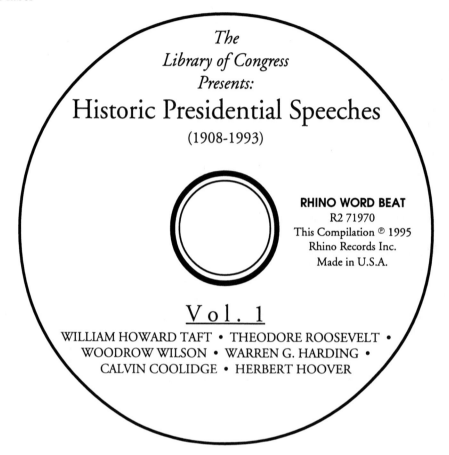

The
Library of Congress
Presents:
Historic Presidential Speeches
(1908-1993)

RHINO WORD BEAT
R2 71970
This Compilation ℗ 1995
Rhino Records Inc.
Made in U.S.A.

Vol. 1
WILLIAM HOWARD TAFT • THEODORE ROOSEVELT •
WOODROW WILSON • WARREN G. HARDING •
CALVIN COOLIDGE • HERBERT HOOVER

Copy of p. 1 in booklet

Vol. 1

1. **WILLIAM HOWARD TAFT**
What Constitutes An Unlawful Trust
Hot Springs, VA (8/5/08)
First issued on Victor 31710
(Courtesy The RCA Records Label, under license from BMG Direct)

2. **WILLIAM HOWARD TAFT**
Democratic Policy Prevents Restoration Of Prosperity
Hot Springs, VA (8/5/08)
First issued on Victor 5555
(Courtesy The RCA Records Label, under license from BMG Direct)

3. **THEODORE ROOSEVELT**
The "Abyssinian Treatment" Of Standard Oil
Emporia, KS (9/22/12)
First issued on Victor 35249
(Courtesy The RCA Records Label, under license from BMG Direct)

4. **THEODORE ROOSEVELT**
Why The Trusts And Bosses Oppose The Progressive Party
Emporia, KS (9/22/12)
First issued on Victor 35250
(Courtesy The RCA Records Label, under license from BMG Direct)

5. **WOODROW WILSON**
The Third Party
New York, NY (9/24/12)
First issued on Victor 35251-A
(Courtesy The RCA Records Label, under license from BMG Direct)

6. **WOODROW WILSON**
To The Farmers
New York, NY (9/24/12)
First issued on Victor 35252-A
(Courtesy The RCA Records Label, under license from BMG Direct)

7. **WARREN G. HARDING**
Americanism
New York, NY (6/29/20)
First issued on Nation's Forum NF 15

8. **WARREN G. HARDING**
Liberty Under The Law
New York, NY (8/6/20)
First issued on Nation's Forum NF 25

9. **WARREN G. HARDING**
Nationalism And Americanism
New York, NY (8/6/20)
Unissued recording made by Nation's Forum [matrix 49878]

10. **CALVIN COOLIDGE**
Inaugural Address (Excerpts)
Washington, DC (3/4/25)
From experimental recordings made by Western Electric [matrices 51775-81]

11. **HERBERT HOOVER**
Radio Address To The Nation On Unemployment Relief
Fort Monroe, VA (10/18/31)
Unissued recording made by Victor [matrix cve 70860-1]
(Courtesy The RCA Records Label, under license from BMG Direct)

All speeches on *Vol. 1* selected by the staff at The Library Of Congress

Example 15. The Library of Congress Presents Historic Presidential Speeches, 1908-1993

Copy of p. 2 in booklet

Vol. 2

1. FRANKLIN D. ROOSEVELT
The First "Fireside Chat" - An Intimate Talk With The People Of The United States On Banking
Washington, DC (3/12/33)
(Courtesy Franklin Delano Roosevelt Library)

2. FRANKLIN D. ROOSEVELT
"We Have Only Just Begun To Fight" Campaign Address
Madison Square Garden, New York, NY (10/31/36)
(Courtesy Franklin Delano Roosevelt Library)

3. HARRY S. TRUMAN
Address Upon Accepting The Democratic Nomination For President
Democratic National Convention, Philadelphia, PA (7/15/48)
(Courtesy Harry S. Truman Library)

All speeches on *Vol. 2* selected by the staff at The Library Of Congress

Vol. 3

1. DWIGHT D. EISENHOWER
Farewell Radio And Television Address To The American People
Washington, DC (1/17/61)
Speech selected by the staff at The Library Of Congress

2. JOHN F. KENNEDY
Commencement Address At American University
American University, Washington, DC (6/10/63)
Speech selected by Theodore Sorensen & approved by Jacqueline Bouvier Onassis

3. LYNDON B. JOHNSON
Remarks At The University Of Michigan
University Of Michigan, Ann Arbor, MI (5/22/64)
Speech selected by Lady Bird Johnson
(Courtesy Lyndon Baines Johnson Library)

Vol. 4

1. RICHARD NIXON
Address To The Nation On The War In Vietnam
Washington, DC (11/3/69)
Speech selected in accordance with President Nixon's opinion in his book *In The Arena* (Simon & Schuster, 1990)
(Courtesy Richard Nixon Project)

2. GERALD R. FORD
Remarks On Taking The Oath Of Office
Washington, DC (8/9/74)
Speech selected by President Ford
(Courtesy Gerald R. Ford Library)

3. JIMMY CARTER
"Energy And National Goals" Address To The Nation
Washington, DC (7/15/79)
Speech selected by President Carter
(Courtesy James Earl Carter Center)

Copy of p. 3 in booklet

Vol. 5

1. RONALD REAGAN
Remarks To The Students And Faculty At Moscow State University
Moscow State University, Moscow, USSR (5/31/88)
Speech selected by President Reagan
(Courtesy National Archives Presidential Library)

2. GEORGE BUSH
Remarks To The Residents Of Leiden
Leiden, The Netherlands (7/17/89)
Speech selected by President Bush
(Courtesy White House & National Archive Presidential Library)

Vol. 6

1. WILLIAM J. CLINTON
Remarks To The Convocation Of The Church Of God In Christ
Memphis, TN (11/13/93)
Speech selected by President Clinton
(Courtesy White House & National Archive Presidential Library)

Example 15. The Library of Congress Presents Historic Presidential Speeches, 1908-1993

```
Type: i    ELvl: I    Srce: d    Audn:       Ctrl:       Lang: eng
BLvl: m    Form:      Comp: nn   AccM: i     MRec:       Ctry: cau
Desc: a    FMus: n    LTxt: l    DtSt: s     Dates: 1995,
 1 010
 2 040      XXX ǂc XXX
 3 007      s ǂb d ǂd z ǂe m ǂf n ǂg g ǂh n ǂi n ǂn u
 4 028 02   R2-71970 ǂb Rhino Word Beat
 5 090      E176.1 ǂb .L4 1995
 6 049      XXXX
 7 245 04   The Library of Congress presents historic presidential speeches,
1908-1993 ǂh [sound recording].
 8 246 30   Historic presidential speeches, 1908-1993
 9 246 30   Historic presidential speeches
10 260      Los Angeles : ǂb Rhino Records, ǂc p1995.
11 300      6 sound discs : ǂb digital ; ǂc 4 3/4 in. + ǂe 1 booklet (56 p. :
ill. ; 26 cm.).
12 508      Compilation produced by Samuel Brylawski and Cooper C. Graham of
the Library of Congress, Motion Picture, Broadcasting, and Recorded Sound
Division ; essays by James H. Billington, Samuel Brylawski, Kathleen Hall
Jamieson, and Cooper C. Graham.
13 538      Compact discs.
14 500      Booklet contains program notes, historical commentary,
bibliography, and time tables.
15 520      Speeches feature the actual voices of seventeen American
presidents from 1908 to 1993. They were selected by the staff of the Library
of Congress, surviving first ladies, and the living presidents and their
staffs.
16 505 0    v. 1. What constitutes an unlawful trust ; Democratic policy
prevents restoration prosperity / William Howard Taft -- The "Abyssinian
treatment" of Standard Oil (1912) ; Why the trust and bosses oppose the
Progressive Party (1912) / Theodore Roosevelt -- The third party ; To the
farmers / Woodrow Wilson -- Americanism ; Liberty under the law ; Nationalism
and Americanism / Warren G. Harding -- Inaugural address (excerpts) / Calvin
Coolidge -- Radio address to the nation on unemployment relief / Herbert
Hoover.
17 505 0    v. 2. The first "Fireside chat" : an intimate talk with the people
of the United States on banking ; We have only just begun to fight : campaign
address / Franklin D. Roosevelt -- Address upon accepting the Democratic
nomination for president / Harry S. Truman.
18 505 0    v. 3. Farewell radio and television address to the American people
/ Dwight D. Eisenhower -- Commencement address at American University / John
F. Kennedy -- Remarks at the University of Michigan / Lyndon B. Johnson.
19 505 0    v. 4. Address to the nation on the war in Vietnam / Richard Nixon
-- Remarks on taking the oath of office / Gerald R. Ford -- Energy and
national goals : address to the nation / Jimmy Carter.
20 505 0    v. 5. Remarks to the students and faculty at Moscow State
University / Ronald Reagan -- Remarks to the residents of Leiden / George
Bush.
21 505 0    v. 6. Remarks to the convocation of the Church of God in Christ /
William J. Clinton.
22 650 0    Campaign speeches ǂz United States.
23 650 0    Speeches, addresses, etc., American.
```

Example 15. The Library of Congress Presents Historic Presidential Speeches, 1908-1993

```
24 651  0  United States ‡x Politics and government ‡y 20th century.
25 650  0  Political oratory ‡z United States.
26 700  1  Brylawski, Samuel.
27 700  1  Graham, Cooper C., ‡d 1938-
28 700  1  Billington, James H.
29 700  1  Jamieson, Kathleen Hall.
30 700  1  Taft, William H. ‡c (William Howard), ‡d 1857-1930.
31 700  1  Roosevelt, Theodore, ‡d 1858-1919.
32 700  1  Wilson, Woodrow, ‡d 1856-1924.
33 700  1  Harding, Warren G. ‡q (Warren Gamaliel), ‡d 1865-1923.
34 700  1  Coolidge, Calvin, ‡d 1872-1933.
35 700  1  Hoover, Herbert, ‡d 1874-1964.
36 700  1  Roosevelt, Franklin D. ‡q (Franklin Delano), ‡d 1882-1945.
37 700  1  Truman, Harry S., ‡d 1884-1972.
38 700  1  Eisenhower, Dwight D. ‡q (Dwight David), ‡d 1890-1969.
39 700  1  Kennedy, John F. ‡q (John Fitzgerald), ‡d 1917-1963.
40 700  1  Johnson, Lyndon B. ‡q (Lyndon Baines), ‡d 1908-1973.
41 700  1  Nixon, Richard M. ‡q (Richard Milhous), ‡d 1913-
42 700  1  Ford, Gerald R., ‡d 1913-
43 700  1  Carter, Jimmy, ‡d 1924-
44 700  1  Reagan, Ronald.
45 700  1  Bush, George, ‡d 1924-
46 700  1  Clinton, Bill, ‡d 1946-
47 710  2  Library of Congress. ‡b Motion Picture, Broadcasting, and Recorded
Sound Division.
```

Comments

General: These items had gold lettering on deep maroon background. We could not get a clear photograph or reproduction of them.

Cataloging: This is cataloged as a set, but we could also catalog each disc separately.

We are limited by the OCLC limit of 50 separate lines in a record (the numbered lines at left) and the limit of 30 separate fields within the 7XX tag group. Cataloging each disc separately would be more work, but would provide more information for our patrons, as well as more access points for their searches, because we could include more information about each speech, such as the length, date, and location. We could then include the title of each speech in an added entry.

The title proper begins with the words "The Library of Congress presents ..." A 246 is used for the variant titles that patrons might suppose to be the "real" titles.

Rules for notes: 6.7B6, 6.7B10, 6.7B11, 6.7B17, 6.7B18 (v. 1-6)

Access: The authority record for Richard Nixon does not include a death date. I wish we could include one when we know it instead of having to follow an authority record that does not include the date.

MARC coding/tagging: Notice the "Compact disc" note is now in field 538.

Processing: These compact discs should not be labeled in any way except one may write with a "Sharpie" pen on the clear band at the center of the disc. No labels of any type should be applied.

Example 16. Wynton Marsalis

Plastic container and compact disc

Back of the container

FATHER TIME**
— Wynton Marsalis
_____

I'LL BE THERE WHEN
THE TIME IS RIGHT**
— Herbie Hancock
_____

RJ*
— Ron Carter
_____

HESITATION*
— Wynton Marsalis
_____

SISTER CHERYL*
— Tony Williams
_____

WHO CAN I TURN TO
(WHEN NOBODY NEEDS ME)*
— L. Bricusse & A. Newley
_____

TWILIGHT**
— Wynton Marsalis
_____

CK 37574
© CBS Inc./℗ CBS Inc.

Produced by Herbie Hancock
Executive Producer: George
Butler

* Recorded in Japan at CBS/Sony
Studios, Shinanomachi,
Roppongi, Tokyo
Engineer: Tomoo Suzuki/2nd
Engineers: Tomita, Ohno,
S. Watanabe

** Recorded in New York at
CBS Recording Studios
Engineer: Tim Geelan
2nd Engineer: Nancy Byers

Production Coordinator:
Tony Meilandt

Special Thanks to Lee Ethier,
Bryan Bell, Rachel McBeth,
Dr. George Butler

Design: John Berg

Photography: William Coupon

Disc label

Example 16. Wynton Marsalis

```
Type: j  ELvl: I  Srce: d  Audn:     Ctrl:     Lang: N/A
BLvl: m  Form:     Comp: jz  AccM: f  MRec:     Ctry: nyu
Desc: a  FMus: n   LTxt:     DtSt: s  Dates: 1982,
 1 010
 2 040       XXX ‡c XXX
 3 007       s ‡b d ‡d f ‡e s ‡f n ‡g g ‡h n ‡i n ‡m e ‡n u
 4 024 1     7464375742
 5 028 02    CK 37574 ‡b CBS
 6 090       M1366 ‡b .M3 1982
 7 049       XXXX
 8 100 1     Marsalis, Wynton, ‡d 1961-
 9 245 10    Wynton Marsalis ‡h [sound recording] / ‡c produced by Herbie
Hancock.
10 260       N[ew] Y[ork], N.Y. : ‡b CBS, ‡c p1982.
11 300       1 sound disc : ‡b digital ; ‡c 4 3/4 in.
12 500       Jazz ensembles.
13 511 0     Branford Marsalis, saxophone ; Jeff Watts or Tony Williams, drums
; Kenny Kirkland or Herbie Hancock, piano ; Ron Carter, Charles Fambrough or
Clarence Seay, double bass ; Wynton Marsalis, trumpet.
14 518       Recorded in Japan at CBS/Sony Studios and in New York at CBS
Recording Studios.
15 538       Compact disc.
16 500       Program notes by Stanley Crouch in container.
17 505 0     Father Time / W. Marsalis -- I'll be there when the time is right
/ H. Hancock -- RJ / Ron Carter -- Hesitation / W. Marsalis -- Sister Cheryl
/ T. Williams -- Who can I turn to (when nobody needs me) / L. Bricusse, A.
Newley -- Twilight / W. Marsalis.
18 650  0    Jazz ‡y 1981-1990.
19 700 1     Carter, Ron, ‡d 1937-
20 700 1     Fambrough, Charles.
21 700 1     Hancock, Herbie, ‡d 1940-
22 700 1     Kirkland, Kenny.
23 700 1     Marsalis, Branford.
24 700 1     Seay, Clarence.
25 700 1     Watts, Jeffrey.
26 700 1     Williams, Tony, ‡d 1945-
27 700 1     Crouch, Stanley.
28 700 12    Marsalis, Wynton, ‡d 1961- ‡t Father time.
29 700 12    Hancock, Herbie, ‡d 1940- ‡t I'll be there when the time is right.
30 700 12    Carter, Ron, ‡d 1937- ‡t RJ.
31 700 12    Marsalis, Wynton, ‡d 1961- ‡t Hesitation.
32 700 12    Williams, Tony, ‡d 1945- ‡t Sister Cheryl.
33 700 12    Bricusse, Leslie. ‡t Who can I turn to.
34 700 12    Marsalis, Wynton, ‡d 1961- ‡t Twilight.
```

Example 16. Wynton Marsalis

Comments

General: This is a collection of works by different persons, with a collective title. The principal performer is chosen as main entry according to rule 21.23.

Cataloging: Place is given on the item as NY NY, so the completion of the name of the city is bracketed into the bibliographic record.

Rules for notes: 6.7B1, 6.7B6, 6.7B7, 6.7B10, 6.7B11, 6.7B18.

Access: A date is no longer added to the author-title analytics according to LCRI 21.30M.

MARC coding/tagging: Field 024 is for the UPC code on the item.

Other coded music information could be supplied in fields 048 and elsewhere, but I am not knowledgeable enough about music to feel comfortable supplying these fields.

Example 17. Great Scenes From Macbeth

Record jacket, disc, and text

Label from disc, side one

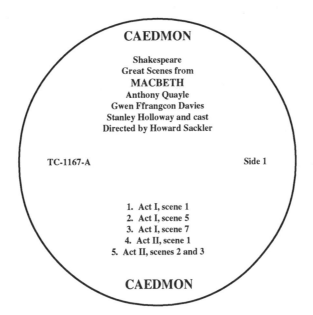

CAEDMON

Shakespeare
Great Scenes from
MACBETH
Anthony Quayle
Gwen Ffrangcon Davies
Stanley Holloway and cast
Directed by Howard Sackler

TC-1167-A   Side 1

1. Act I, scene 1
2. Act I, scene 5
3. Act I, scene 7
4. Act II, scene 1
5. Act II, scenes 2 and 3

CAEDMON

Example 17. Great Scenes From Macbeth

```
Type: i   ELvl: I   Srce: d   Audn: d   Ctrl:     Lang: eng
BLvl: m   Form:     Comp: nn  AccM:     MRec:     Ctry: nyu
Desc: a   FMus: n   LTxt: d   DtSt: s   Dates: 1963,
 1 010
 2 040      XXX ǂc XXX
 3 007      s ǂb d ǂd b ǂe m ǂf m ǂg e ǂh n ǂi n ǂn u
 4 028 02   TC-1167 ǂb Caedmon
 5 090      PR2823 ǂb .A35 1963
 6 049      XXXX
 7 100 1    Shakespeare, William, ǂd 1564-1616.
 8 240 10   Macbeth. ǂk Selections
 9 245 10   Great scenes from Macbeth ǂh [sound recording] / ǂc Shakespeare.
10 260      New York : ǂb Caedmon, ǂc [1963]
11 300      1 sound disc : ǂb analog, 33 1/3 rpm ; ǂc 12 in. + ǂe 1 booklet (24
p. ; 28 cm.)
12 511 0    Starring Anthony Quayle ; Gwen Ffrangcon Davies ; Stanley Holloway
; with supporting cast ; directed by Howard Sackler.
13 500      "From American Shakespeare 7th annual festival award winning
series"--Album cover.
14 500      Text of the recording inserted; synopsis on container.
15 505 0    Act I, scene 1 -- Act I, scene 5 -- Act 1, scene 7 -- Act II,
scene 1 -- Act II, scenes 2 and 3 -- Act III, scene 4 -- Act IV, scene 1 --
Act V, scene 1 -- Act V, scene 5 -- Act 5, scene 7.
16 600 00   Macbeth, ǂc King of Scotland, ǂd 11th cent. ǂx Drama.
17 650  0   English drama ǂy 16th century.
18 700 1    Quayle, Anthony, ǂd 1913-
19 700 2    Ffrangcon-Davies, Gwen, ǂd 1891-1992.
20 700 1    Holloway, Stanley.
```

Comments

General: This example shows the usefulness of the uniform title. All versions of Macbeth are brought together with the uniform title, regardless of the wording or spelling or language of the chief source of information. This was especially important in the days of the card catalog.

Cataloging: Rule numbers for notes are 6.7B6, 6.7B7, 6.7B11, 6.7B18.

MARC coding/tagging: "AccM" is not coded unless the material for which a code may be assigned is mentioned in a note and is substantial or unique and could not be found in a standard reference work.

Example 17. Great Scenes From Macbeth

```
Shakespeare, William, 1564-1616.
   [Macbeth. Selections]
   Great scenes from Macbeth [sound recording] /
Shakespeare. -- New York, N.Y. : Caedmon, [1963].
   1 sound disc : analog, 33 1/3 rpm ; 12 in. + 1
booklet (24 p. ; 28 cm.).

   Caedmon: TC 1167.
   Anthony Quayle, Gwen Ffrangcon Davies, Stanley
Holloway, and cast ; directed by Howard Sackler.
   "From American Shakespeare 7th annual festival
award winning series"--Album cover.

   1. English drama--Early modern and Elizabethan,
1500-1600.  I. Ffrangcon-Davies, Gwen, ‡d 1891-
1992.  II. Holloway, Stanley.  III. Quayle,
Anthony, 1913-  IV. Sackler, Howard.  V. Title.
VI. Title: Macbeth.
```

Comments

General: Some examples are shown in card form in this book, as some users do still have card catalogs or shelflists.

How would you catalog these cassettes?

Two albums of cassettes

Cassette label

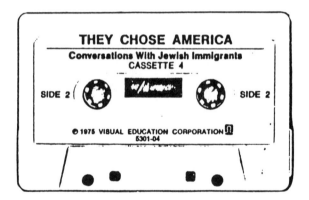

These two packages (volumes 1 and 2) each contain six cassettes, and each cassette has its own title. The set includes interviews with Jewish immigrants as well as with immigrants from China, Ireland, Italy, Mexico, Poland, Cuba, Germany, Greece, Hungary, Japan, Finland, Norway, Denmark, and Sweden. The immigrants arrived in America between 1902 and 1968.

Chapter 6

VIDEORECORDINGS

AACR 2 Chapter 7

This chapter includes examples of cataloging for all types of videorecordings. For motion picture examples, see an earlier edition of this book; the only difference in cataloging is in the physical description of the item and one or two notes.

Special Rules for Cataloging Motion Pictures and Videorecordings

In this section the special rules for cataloging motion pictures and videorecordings will be discussed. For rules and/ or areas not discussed here, see chapter 2 of this book. Parts of some of the rules are given; the user is referred to the rules themselves for complete text and examples. All of the Library of Congress rule interpretations for this chapter are included.

• *Archival Moving Image Materials: A Cataloging Manual*, compiled by Wendy White-Henson. (Washington, D.C.: Library of Congress, 1984).

Excerpts from AMIM are included in this chapter. I found some of its explanations especially helpful.

• *Cataloging Motion Pictures and Videorecordings*, by Nancy B. Olson. (Lake Crystal, Minn.: Soldier Creek Press, 1991).

• *... 1996 Update*. (Lake Crystal, Minn.: Soldier Creek Press, 1996).

Forty examples with considerable discussion. Update adds information on format integration, changes and corrections to original publication, and one example with discussion of interactive multimedia.

• *Cataloging Musical Moving Image Material*, edited by Lowell E. Ashley. (Canton, Mass.: Music Library Association, 1996).

Forty-two examples in MARC format with discussion of descriptive cataloging, main and added entries, subject access, and classification. Very useful.

Chief Source of Information

The chief source of information for motion pictures and videorecordings is the material itself, including all title and credits frames, regardless of location of those title and credits frames. Information at the end of a film is equal in status to that at the beginning of the film.

Title and Statement of Responsibility Area
MARC field 245

Title proper

A problem with film titles is that of "so-and-so presents" and other information appearing before the title, as discussed in chapter 2 of this book.

Television series and movie serials might have segment, part, or individual titles and/or numbers in addition to the series title. *Archival Moving Image Materials (AMIM)* suggests the following methods of handling these titles, which you might want to consider. As always, your cataloging should be based on your patrons' needs. The practice suggested here is one method that could be used. The same type of access is provided if the name of the series and episode number are used as a series statement.

Enter the following types of moving image material under their series and episode, part, individual, or segment titles: television series, theatrical serials, newsreels, and educational and technical series that are intended to be viewed consecutively (if this can be determined). The principle that the primary access point includes both the series and episode titles is a cataloging standard in archives for several reasons. In most cases individual titles of parts or episodes are almost meaningless without the title of the series or serial to which they are subordinate. Placing series title and episode title in two different places in a catalog description is confusing and misleading to users.

Examples: Mary Tyler Moore. Chuckles bites the dust.
General Hospital. No. 237.
The March of Time. Vol. 14, no. 18, Watchdogs of the mail.

As noted above, enter television series programs by the series and episode title, separated by a period, space. The name of a news program (or part of the program name) is often the same as the company that produced it and is capitalized because it is a corporate body name.

Example: CBS News special report. The Duke, 1907-1979.

In addition to a series title and a title of an individual segment or episode, a television series title may also include a title for a subseries, i.e., a series within a series. A subseries is a group of programs which appears in conjunction with another, more comprehensive, series of which the subseries forms a part. Though they may not formally be designated a subseries, a group of programs with the same title that is subordinate to or part of a larger series is treated as a subseries.

Example: ABC scope. The Vietnam War. How much dissent?
ABC scope. The Vietnam War. Children of war.

In television particularly, but not exclusively, there may be a secondary series title that more broadly identifies the context of a particular series title. An example would be public television's programming group, Masterpiece Theater, which includes separate series such as *Upstairs, Downstairs*, and of course individual episodes within the series.

Theatrical serials are always intended to be viewed in a specified order.

Example: Captain Midnight. Chapter 14, Scourge of revenge.

An educational or technical series title and episode title should be considered the title proper when it can be determined that the work is part of a series intended to be viewed consecutively or as a group, or that the episodes or segments build upon one another in a cumulative manner.

AMIM (cont.)

The presence of numbers is one of the major, though not the only, indicators of this situation. Segments that are quite short and that are intended to be viewed together, rather than independently, should be described using their series and segment title. Good judgment must be exercised in making the determination to describe a work using both the series and segment or episode titles.

> *Examples:* Biblical masterpieces. Song of Songs.
> Music as a language. Music as emotion.
> Music as a language. Music as sound.
> The Nature of communism. No. 1, Introduction to the course.

(*AMIM* p. 25-29)

Statement of responsibility

Another problem in film cataloging is the proliferation of credits given on the title and credits frames. Early films usually listed one producer, one director, and one production company, together with the writers and the cast. Now films give credit to many corporate bodies, and the producer and director functions seem to be done by committees.

Several rule interpretations guide us in deciding which names go in the statement of responsibility, which go in the credits note, and which are to be ignored.

> **7.1F1.** (*Amendments 1993*) Transcribe statements of responsibility relating to those persons or bodies credited in the chief source of information with a major role in creating a film (e.g., as producer, director, animator). Give all other statements of responsibility (including those relating to performance) in notes.
> **LCRI 7.1F1.** Primarily this means giving the names of corporate bodies credited with the production of the work. Personal names should also be transcribed when the person's responsibility is important in relation to the content of the work. For example, names of persons who are producers, directors, and writers are given in most instances; the name of an animator is given if animation is a significant feature of the work; the name of a photographer is given if the work is a travelog. (*CSB* 11)
> **LCRI 7.1F1.** When deciding whether to give names in the statement of responsibility or in a note, generally give the names in the statement of responsibility when the person or body has some degree of overall responsibility; use the note area for others who are responsible for only one segment or one aspect of the work. Be liberal about making exceptions to the general policy when the person's or body's responsibility is important in relation to the content of the work, i.e., give such important people and bodies in the statement of responsibility even though they may have only partial responsibility. For example, the name of a rock music performer who is the star of a performance on a videorecording may be given in the statement of responsibility even if his/her responsibility is limited to the performance.

```
Ain't that America / John Cougar Mellencamp
```

> Normally the Library of Congress considers producers, directors, and writers as having some degree of overall responsibility and gives them in the statement of responsibility. (*CSB* 36)

Richard Thaxter, Library of Congress, discusses this matter further:

> There is a larger issue here; that is, whether an agency which causes a film to be made should be given in the statement of responsibility. In general I think the answer is yes. If one body hires another to produce a film, one can usually assume that the originating agency will have a role in determining the intellectual and artistic content of the finished product. If we decide this is the case then we give both bodies in the statement of responsibility.

At the other end of the spectrum from those works created by one body under the direction of another, are films, etc., for which one agency merely provides funding for another body, or individual, who then produces the work. In this case we do not usually record the name of the sponsor. This would almost always be true in the case of "Made possible by a grant from ..." There are, of course, many situations that fall between the two obvious cases mentioned above, and in the borderline situations catalogers must make a judgment based on interpretation of statements in the work and knowledge of the bodies involved.

Statements found on the actual items are often ambiguous; it often is difficult to determine the relationship of a body to the work in hand (Online Audiovisual Catalogers. *Newsletter*, 3 (Sept. 1983), 11).

Another question in this same article refers to the phrase "produced in cooperation with." Thaxter says this phrase may be included in the statement of responsibility.

> **7.1F3.** If a statement of responsibility names both the agency responsible for the production of a motion picture or videorecording and the agency for which it is produced, give the statement as found.

This instruction to "Give the statement as found" is particularly useful whenever a confusing statement is found on a chief source of information.

The following excerpts from *Archival Moving Image Materials* may be helpful.

> A statement of responsibility is a statement, transcribed from the material being described, accompanying material, or from secondary sources, which relates all those corporate bodies and persons credited with participation in the original production of a moving image work and who are considered to be of major importance to the work. Credits and their functions are synonymous with the concept of statement of responsibility.
>
> Standard cataloging practice for archival moving image material is to give the production company as the first statement of responsibility. With few exceptions, such as amateur-produced material and the instances in which an individual does in fact perform all production activities, the production company is responsible, in a broad sense, for the overall creation of the work. The production company often serves as the coordinating body responsible for the participation of all persons and other companies in the production of a moving image work (*AMIM*, p.48).
>
> Because responsibility for moving image materials is most often complex and highly diverse, archives—particularly those with special interests—should determine the types of functions they wish to include in this area. These functions may vary from institution to institution according to the types of moving image material. For example, an archive holding television material would probably consider the function of producer more important than that of director. The opposite would be the case for archives whose collections are comprised of motion picture material (*AMIM*, p.49).
>
> With the exception of production company, which is always the first statement of responsibility for moving image material, the order of the statements of responsibility should be determined by the requirements of individual archives (*AMIM*, p.50).
>
> Choose the credit function/type of responsibility terms as found on the item unless [it is misleading] (*AMIM*, p.51).
>
> If a statement of responsibility names both the production company and the sponsor or agency for which it is produced, give the production company first. The word "presents" may imply the function of sponsor. Use the terminology on the item unless it is misleading; use judgment to distinguish corporate bodies that are sponsors from those that are production companies. Likewise, use judgment to distinguish bodies whose contribution is significant, e.g., providing major funding, from those whose participation is minor (*AMIM*, p.52).

In some cases, the same credit term has been used for differing functions during different periods of history, [and] in different parts of the moving image industry. For example, the use of the credit term, "presents," has been and continues to be ambiguous (*AMIM*, p. 53).

Edition Area
MARC field 250

Versions of feature films are being released as videorecordings. Each version is an edition, and the wording on the item is used as an edition statement.

```
250      Restored version.
250      Color version.
250      25th anniversary ed.
250      Letterbox format.
250      DVS version.
250      Director's cut.
250      Unrated version.
```

Publication, Distribution, Etc., Area
MARC field 260

The prescribed sources of information for area 4 include the chief source of information (the title and credits screens) and any accompanying material. Accompanying material would include a teacher's guide, but not the container of a videocassette. Therefore, any information taken from the container of a videocassette must be bracketed. In 1997 the Joint Steering Committee approved adding the container as a prescribed source of information but we may not use this decision until the rule change is published by ALA.

Place of publication

The place of publication or distribution for videocassettes is given only on the container in many cases. If so, it must be bracketed.

Publisher/distributor

Moving image materials are not published or distributed in the traditional manner of books and periodicals. The agency which most nearly matches the function of publisher for books, is, for films, the distributor or releasing company. (*AMIM*, p. 80).

7.4D1. (*Amendments 1993*) Give the name of the publisher, etc., and, *optionally* the name of the distributor, releasing agency, etc., and/or production agency or producer not named in the statements of responsibility (see 7.1F) as instructed in 1.4D.

The intent of this rule, according to Richard Thaxter, is to provide a way to get a name in this area that could not be entered in the statement of responsibility. We can record a producer's name, if that producer is also the distributor, in both places. The name of the publisher or distributor usually appears on the first of the title/credits frames of the motion picture or video.

Dates

Videos that are copies of feature films normally carry several dates. The date that goes in this area (MARC field 260 ǂc) is that of publication/distribution of the video you are cataloging. Look for the latest date you can find anywhere on the item — credits screens, cassette label, container — and assume it represents the publication date of the item in hand. It is bracketed if it comes from the container (not a prescribed source) or if it is an assumed date.

The original copyright date for the motion picture is given in the edition and history note under rule 7.7B7. There may be other dates representing colorization of a film, later editing of a film, or adding closed-captioning or describing the video. There may be dates on the container representing the copyright date of the design of the package, or the release of the version in hand, or for copyright renewal. Again, look for the latest date as evidence of publication, and the original copyright date of the film as well as the copyright date of the version in hand if anything was added and/or changed from the original film.

The date of publication of the item in hand goes in field 260; other dates go in edition and history notes and may be used in the fixed fields.

Dates in fixed fields

If the video is an original work, it will be date type "s" with its date in the fixed field "Dates:".

If the video is a new edition of an older work, it is treated as a new or original work. To be a new edition, it must have some change in content (material added or removed), or a change in language (closed-captioning or descriptive video added, sound track in Spanish added, etc.), or be colorized, or otherwise changed.

If the only change is to copy a film onto video, then it may be treated as date type "p" with the date of publication/ distribution as the first date and the date of original production as the second date in the fixed fields.

If you have the date of publication/distribution and a copyright date for the original item, and nothing has been changed, and the medium is the same, then use date type "t" for copyright.

Physical Description Area
MARC field 300

Extent of item

The following terms are to be used for specific material designation. A more specific term may be used if needed.

> film cartridge
> film cassette
> film loop
> film reel
> videocartridge
> videocassette
> videodisc
> videoreel

Playing time

7.5B2. Give the playing time of a motion picture or videorecording as instructed in rule 1.5B4.

```
300      1 videocassette (57 min.)
300      2 film reels (ca. 25 min. each)
300      1 film loop (3 min., 27 sec.)
```

The type of video (i.e., Beta, VHS, etc.) is no longer named here, but is given in a note.

Playing time for videodiscs

If the videodisc is of moving images, give the playing time as shown above.

```
300      1 videodisc (42 min.)
300      1 videodisc (ca. 120 min.)
```

If the videodisc consists of frames of still images, give the playing time if stated. If the number of frames is available, that information may be given.

```
300      1 videodisc (32,242 fr.)
```

If the videodisc has both still and moving images, the playing time may be given in this area, or the playing time and number of still frames may be given in a note.

Other physical details:

> **7.5C1.** Give the following details, as appropriate, in the order set out here:

> aspect ratio and special projection characteristics (motion pictures) [archival]
> sound characteristics
> colour
> projection speed (motion pictures) [if not standard for the item]

If a film has stereo sound or other specialized sound information, that information is recorded in a note rather than as part of Area 5.

Series Area
MARC fields 4XX

Prescribed sources of information for the series area are the chief source of information and accompanying material. This does not include the video container. If the series statement is taken from the container it must be bracketed.

```
440   5   [The Rodgers & Hammerstein collection]
```

Notes Area
MARC fields 5XX

Notes permitted in this chapter are:

7.7B1.   Nature or form
7.7B2.   Language
7.7B3.   Source of title proper
7.7B4.   Variations in title
7.7B5.   Parallel titles and other title information
7.7B6.   Statements of responsibility
7.7B7.   Edition and history
7.7B9.   Publication, distribution, etc., and date
7.7B10. Physical description
7.7B11. Accompanying material
7.7B12. Series
7.7B13. Dissertations
7.7B14. Audience
7.7B16. Other formats

7.7B17. Summary
7.7B18. Contents
7.7B19. Numbers
7.7B20. Copy being described, library's holdings, and restrictions on use
7.7B21. "With" notes

Notes may be combined.

```
500     Senator Hubert H. Humphrey speaks at a workshop
held July 6, 1977, at Mankato State University, on the
use of politics and the applications of power in
advancing the program, objectives, and goals of
handicapped and disabled persons.
```

7.7B1. Nature or form of a motion picture or videorecording (MARC field 500)

To be used to name or explain the form of the item as necessary.

```
500     An experimental film.
500     Documentary.
```

7.7B2. Language (MARC field 546)

The range of information that may be expressed in language notes has been expanded with recent discussions and decisions. The note was originally used for the language of the item—if the sound track of a film was in German, we said that in a note under rule 7.7B2.

An example was added to 7.7B2 in 1986 through an LCRI saying "Closed-captioned for the hearing impaired" and this was changed by JSC in 1995 to "Closed-captioned" after determining that this technique was used to add captions for the hearing impaired, but also was used for other purposes.

Many questions were raised on Autocat during 1996 about videos with captions (both closed and open), videos described by Descriptive Video Service, intertitles, videos that are signed, etc. After a number of discussions, Glenn Patton of OCLC clarified the problem as follows: "What I think we're looking at here is a continuum of the language aspects of moving image materials that moves from title cards and intertitles in silent films, to dubbing in another language, to subtitles in another language, to subtitles in the same language (which is really what traditional closed-captioning is), to signing in the same or another language, to audio description, etc." He goes on to mention videos with sound track in English but closed captions in Spanish. (e-mail 7 Feb. 1997)

As a result of these discussions, LC agreed that notes about any of these aspects of language would be coded as language notes using MARC field 546. A further series of discussions led OCLC to agree that a captioned film and the same film without captioning should be on separate bibliographic records in OCLC, as they are different editions of the title.

Closed-captioning is indicated on a package by a symbol that looks like a television set with a tail. The words "captioned" or "closed captioned" or the letters "cc" in a box sometimes are used in addition to, or instead of, the symbol. Either one of these symbols may appear on the spine of the video container with no other information given.

The Descriptive Video Service provides a description of the setting and action of a film for those who cannot see, using the second audio track of the video. The symbol for these shows sound waves coming from a speaker, and is reproduced here with the closed captioning symbols. Nearly every TV and VCR manufactured after 1988 is designed with a SAP (second audio program) switch that is needed for the DVS videos. Units made after September 1993 have a switch to display closed captions. Catalogers need to find those switches for use when previewing videos.

Figure 3

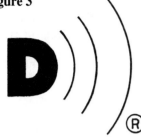  

```
546      Described for the visually handicapped.
546      Closed-captioned.
546      Sound track in German; subtitles in English.
```

7.7B3. Source of title proper (MARC field 500)

To be used if the title proper is taken from other than the chief source of information.

```
500      Title from container.
500      Title supplied by cataloger.
```

7.7B4. Variations in title (MARC fields 246, 500)

To be used to note any title appearing on the item that differs significantly from the title proper. If the title applies to the entire work, use field 246.

> **LCRI 7.7B4.** When considering 7.7B4 for a variation in title, decide first whether an added title entry is needed under the variant title. Decide this primary issue by consulting 21.2. If the variation in title is as great as the differences in titles described in 21.2, make the added entry and justify the added entry by means of a note formulated under 7.7B4, otherwise, do not apply 7.7B4. (*CSB* 13)

```
246 1    ǂi Title on cartridge and container: ǂa
Trisecting a straight line with triangles
```
   (*Title proper:* Trisecting a line with triangles)

7.7B5. Parallel titles and other title information (MARC fields 246, 500)

To be used for parallel titles and important other title information not recorded in the title and statement of responsibility area.

```
246 1    ǂi Title on manual: ǂa Getting ready to read and add
```
   (*Title proper:* Préparation à la lecture et à l'addition)

7.7B6. Statements of responsibility (MARC fields 500, 508, 511)

To be used to record important information not recorded in the statement of responsibility area.

Cast: List, in MARC field 511, featured players, performers, narrators, and/or presenters. First indicator "1" generates the display constant "Cast:"

```
511 0    Narrator: Walter Cronkite.
511 1    Gene Kelly, Donald O'Connor, Debbie Reynolds, Jean
Hagen, Millard Mitchell, Cyd Charisse.
```

Credits: List, in MARC field 508, persons other than the cast who have contributed to the artistic and technical production of a motion picture or videorecording and who are not named in the statement of responsibility. Do not include assistants, associates, etc., or any other persons making only a minor contribution. Preface each name or group of names with a statement of function.

```
508      Credits: Screenplay, Harold Pinter ; music, John
Dankworth ; camera, Gerry Fisher ; editor, Reginald Beck.
```

Notice the punctuation within the note. This type of spacing and punctuation is used because this formal note contains statement of responsibility information.

Notice also this note does not have the function and name information in the same order as that used in the 6.7B6 note. The film note has function followed by name. The music note has name followed by function. The difference is based on tradition. It would not be wrong to do it either way.

> The difference has been in place for several decades. I see some sense in both cases: screen credits usually give function first; music credits tend to put the name in primary position, "probably because normally the names are rather well known." The notes we make are more or less copied from what appears, as far as order is concerned, and there are different conventions for order from one kind of material to another. (Ben R. Tucker, letter to the author, 17 Dec. 1984).

> **LCRI 7.7B6.** For audiovisual items, generally list persons (other than producers, directors, and writers) or corporate bodies who have contributed to the artistic and technical production of a work in a credits note (see RI 7.1F1).
>
> Give the following persons or bodies in the order in which they are listed below. Preface each name or group of names with the appropriate term(s) of function:
>
> > photographer(s), camera, cameraman/men, cinematographer,
> > animator(s),
> > artist(s), illustrator(s), graphics,
> > film editor(s), photo editor(s), editor(s),
> > narrator(s), voice(s),
> > music,
> > consultant(s), adviser(s).
>
> Do not include the following persons or bodies performing these functions:
>
> > assistants or associates,
> > production supervisors or coordinators,
> > project or executive editors,
> > technical advisers or consultants,
> > audio or sound engineers,
> > writers of discussion, program, or teacher's guides,
> > other persons making only a minor or purely technical contribution.

(*CSB* 22)

Richard Thaxter commented on this LCRI: "The list of persons to include and the order in which they should go is neither prescriptive nor exhaustive. The list in rule interpretation 7.7B6 was designed to solve data sheet cataloging problems at LC" (Online Audiovisual Catalogers. *Newsletter,* 3 (Sept. 1983), 10).

7.7B7. Edition and history (MARC field 500)

To be used for information about earlier editions, or the history of the item being cataloged.

LCRI 7.7B7. When an item is known to have an original master in a different medium and the production or release date of the master is more than two years earlier than that of the item being cataloged, give an edition/history note.

```
Originally produced as motion picture in [year]
Originally issued as filmstrip in [year]
```

Make a similar note when an item is known to have been previously produced or issued (more than two years earlier) if in a different medium, but the original medium is unknown.

```
Previously produced as motion picture in [year]
Previously issued as slide set in [year]
```

If the date of production or release of an original master or an earlier medium is unknown or if the difference between its production or release date and the production or release date of the item being cataloged is two years or less, indicate the availability of the other medium or media in a note according to 7.7B16.

Note: The use of production versus release dates is left to the cataloger's judgment. Make the note that seems best to give information about either production or release of other formats on a case-by-case basis. (*CSB* 15)

See also the discussion on the above topic in chapter 2 of this book.

```
500     Issued in 1945 as motion picture.
500     Revised version of the filmstrip issued in 1967 under the
same title.
```

7.7B9. Publication, distribution, etc., and date (MARC field 500)

To be used for important information not recorded in the publication, distribution, etc., area.

LCRI 7.7B9. When a foreign firm, etc., is given in the source as emanator or originator, do not assume that the item was either made or released in that country if not so stated. Instead use the note

```
A foreign film (Yugoslavia)
```

For a U.S. emanator and a foreign producer or a foreign emanator and a U.S. producer, do not make the note. (*CSB* 13)

7.7B10. Physical description (MARC fields 500, 538)

Different physical description characteristics may be given in the notes. The most common notes are explained here.

```
500     Sepia print.
500     Technicolor.
```

Stereo sound is indicated in a note rather than in area 5.

Dolby sound is indicated on the container by the Dolby symbol of back-to-back upper-case Ds in an oblong, or by the word "stereo" enclosed in a pair of Ds. The container may say Dolby stereo, Dolby system, Dolby surround, or other wording. The presence of Dolby sound is to be indicated in a note.

Figure 4

▯STEREO▯

▯◖ DOLBY SYSTEM ®

The videorecording system (VHS, Beta, LaserVision, etc.) is given in a note rather than in area 5. If desired, this information may be given as the first note in the bibliographic record, according to rule 1.7B of the 1988 revision. Give the information as found on the item. The abbreviation "stereo." ends in a period.

```
538     VHS hi-fi stereo., Dolby system, on linear tracks.
538     VHS hi-fi, Dolby stereo.
538     VHS hi-fi, stereo., Dolby surround, videophonic sound
digitally duplicated.
538     LaserVision CAV.
538     U-matic.
538     Beta.
```

Other notes, for archival cataloging, deal with length of film or tape in feet, type of color, form of print, film base, generation of copy, special projection requirements, and any other physical details important for use or preservation.

7.7B11. Accompanying material (MARC field 500)

To be used for any important information not given in the accompanying material part of area 5.

```
500     Guide includes bibliography.
```

7.7B12. Series (MARC field 500)

To be used for any important information not recorded in the series area.

```
500     Formerly issued as part of series: The Atlantic
community.
```

7.7B13. Dissertations (MARC field 502)

To be used for the standard dissertation note when applicable.

```
502     Thesis (Ed. Sp.)--Mankato State University, 1982.
```

7.7B14. Audience (MARC field 521)

To be used to record the intended audience of a work; use this note only if the information is stated on the item. Do not attempt to judge the audience for an item. If no indicator, the display constant "Audience:" will be generated. First indicator "8" is used when no display constant is wanted.

```
521     Grade 3-4.
521 8   MPAA rating: R.
```

7.7B16. Other formats (MARC field 530)

To be used to list other formats in which the work is available. The Library of Congress lists all formats available commercially.

> 530   Issued also as 1/2 in. Beta I videocassette.

7.7B17. Summary (MARC field 520)

To be used for a brief objective summary of the content of the item. Do not use a summary if the rest of the bibliographic record provides enough information.

> 520   A documentary of the history of the brewing industry in
> Mankato, Minn.

7.7B18. Contents (MARC fields 505, 500)

To be used for a formal (field 505) or informal (field 500) listing of the contents of the item.

> 505 0   1. Who killed Jesus Christ? -- 2. Let His blood fall on
> our heads -- 3. And on the heads of our children -- 4. Calvary.
> The verdict.

7.7B19. Numbers (MARC field 500)

To be used to list any important number appearing on the item other than those to be recorded in the 02X fields. The number may be in quotes with a source named if not from one of the authorized sources for this field.

A manufacturer's number for videorecordings is recorded in field 028 with first indicator "4." It does not end in a period.

> 500   "RGA 42-95."
> 028 40   909 ǂb Walt Disney Home Video

7.7B20. Copy being described, library's holdings, and restrictions on use (MARC fields 506, 590)

Field 506 is used for general restrictions on use of an item.

> 506   "For private home use only."
> 506   Licensed for individual viewing only.

Field 590 is used for any notes applicable only to the particular copy of the item being described. It also is used for local library restrictions on the material being described or for information of use only to patrons of the local library.

> 590   To be used by nursing students only.
> 590   Rights to this broadcast expire with the life of this
> tape.

7.7B21. "With" notes (MARC field 501)

To be used for "with" notes.

> 501   In cassette with: Saga of the whale.

Main Entry

There has been recent controversy about the choice of main entry for some types of videos. Some music people argue that a video of a performance should carry the same main entry as the score or sound recording of that performance. Videos usually have one or more corporate bodies and many people involved in the production, direction, editing, and other aspects of creating the production that is filmed. The rules direct us, when responsibility is diffuse, to enter under title. *Cataloging Musical Moving Image Material*, edited by Lowell E. Ashley (Canton, Mass.: Music Library Association, 1996), gives a clear and fair history of this problem, and directs users to follow the rules as written while working to bring about any changes needed. It states:

> A moving image work which is deemed to be a work of mixed responsibility and which is shown to be such in its bibliographic description is entered under title, except one which qualifies for entry under a corporate body under AACR2 21.1B2 or a principal performer under LCRI 21.23C (music videos). (p. 5)

It is rare to encounter a commercial video that is wholly the work of one person; it is even more rare to find a video that would receive corporate main entry. To receive corporate main entry, the item must "emanate" from the corporate body and fall into one of the six categories specified in 21.1B2; if there is any doubt, it is entered under title.

In the days of card catalogs, one might want all manifestations of a work to carry the same main entry and file together in a card catalog. Now, with online catalogs, access by composer or uniform title or librettist or whatever/whomever is easily provided, so that bibliographic records for all manifestations of a work are easily accessible by a composer search or any other search desired.

An LCRI in 1989 (*CSB* 45) directed us to apply rules 21.23C1 and 21.23D1 to "videorecordings that contain collections of music performed by a principal performer." This LCRI is used in the Madonna example (ex. 34) later in this chapter.

Genre Access

Genre headings are discussed briefly in an earlier chapter of this book. They are most useful when cataloging videos, particularly when cataloging videos of feature films.

Genre headings provide access to the form of an item, or the form of the content of the item, rather than to the subject matter covered by the item being cataloged.

The Library of Congress list of subject headings has always intermingled true subject headings with genre headings; indeed, the same term is frequently used for both concepts, leading to some confusion. Do you want a work about "Video recordings for the hearing impaired" or do you want a video that is to be used by someone with that impairment? The same heading applies to both. "Comedy films," "Detective and mystery films," "Western films" and many similar headings apply equally well to works about the subject, bibliographies of works on the subject, a filmographies, or the films themselves.

The Library of Congress does not use distinctive coding for genre headings at this time.

The following examples show some genre headings coded appropriately:

```
655  7  Video recordings for the hearing impaired ǂ2 lcsh
655  7  Video recordings for the visually handicapped ǂ2 lcsh
655  7  Sign language ǂ2 lcsh
655  7  Science fiction films ǂ2 lcsh
655  7  Star Trek films ǂ2 lcsh
```

Example 18. A Star is Born

This video presents a number of cataloging problems. The container and the videocassette label say "restored version" and the container explains the story of the film. The original 181-minute film was cut to 153 minutes before release. Most of the missing footage was recovered in the 1987 restoration, and still photographs with narration were used for the scenes not found. The restored version is an edition of the original 1954 film.

This same story has been made into film three different times, each with the same title. The first was made in 1937, with Janet Gaynor, Frederick March, and Adolphe Menjou. The second is the one cataloged here, made in 1954 with Judy Garland, James Mason, and Jack Carson. The third was made in 1976 with Barbra Streisand, Kris Kristofferson, and Gary Busey.

A uniform title main entry is needed for each, with the date added to distinguish among them. This restored version needs both the original date (1954) and the version information to distinguish it from the original 1954 version, also available on videocassette.

Uniform titles for the three versions, and for the restored version, would be as follows:

```
Star is born (1937)
Star is born (1954)
Star is born (1954 : Restored version)
Star is born (1976)
```

If your library only owned one of these, and there were no conflict in your catalog, you might choose not to use the uniform title main entry.

Cassette label   **Side of box**

From front of box

Restored Version

JUDY GARLAND · JAMES MASON "A STAR IS BORN"
Also Starring JACK CARSON · CHARLES BICKFORD · Screenplay by MOSS HART
Selected Songs: Music by HAROLD ARLEN · Lyrics by IRA GERSHWIN
Musical Direction by RAY HEINDORF · Produced by SIDNEY LUFT
Directed by GEORGE CUKOR

From Warner Bros. A Warner Communications Company

From back of box

"Dolby" and the ⫿⫿ are trademarks of Dolby Laboratories Licensing Corporation.
The linear audio tracks on this tape have been encoded with Dolby B-type noise reduction.
Program Content & Photography ©1954 Warner Bros. Pictures Inc.
Renewed ©1982 Warner Bros. Inc.
Artwork ©1983 Warner Bros. Inc.
Package Design & Summary ©1987 Warner Home Video Inc.
A Subsidiary of Warner Bros. Inc. A Warner Communications Company
4000 Warner Blvd., Burbank, CA 91522. All rights reserved.

Example 18. A Star is Born

Transcription of major title and credits screens

Warner Home Video

Warner Bros Pictures

Judy Garland

James Mason

in

A Star is Born

[other cast]

Screen Play by Moss Hart

Based on
the Dorothy Parker, Alan Campbell
Robert Carson Screen Play
From a Story by
William A. Wellman and Robert Carson

New Songs
Music by Harold Arlen
Lyrics by Ira Gershwin

Musical Direction by Ray Heindorf

Produced by Sidney Luft

Directed by George Cukor

Example 18. A Star is Born

```
Type: g   ELvl: I   Srce: d   Audn: g   Ctrl:       Lang: eng
BLvl: m   TMat: v   GPub:     AccM:     MRec:       Ctry: cau
Desc: a   Time: 176 Tech: l   DtSt: s   Dates: 1987,
 1 040      XXX ǂc XXX
 2 007      v ǂb f ǂd c ǂe b ǂf a ǂg h ǂh o ǂi s
 3 028 40   11335 ǂb Warner Home Video
 4 090      PN1995.9.M86 ǂb S7 1954a
 5 049      XXXX
 6 130 0    Star is born (1954 : Restored version)
 7 245 12   A star is born ǂh [videorecording] / ǂc Warner Bros. Pictures ;
screen play by Moss Hart ; produced by Sidney Luft ; directed by George
Cukor.
 8 250      Restored version.
 9 260      [Burbank, CA] : ǂb Warner Home Video, ǂc [1987].
10 300      2 videocassettes (176 min.) : ǂb sd., col. ; ǂc 1/2 in.
11 511 1    Judy Garland, James Mason, Jack Carson, Charles Bickford.
12 508      Music, Harold Arlen ; lyrics, Ira Gershwin.
13 500      "Based on the Dorothy Parker, Alan Campbell, Robert Carson
screenplay from a story by William A. Wellman and Robert Carson."
14 500      Originally released as motion picture in 1954.
15 538      VHS hi-fi, Dolby stereo.
16 521 8    MPAA rating: PG.
17 520      A classic story of fame, innocence, and destruction, as a matinee
idol (Mason) falls in love with a young girl (Garland) and propels her to
stardom.
18 650 0    Feature films.
19 650 0    Musical films.
20 650 0    Motion picture actors and actresses.
21 700 1    Hart, Moss, ǂd 1904-1961.
22 700 1    Luft, Sid.
23 700 1    Cukor, George Dewey, ǂd 1899-
24 700 1    Garland, Judy.
25 700 1    Mason, James, ǂd 1909-
26 700 1    Carson, Jack, ǂd 1910-1963.
27 700 1    Bickford, Charles, ǂd 1899-1967.
28 700 1    Arlen, Harold, ǂd 1905-1986.
29 700 1    Gershwin, Ira, ǂd 1896-
30 710 2    Warner Bros. Pictures.
31 710 2    Warner Home Video (Firm).
```

Comments

Cataloging: "Restored version" is used as the edition statement for this video.

The place and date of publication are bracketed because they do not appear in the film credits; they are on the container.

Rules for notes: 7.7B6 (1st), 7.7B6 (2nd), 7.7B7, 7.7B7, 7.7B10f and a, 7.7B14.

Access: The parenthetical qualifier in field 130 is not separately subfielded. Each system has its own way of handling indexed fields with parenthetical qualifiers. Make sure you know what your local system does and how to retrieve information from these fields.

The first two subject headings are genre headings. I use the date the film was made in the classification number rather than the date the item being cataloged was distributed, so patrons are not misled by thinking this is a new work. I added "a" to the date to indicate it is not quite the same as the work we own without the "a".

Example 18. A Star is Born

   Processing: A library would want to repackage this in a sturdy container. We use plastic containers that have clear sleeves on the outside. The original box is cut into pieces and the front, back, and spine are inserted into these sleeves. With this packaging we do not lose any of the important (and attractive) information on the package, and the cassettes are protected from dust.

   Do NOT sensitize or desensitize videocassettes. They are magnetic.

Example 19. The Sound of Music

On the overwrap

> Silver Anniversary Edition

On the front of the box

> Silver Anniversary

Also on the box

> THE RODGERS & HAMMERSTEIN COLLECTION

Transcription of significant title and credits screens

CBS Fox Video
c1990

[sales pitch for Rodgers & Hammerstein Collection of videos]

Stereo Surround

[Interview with Robert Wise]

20th Century Fox

A Robert Wise Production of
Rodgers and Hammerstein's

**The
Sound of Music**

starring
Julie Andrews
Christopher Plummer
…
Music by Richard Rodgers
Lyrics by Oscar Hammerstein II
Additional Words and Music by
Richard Rodgers

Music supervised, arranged, and conducted by Irwin Kostal

From the stage musical with music and lyrics by
Richard Rodgers and Oscar Hammerstein II

Book by Howard Lindsay and Russel Crouse

originally produced on the stage by
Leland Hayward, Richard Halliday, Richard Rodgers, and Oscar Hammerstein II

Screenplay by Ernest Lehman

Directed by Robert Wise

Example 19. The Sound of Music

```
Type: g  ELvl: I   Srce: d   Audn: g    Ctrl:      Lang: eng
BLvl: m  TMat: v   GPub:     AccM:      MRec:      Ctry: nyu
Desc: a  Time: 175 Tech: l   DtSt: s    Dates: 1990,
 1 040      XXX ǂc XXX
 2 007      v ǂb f ǂd c ǂe b ǂf a ǂg h ǂh o ǂi s
 3 090      PN1995.9.M86 ǂb R6 1965a
 4 049      XXXX
 5 245 00   Rodgers and Hammerstein's the sound of music ǂh [videorecording] /
ǂc 20th Century-Fox ; directed by Robert Wise ; screenplay by Ernest Lehman.
 6 246 30   Sound of music
 7 250      [Silver anniversary ed.].
 8 260      [New York, NY] : ǂb CBS/Fox Video, ǂc c1990.
 9 300      2 videocassettes (175 min.) : ǂb sd., col. ; ǂc 1/2 in.
10 440 5    [The Rodgers & Hammerstein collection]
11 538      VHS format, stereo.
12 546      Closed-captioned.
13 511      Julie Andrews, Christopher Plummer, Richard Haydn, Peggy Wood,
Eleanor Parker, Charmian Carr, the Bil Baird Marionettes.
14 508      Music by Richard Rodgers, lyrics by Oscar Hammerstein II, with
additional words and music by Richard Rodgers ; music supervised, arranged,
and conducted by Irwin Kostal.
15 500      Originally released as motion picture in 1965.
16 500      Based on the stage musical with music and lyrics by Richard
Rodgers and Oscar Hammerstein II, book by Howard Lindsay and Russel Crouse,
which was based on the lives of the Trapp Family Singers.
17 521 8    MPAA rating: G.
18 520      A young girl named Maria is uncertain about her decision to enter
a religious order. While deciding what to do, she becomes the governess of
the seven Von Trapp children who live with their widowed father, a former
captain in the Austrian navy. Set in Austria just before its takeover by the
Nazis in 1938.
19 500      Feature preceded by 1990 interview with director Robert Wise and
by advertisement for titles in the CBS/Fox Rodgers & Hammerstein collection.
20 650  0   Musical films.
21 610 20   Trapp Family Singers ǂx Drama.
22 650  0   Vocation (in religious orders, congregations, etc.).
23 651  0   Austria ǂx History ǂy 1918-1938.
24 650  0   Video recordings for the hearing impaired.
25 700 1    Wise, Robert, ǂd 1914-
26 700 1    Lehman, Ernest, ǂd 1915-
27 700 1    Andrews, Julie.
28 700 1    Plummer, Christopher.
29 700 1    Haydn, Richard, ǂd 1905-
30 700 1    Wood, Peggy, ǂd 1892-1978.
31 700 1    Parker, Eleanor, ǂd 1922-
32 700 1    Carr, Charmian.
33 700 1    Rodgers, Richard, ǂd 1902-
34 700 1    Hammerstein, Oscar, ǂd 1895-1960.
35 700 1    Lindsay, Howard, ǂd 1889-1968.
36 700 1    Crouse, Russel, ǂd 1893-1966.
37 710 2    Twentieth Century-Fox Film Corporation.
38 710 2    CBS Fox Video.
```

Example 19. The Sound of Music

```
39 710 2   Bil Baird Marionettes.
40 710 2   Argyle Enterprises.
41 710 2   CBS Fox Video.
```

Comments

General: This video was one of the first of the anniversary editions of motion pictures.

Cataloging: The title proper is as it appears on the title screens, with the personal possessive "Rodgers and Hammerstein's" preceding the "real" title. It must be transcribed as such according to the LCRI for film titles. A 246 is used for the "real" title and both are retrievable in any online system.

The edition and series information came from the box rather than the title and credits screens, so, if used, must be recorded in brackets.

Rules for notes: 7.7B10 (moved to first position), 7.7B2, 7.7B6, 7.7B6, 7.7B7, 7.7B7, 7.7B14, 7.7B17, 7.7B18. One could add a contents note and added entries for the songs.

Access: I used subject headings for type of film (genre), for the setting and time period (Austria ...), for the closed-captioning, for the Trapp Family, and for religious vocation. I make personal added entries in the order names appear in the bibliographic description, as it is easier to check to see if I've missed anyone. I make added entries for all corporate bodies named.

This film could be classed in the number for the Trapp Family Singers, or with history of Austria during the time period 1938.

MARC coding/tagging: "Ctry" in the fixed field is coded for country of production of the motion picture rather than place of distribution of the item in hand.

I carefully arrange the notes in the order of the AACR 2 rules. The order makes sense to me, as it arranges notes in the same order as areas 1-6 of the bibliographic description. Systems that rearrange these notes in order of MARC tag negate our careful work.

Example 20: Singin' in the Rain

The VHS, CAV, and CLV versions of Singin' in the Rain

Transcription of title and credits screens

MGM/UA Home Video

Metro Goldwyn Mayer

| Gene | Debbie | Donald |
| Kelly | Reynolds | O'Connor |

in

Singin' In The Rain

with

| Jean | Millard |
| Hagen | Mitchell |

Cyd
Charisse

Story and Screen Play by
Adolph Green and Betty Comden

Suggested by the Song "Singin' in the Rain"

Songs:
Lyrics by Arthur Freed
Music by Nacio Herb Brown

Example 20: Singin' in the Rain

Produced by Arthur Freed

Directed by Gene Kelly and Stanley Donen

The CAV and CLV videodiscs have the following additional credits at the beginning of the title and credits frames:

Criterion
MGM/UA Home Video
Turner

```
Type: g    ELvl: I    Srce: d    Audn: g    Ctrl:      Lang: eng
BLvl: m    TMat: v    GPub:      AccM:      MRec:      Ctry: cau
Desc: a    Time: 103  Tech: l    DtSt: s    Dates: 1990,
 1 040       XXX ǂc XXX
 2 007       v ǂb d ǂd c ǂe g ǂf a ǂg i ǂh z ǂi u
 3 028 40    CC1210L ǂb Voyager
 4 090       PN1995.9.M86 ǂb S4 1952a
 5 049       XXXX
 6 245 00    Singin' in the rain ǂh [videorecording] / ǂc Metro Goldwyn Mayer ;
produced by Arthur Freed ; directed by Gene Kelly and Stanley Donen ; story
and screen play by Adolph Green and Betty Comden.
 7 246 3     Singing in the rain
 8 260       [Santa Monica, Calif.: ǂb Distributed by the Voyager Company, ǂc
1990].
 9 300       1 videodisc (103 min.) : ǂb sd., col. ; ǂc 12 in.
10 440 0     Criterion collection ; ǂv 52A
11 511       Gene Kelly, Debbie Reynolds, Donald O'Connor, Jean Hagen, Millard
Mitchell, Cyd Charisse.
12 508       Lyrics by Arthur Freed ; music by Nacio Herb Brown.
13 500       Originally released as a motion picture in 1952.
14 538       Extended play (CLV)
15 521 8     MPAA rating: G.
16 520       Musical comedy parody of Hollywood's transition to talking
pictures in the 1920s.
17 650  0    Feature films.
18 650  0    Musical films.
19 650  0    Sound motion pictures ǂx History.
20 700 1     Freed, Arthur, ǂd 1894-1973.
21 700 1     Kelly, Gene, ǂd 1912-
22 700 1     Donen, Stanley.
23 700 1     Green, Adolph.
24 700 1     Comden, Betty.
25 700 1     Reynolds, Debbie.
26 700 1     O'Connor, Donald, ǂd 1925-
27 700 1     Hagen, Jean, ǂd 1924-1977.
28 700 1     Mitchell, Millard, ǂd 1900-1953.
29 700 1     Charisse, Cyd.
30 710 2     Metro-Goldwyn-Mayer.
31 710 2     Voyager Company.
```

Example 20: Singin' in the Rain

Comments

General: The photograph here shows three versions of Singin' in the Rain, VHS videocassette and CAV and CLV videodiscs. The complete MARC record shows the complete bibliographic record for the CLV video disc. This two-sided videodisc may be searched by "chapters" of the film.

The CAV disc allows random access, slow and fast motion, and freeze frame functions. It includes supplementary material on side 4 of the 2 videodiscs in its package.

Cataloging: If you had all three of these in your collection, you would need to set up uniform titles for each.

Access: The manufacturer's number is put in field 028, just as for sound recordings, but with indicator "4" to indicate this is a videorecording number.

This film could be classed with history of motion pictures rather than in the number I used for musicals.

Cataloging for CAV videodisc:

Much of the bibliographic record would be the same for both CAV and CLV discs. The series number for the CAV version is 52 rather than the 52A for the CLV version. The CAV version has 2 videodiscs rather than 1, but we do not know how many minutes the total package runs. Field 538 would, using the words on the item, say "Full feature format (CAV)."

Added fields (and these would require additional added entries as well):

```
500     Audio essay by Ronald Haver is on the second audio track.
500     Following the film are original film versions of the
songs Singin' in the rain (Cliff Edwards), Beautiful girl (Bing
Crosby), and You were meant for me (Charles King and Anita Page).
```

Also included are an early demonstration of talking movies, and an outtake from the film.

Example 21. Cathedral

Information on the back of the box

CATHEDRAL

The Story of Its Construction

The illustrator par excellence, David Macaulay, serves as your host in this highly-praised special, originally aired on PBS and based on his internationally celebrated book.

"CATHEDRAL is a delight…a great plum pudding of a program."—The New York Times

Based on the award-winning book by David Macaulay, CATHEDRAL uses live-action film and cinema-quality animation to illustrate the planning, building, and cultural importance of the Gothic cathedral. Filmed on location at eight awe-inspiring churches, this wonderful film provides a look at Gothic cathedrals throughout France, while animated portions inspired by Macaulay's acclaimed line drawings trace the design and construction of an imaginary but historically accurate cathedral near Paris.

The locations include: Amiens, Chartres, Bourges, Reims, Beauvais, Notre-Dame de Paris and the Royal Abbey Church of St. Denis.

© 1985, UNICORN PROJECTS INC. DISTRIBUTED BY DORSET VIDEO.

Host
David Macaulay, with French actress
Caroline Berg

Narrator
Derek Jacobi (animated sequences)

Animation
Animation Partnership Ltd. London

Producer
Unicorn Projects, Inc., Washington, DC
Presented on PBS by WGBH Boston

Underwriters
National Endowment for the Humanities and
the Arthur Vining Davis Foundations

Project Advisors
John Baldwin, Johns Hopkins University
William Clark, Queens College
David Herlihy, Harvard University
Robert Mark, Princeton University
Gabrielle M. Spiegel, University of Maryland

Illustration from CATHEDRAL by David Macaulay
© 1973. Published by Houghton Mifflin Company

Example 21. Cathedral

Transcription of significant title and credits screens

The National Endowment for the Humanities
The Arthur Vining Davis Foundations
Unicorn Projects
A Unicorn Project

Cathedral

Based on the book by David Macaulay
with David Macaulay and Caroline Beny

Executive Producer Ray Hubbard

Written and Produced by Mark Olshaker and Larry Klein

Animation Created and Directed by Tony White

Original Music Score by Ian Llande and Steve Parr

Live Action Sequences by Carl Gover Associates
Directed by Tim King
Producer Colin Leighton
c1985

Example 21. Cathedral

```
Type: g   ELvl: I   Srce: d   Audn: g   Ctrl:        Lang: eng
BLvl: m   TMat: v   GPub:     AccM:     MRec:        Ctry: enk
Desc: a   Time: 058 Tech: c   DtSt: s   Dates: 1985,
```

```
 1 040      XXX ǂc XXX
 2 007      v ǂb f ǂd c ǂe b ǂf a ǂg h ǂh o ǂi u
 3 020      1556583362
 4 090      NA5543 ǂb .C3 1985
 5 049      XXXX
 6 245 00   Cathedral ǂh [videorecording] / ǂc Unicorn Projects ; written and
produced by Mark Olshaker and Larry Klein ; animation created and directed by
Tony White ; live action sequences by Carl Gover Associates ; directed by Tim
King ; producer, Colin Leighton.
 7 260      [England? : ǂb Dorset Video], ǂc c1985.
 8 300      1 videocassette (58 min.) : ǂb sd., col. ; ǂc 1/2 in.
 9 508      Music, Ian Llande, Steve Parr.
10 500      Based on the book by David Macaulay.
11 500      Originally produced for television in 1985.
12 538      VHS.
13 520      Follows, through animation, the planning and construction of a
Gothic cathedral in the imaginary French town of Beaulieu during the
thirteenth century. In live-action sequences David Macaulay and Caroline Beny
explain why and how the great cathedrals of Europe were built.
14 650  0   Cathedrals ǂz France.
15 650  0   Architecture, Gothic ǂz France.
16 700 1    Olshaker, Mark, ǂd 1951-
17 700 1    Klein, Larry, ǂd 1929-
18 700 1    White, Tony, ǂd 1947-
19 700 1    King, Tim.
20 700 1    Leighton, Colin.
21 700 1    Llande, Ian.
22 700 1    Parr, Steve.
23 700 1    Beny, Caroline.
24 700 1    Macaulay, David. ǂt Cathedral.
25 710 2    Unicorn Projects, Inc.
26 710 2    Carl Gover Associates.
27 710 2    Dorset Video (Firm)
```

Comments

General: This video has both animated and live action portions, resulting in twice the normal number of credits for producer, director, etc. The video was originally produced for television, then sold in the 60-minute version, and in a 30-minute edited version. It is based on a book of the same title.

Cataloging: Nowhere on the item or its packaging does it indicate any location for Dorset Video, which is named only on the container. We assume it was produced in England and place both "England" and "Dorset Video" in brackets.

Access: It was difficult to read some of the names in the credits. When they can't be verified in the authority file, I do the best I can. The container gave a name as Caroline Berg. The credits were blurred. The authority file had a Caroline Beny who seemed to fit, so I used that.

MARC coding/tagging: In the fixed fields, "Tech" is coded "c" for a combination of animation and live action.

Example 22. Frosty the Snowman

Distribution information on the container with ISBN

```
┌─────────────────────────────────────────────┐
│                              ISBN 1-55658-336-2  │
│  Christmas Classics          Exclusively Distributed By │
│                              MCA DISTRIBUTING CORP.   │
│  S • E • R • I • E • S                            │
│                         0   1223-27311-3    3    │
└─────────────────────────────────────────────┘
```

Transcription of most title and credits screens

Family Home Entertainment

Rankin/Bass Present

Frosty the Snowman

Told & Sung by Jimmy Durante

Starring Billy DeWolfe as The Magician

and

Jackie Vernon as "Frosty"

Produced & Directed by Arthur Rankin, Jr. & Jules Bass

Written by Romeo Mueller

Example 22. Frosty the Snowman

```
Type: g   ELvl: I   Srce: d   Audn: g   Ctrl:       Lang: eng
BLvl: m   TMat: v   GPub:      AccM:     MRec:       Ctry: cau
Desc: a   Time: 030 Tech: a   DtSt: s   Dates: 1989
 1 040       XXX ǂc XXX
 2 007       v ǂb f ǂd c ǂe b ǂf a ǂg h ǂh o ǂi u
 3 020       1556583362
 4 024       012232731133
 5 090       PN1995.9.C5 ǂb F7 1969
 6 049       XXXX
 7 245 00  Frosty the Snowman ǂh [videorecording] / ǂc produced & directed by
Arthur Rankin, Jr. & Jules Bass ; written by Romeo Muller.
 8 260       [Van Nuys, CA] : ǂb Family Home Entertainment : ǂb [Exclusively
distributed by MCA Distributing Corp., ǂc 1989].
 9 300       1 videocassette (30 min.) ; ǂb sd., col. ; ǂc 1/2 in.
10 440 0   [Christmas classics series]
11 511 0   Told and sung by Jimmy Durante ; Billy DeWolfe as the Magician,
Jackie Vernon as Frosty.
12 500       Based on the song by Steve Nelson.
13 500       Produced for television in 1969.
14 538       VHS.
15 520       When Frosty the Snowman is accidently brought to life, he must
outwit the plans of an evil magician in order to find safety at the North
Pole.
16 650  0  Christmas stories.
17 650  0  Children's films.
18 650  0  Animated films.
19 700  1  Rankin, Arthur.
20 700  1  Bass, Jules.
21 700  1  Muller, Romeo.
22 700  1  Durante, Jimmy.
23 700  1  De Wolfe, Billy, ǂd 1907-1974.
24 700  1  Vernon, Jackie.
25 700  1  Nelson, Steve Edward, ǂd 1907-   ǂt Frosty the Snowman.
26 710  2  Family Home Entertainment (Firm).
```

Comments

General: This animated film was produced for television and later distributed in videocassette.

Cataloging: There is an ISBN on the package, so that is included in the bibliographic record. At the time this was distributed, very few videos carried ISBNs.

The wording about distribution is taken exactly as found on the package. MARC coding/tagging: "Dates" in the fixed field show only the date of the videorecording being cataloged. The date of the original production is given in a note, but that is not the date of the version in hand.

MARC coding/tagging: Field 024 is for the number below the barcode on the container.

Example 23. Damon Runyon's Sorrowful Jones

Transcription from the back of box

PARAMOUNT presents
BOB HOPE • LUCILLE BALL
in DAMON RUNYON'S "SORROWFUL JONES"
with WILLIAM DEMAREST • BRUCE CABOT
THOMAS GOMEZ and introducing MARY ANNE SAUNDERS
Forward narrated by WALTER WINCHELL • Produced by ROBERT L. WELCH
Directed by SIDNEY LANDFIELD • Screenplay by MELVILLE SHAVELSON, EDWARD HARTMANN
and JACK ROSE • Adapted from a story by DAMON RUNYON and a screenplay by
WILLIAM R. LIPMAN, SAM HELLMAN and GLADYS LEHMAN
© 1949 Paramount Pictures Inc. Renewed 1976 by EMKA. All Rights Reserved.

70 UNIVERSAL PLAZA, UNIVERSAL CITY, CA 91608
©1988 MCA Home Video, Inc. All Rights Reserved. Printed in U.S.A.

Transcription of most title and credits screens

MCA Home Video

A Paramount Picture

Bob Hope and Lucille Ball
in
Damon Runyon's

Sorrowful Jones

with
William Demarest
Bruce Cabot
Thomas Gomez
Tom Pedi
Paul Lees
Houseley Stevenson
and introducing
Mary Jane Saunders

Screenplay by Melville Shavelson, Edward Hartmann and Jack Rose

Adapted from a story by Damon Runyon
and a screenplay by William R. Lipman, Sam Hellman, and Gladys Lehman

Produced by Robert L. Welch
Directed by Sidney Lanfield

Example 23. Damon Runyon's Sorrowful Jones

```
Type: g  ELvl: I  Srce: d  Audn: g   Ctrl:      Lang: eng
BLvl: m  TMat: v  GPub:    AccM:     MRec:      Ctry: cau
Desc: a  Time: 088 Tech: l  DtSt: s   Dates: 1988,
```

1	040	XXX ‡c XXX
2	007	v ‡b f ‡d b ‡e b ‡f a ‡g h ‡h o ‡i u
3	090	PN1995.9.C55 ‡b D3 1949
4	049	XXXX
5	245 00	Damon Runyon's Sorrowful Jones ‡h [videorecording] / ‡c a Paramount Picture ; produced by Robert L. Welch ; directed by Sidney Lanfield ; screenplay by Melville Shavelson, Edward Hartmann, and Jack Rose.
6	246 30	Sorrowful Jones
7	260	[Universal City, Calif.] : ‡b MCA Home Video, ‡c 1988.
8	300	1 videocassette (88 min.) : ‡b sd., b&w ; ‡c 1/2 in.
9	538	VHS.
10	511 1	Bob Hope, Lucille Ball, William Demarest, Bruce Cabot, Mary Jane Saunders.
11	511 0	"Forward [sic] narrated by Walter Winchell."
12	508	Music score, Robert Emmett Dolan.
13	500	Adapted from a story by Damon Runyon and a screenplay by William R. Lipman, Sam Hellman and Gladys Lehman.
14	500	Originally produced as motion picture in 1949.
15	520	A penny-pinching Broadway bookie, Sorrowful Jones (Hope) inherits a five-year-old girl on a bet. Big Steve (Cabot) is a bad guy with a horse in the big race, Gladys O'Neill (Ball) is a night club singer friendly with both Hope and Cabot.
16	650 0	Feature films.
17	650 0	Comedy films.
18	650 0	Bookmakers (Gambling).
19	700 1	Welch, Robert, ‡d 1910-
20	700 1	Lanfield, Sidney, ‡d 1898-1972.
21	700 1	Shavelson, Melville, ‡d 1917-
22	700 1	Hartmann, Edward.
23	700 1	Rose, Jack, ‡d 1911-
24	700 1	Hope, Bob, ‡d 1903-
25	700 1	Ball, Lucille, ‡d 1911-1989.
26	700 1	Demarest, William.
27	700 1	Saunders, Mary Jane.
28	700 1	Winchell, Walter, ‡d 1897-1972.
29	700 1	Dolan, Robert Emmett, ‡d 1908-
30	700 1	Runyon, Damon, ‡d 1880-1946.
31	700 1	Lipman, William R.
32	700 1	Hellman, Sam.
33	700 1	Lehman, Gladys.
34	710 2	Paramount Pictures, inc.
35	710 2	MCA Home Video (Firm).

Comments

General: This is another example with a personal possessive appearing before the title.

Cataloging: For all these films, the credits considered most important go in the statement of responsibility. Other credits that you decide should be included go in notes. Cast is always named in a note rather than in the statement of responsibility.

Example 23. Damon Runyon's Sorrowful Jones

　　Access: You might not want or need as many added entries for your patrons — this is one of the decisions you make based on the needs of your patrons.

　　MARC coding/tagging: The note "VHS" can be moved to the first position if you want.

Example 34. Ciao, Italia

Transcription of some title and credits screens

Madonna

Ciao, Italia
Live from Italy

Produced by Riccardo Mario Corato Network
for RAI Radiotelevisione Italiana

Director Egbert Van Hees
ID TV Amsterdam

Live Recording Produced by ID TV Amsterdam
in cooperation with Cinevideogroep

Executive Producer Harry De Winter

Producer Marijke Klasema

Editor Michael Snoway

Example 34. Ciao, Italia

```
Type: g    ELvl: I    Srce: d    Audn: g    Ctrl:      Lang: eng
BLvl: m    TMat: v    GPub:      AccM:      MRec:      Ctry: it
Desc: a    Time: 100  Tech: 1    DtSt: s    Dates: 1988,
 1 040      XXX ǂc XXX
 2 007      v ǂb f ǂd c ǂe b ǂf a ǂg h ǂh o ǂi s
 3 090      M1630.18 ǂb .M3 1988
 4 049      XXXX
 5 100 0    Madonna, ǂd 1957-
 6 245 10   Ciao, Italia ǂh [videorecording] : ǂb live from Italy / ǂc Madonna
; produced by Ricardo Mario ; Corato Network for RAI, Radiotelevisione
Italiana ; director, Egbert Van Hees.
 7 260      [Burbank, Calif. : ǂb Warner Reprise Video, ǂc 1988].
 8 300      1 videocassette (100 min.) : ǂb sd., col. ; ǂc 1/2 in.
 9 500      Concert performance.
10 511 1    Madonna, with vocal and instrumental accompaniment.
11 508      Musical director, Pat Leonard ; concert directed and staged by
Jeffrey Hornaday.
12 500      All songs written by Madonna.
13 538      VHS format, Dolby stereo.
14 505 00   ǂt Open your heart -- ǂt Lucky star -- ǂt True blue -- ǂt Papa
don't preach -- ǂt White heat -- ǂt Causing a commotion -- ǂt Look of love --
ǂg Medley: ǂt Dress you up; ǂt Material girl; ǂt Like a virgin -- ǂt Where's
the party -- ǂt Live to tell -- ǂt Isla bonita -- ǂt Who's that girl -- ǂt
Holiday.
15 650  0   Popular music ǂy 1981-1990.
16 650  0   Rock music ǂy 1981-1990.
17 700 1    Mario, Ricardo.
18 700 1    Van Hees, Egbert.
19 710 2    Corato Network.
20 710 2    Radiotelevisione italiana.
21 710 2    Warner Reprise Video (Firm).
```

Comments

General: This is a filmed concert performance.

Cataloging: This is a work with a collective title and a principal performer. All songs are by the same composer, who is also the principal performer. Main entry is for the composer following rule 21.23B1.

The word "stereo." is not permitted in Area 5 for videorecordings so must be recorded in a note.

Access: I used an enhanced contents note to provide access to the titles of the songs rather than make a composer title analytic for each.

MARC coding/tagging: The fixed field "Ctry" is coded for country of production rather than country of distribution; this is done only for film material.

Example 25a. Honey, I Shrunk the Kids

Back and side of cassette box

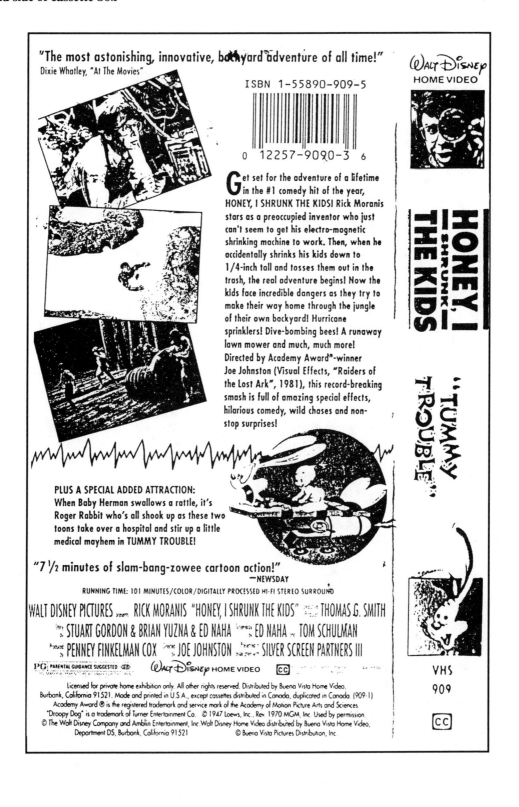

Example 25a: Honey, I Shrunk the Kids

Transcription of title screens and credits

Walt Disney Pictures
presents

in association with
Silver Screen Partners III

Rick Moranis
in

Honey, I Shrunk the Kids

Story by Stuart Gordon, Brian Yuzna, Ed Naha

Screenplay by Ed Naha, Tom Schulman

Produced by Penney Finkelman Cox

Directed by Joe Johnston

```
Type: g    ELvl: I    Srce: d    Audn: g    Ctrl:       Lang: eng
BLvl: m    TMat: v    GPub:      AccM:      MRec:       Ctry: cau
Desc: a    Time: 101  Tech: l    DtSt: s    Dates: 1990,
 1 040      XXX ǂc XXX
 2 007      v ǂb f ǂd c ǂe b ǂf a ǂg h ǂh o ǂi s
 3 020      1558909095
 4 024 1    012257909036
 5 028 40   909 ǂb Walt Disney Home Video
 6 090      PN1995.9.C55 ǂb H6 1989
 7 049      XXXX
 8 245 00   Honey, I shrunk the kids ǂh [videorecording] / ǂc Walt Disney
Pictures ; Silver Screen Partners III ; produced by Penney Finkelman Cox ;
directed by Joe Johnston.
 9 260      [Burbank, CA] : ǂb Walt Disney Home Video ; ǂb [Distributed by
Buena Vista Home Video], ǂc c1990.
10 300      1 videocassette (101 min.) : ǂb sd., col. ; ǂc 1/2 in.
11 538      VHS, stereo.
12 546      Closed-captioned.
13 511 1    Rick Moranis, Matt Frewer, Marcia Strassman, Kristine Sutherland.
14 508      Story by Stuart Gordon, Brian Yuzna, and Ed Naha; screenplay by Ed
Naha and Tom Schulman.
15 521 8    MPAA rating: PG.
16 520      An absent-minded inventor (Moranis) working on a shrinking machine
accidentally shrinks his kids down to 1/4 inch in height. When they are
tossed out with the trash, they have to make their way home through a
backyard that has become a jungle.
```

Example 25a: Honey, I Shrunk the Kids

```
17 500      Preceded by a preview of the movie Dick Tracy.
18 501      With: Tummy trouble.
19 650   0  Inventors.
20 650   0  Science fiction films.
21 650   0  Comedy films.
22 650   0  Video recordings for the hearing impaired.
23 700 1    Cox, Penney Finkelman.
24 700 1    Johnston, Joe.
25 700 1    Moranis, Rick.
26 700 1    Frewer, Matt.
27 700 1    Strassman, Marcia.
28 700 1    Sutherland, Kristine.
29 700 1    Gordon, Stuart.
30 700 1    Yuzna, Brian.
31 700 1    Naha, Ed.
32 700 1    Schulman, Tom.
33 710 2    Walt Disney Pictures.
34 710 2    Silver Screen Partners III.
35 710 2    Walt Disney Home Video.
36 710 2    Buena Vista Home Video.
37 730 02   Dick Tracy (Motion picture)
```

Comments

General: Here are two titles on one cassette with no collective title, and each with its own title and credits frames. They could be cataloged on one bibliographic record with all the information about the cartoon combined into one note, or both titles could be given in the title area with credits for each done in separate notes. I chose to catalog each separately and link them using "with" notes.

MARC coding/tagging: This item has an ISBN recorded in field 020, a UPC barcode recorded in field 024, and a manufacturer's number recorded in field 028.

Example 25b. Tummy Trouble

General credits at beginning of videocassette

Walt Disney Home Video

Walt Disney Pictures

(preview of Dick Tracy)

Transcription of title screens and credits

Walt Disney Pictures
R. K. Maroon presents A Maroon Cartoon in color
© 1990
Walt Disney Pictures and Steven Spielberg present

Tummy Trouble

Animation directed by Rob Minkhoff
Live action directed by Frank Marshall
Produced by Don Hahn
AMBLIN Entertainment
Distributed by
Buena Vista Pictures Distribution, Inc.

Example 25b. Tummy Trouble

```
Type: g   ELvl: I   Srce: d   Audn: g   Ctrl:        Lang: eng
BLvl: m   TMat: v   GPub:     AccM:     MRec:        Ctry: cau
Desc: a   Time: 101 Tech: c   DtSt: s   Dates: 1990,
 1 040       XXX ǂc XXX
 2 007       v ǂb f ǂd c ǂe b ǂf a ǂg h ǂh o ǂi s
 3 020       1558909095
 4 024 1     012257909036
 5 028 40    909 ǂb Walt Disney Home Video
 6 090       PN1995.9.C55 ǂb H6 1989
 7 049       XXXX
 8 245 00    Tummy trouble ǂh [videorecording] / ǂc Walt Disney Pictures ;
Amblin Entertainment ; [presented by] Steven Spielberg ; produced by Don Hahn
; animation directed by Rob Minkhoff ; live action directed by Frank
Marshall.
 9 260       [Burbank, CA] : ǂb Walt Disney Home Video ; ǂb Distributed by
Buena Vista Pictures, ǂc c1990.
10 300       on 1 videocassette (8 min.) : ǂb sd., col. ; ǂc 1/2 in.
11 500       "A Maroon cartoon." Live action in a cartoon setting with both
live and animated characters.
12 546       Closed-captioned.
13 538       VHS, stereo.
14 520       "When Baby Herman swallows a rattle, it's Roger Rabbit who's all
shook up as these two toons take over a hospital and stir up a little medical
mayhem"--Container.
15 501       With: Honey, I shrunk the kids.
16 650  0    Animated films.
17 650  0    Video recordings for the hearing impaired.
18 650  0    Roger Rabbit (Fictitious character)
19 650  0    Baby Herman (Fictitious character)
20 700 1     Spielberg, Steven, ǂd 1947-
21 700 1     Hahn, Don.
22 700 1     Minkhoff, Rob.
23 700 1     Marshall, Frank.
24 710 2     Walt Disney Pictures.
25 710 2     Amblin Entertainment (Firm)
26 710 2     Walt Disney Home Video (Firm)
27 710 2     Buena Vista Pictures.
```

Comments

General: This cataloging of a cartoon allows for patron access to the cartoon characters and other details that would not be easily available if the cartoon were mentioned only in a note on another bibliographic record. This cartoon does have its own credits. There are several Roger Rabbit cartoons, and patrons might like to know about this one.

Cataloging: This pair of examples shows how "With" cataloging works. The note indicates there is another complete bibliographic record for the other title.

Access: The classification number for this title is the same as that for Honey, I Shrunk the Kids. We cannot have two different class numbers on one physical item.

Access to the cartoon characters is provided through subject headings.

Example 26. News Images

Title screen information

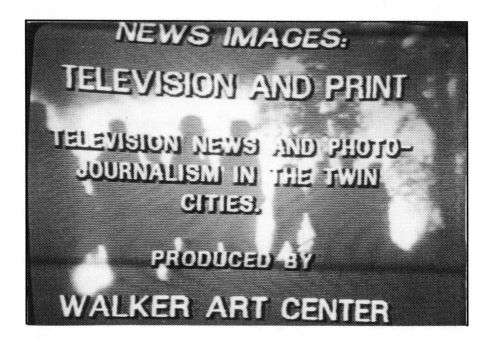

Example 26. News Images

```
Type: g   ELvl: I   Srce: d   Audn: f   Ctrl:       Lang: eng
BLvl: m   TMat: v   GPub:     AccM:     MRec:       Ctry: mnu
Desc: a   Time: 015 Tech: l   DtSt: s   Dates: 1978,
 1 040      XXX ‡c XXX
 2 007      v ‡b f ‡d c ‡e b ‡f a ‡g h ‡h o ‡i u
 3 090      PN4888.T4 ‡b N4 1978
 4 049      XXXX
 5 245 00   News images ‡h [videorecording] : ‡b television and print :
television news and photojournalism in the Twin Cities / ‡c produced by
Walker Art Center with the assistance of WCCO-TV ; director, Charles Helm ;
producer and script writer, Maud Lavin.
 6 246 30   News images, television and print
 7 246 30   Television and print
 8 246 30   Television news and photojournalism in the Twin Cities
 9 260      Minneapolis : ‡b Walker Art Center, ‡c c1978.
10 300      1 videocassette (15 min.) : ‡b sd., col. ; ‡c 1/2 in.
11 511 0    Narrator, Dave Moore.
12 538      VHS.
13 520      Describes and compares television journalism and press photography
using examples of Minneapolis and St. Paul news items.
14 650  0   Photojournalism.
15 650  0   Television broadcasting of news.
16 700 1    Helm, Charles.
17 700 1    Lavin, Maud.
18 700 1    Moore, Dave, ‡d 1924-
19 710 2    Walker Art Center.
20 710 2    WCCO-TV (Television station : Minneapolis, Minn.)
```

Comments

General: This was a problem in deciding what to use for title proper. I added enough 246 fields so that any title one searched should retrieve this record.

Example 27. Henry Ford Museum & Greenfield Village

Cassette label

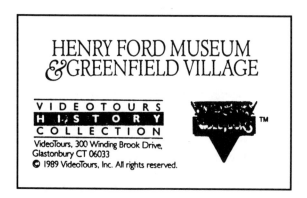

Videocassette and box

Example 27. Henry Ford Museum & Greenfield Village

Transcription of title and credits frames

Produced by Wave, Inc.

Executive Producer
Dennis T. Allen

Produced by
Charles H. Slatkin

Directed by
Charles H. Slatkin

Principal photography
Charles H. Slatkin

Narrated by
Don Wescott

Written by
Fred Bauer

Associate Producer
Scot M. Broderick

Edited by
David F. Schirmer
David M. Eells

Original Music by
Jeff Loeb

Example 27: Henry Ford Museum & Greenfield Village

```
Type: g    ELvl: I    Srce: d   Audn: g    Ctrl:      Lang: eng
BLvl: m    TMat: v    GPub:     AccM:      MRec:      Ctry: ctu
Desc: a    Time: 030  Tech: 1   DtSt: s    Dates: 1989,
```

```
 1 040       XXX ‡c XXX
 2 007       v ‡b f ‡d c ‡e b ‡f a ‡g h ‡h o ‡i u
 3 090       T180.D4 ‡b H4 1989
 4 049       XXXX
 5 245 00    Henry Ford Museum & Greenfield Village ‡h [videorecording] / ‡c
produced by Wave, Inc. ; produced and directed by Charles H. Slatkin ;
written by Fred Bauer.
 6 246 3     Henry Ford Museum and Greenfield Village
 7 246 30    Henry Ford Museum
 8 246 30    Greenfield Village
 9 260       Glastonbury, Conn. : ‡b VideoTours, ‡c c1989.
10 300       1 videocassette (30 min.) : ‡b sd., col. ; ‡c 1/2 in.
11 440 0     VideoTours history collection
12 538       VHS, stereo.
13 520       Provides a behind-the-scenes tour of the Henry Ford Museum and
Greenfield Village located in Dearborn, Mich. Greenfield Village includes the
homes and work places of Thomas Edison, the Wright brothers, Noah Webster and
others. The Henry Ford museum shows how living conditions of the American
people have changed over the decades through displays of things used in homes
and workplaces-from egg beaters to automobiles.
14 610 20    Henry Ford Museum and Greenfield Village.
15 651  0    United States ‡x History.
16 650  0    Historical museums ‡z Michigan ‡z Dearborn.
17 710 2     Henry Ford Museum and Greenfield Village.
18 710 2     VideoTours, Inc.
```

Comments

 General: I keep trying to find a video that would be given corporate main entry, but haven't found one yet. It would need to be about the corporation, issued by the corporation, but not be a public relations film.

 Cataloging: While the labels used the abbreviation "CT" the title and credits screens used "Conn.," so Conn. is what is used in the place of publication.

Example 28. Out of the Closet

Transcription of title and credits frames:

Moore on Sunday
Produced and Written by Jim Hayden
A Presentation of the Public Affairs Unit
WCCO Television News

```
Type: g   ELvl: I    Srce: d   Audn: e   Ctrl:      Lang: eng
BLvl: m   TMat: v    GPub:     AccM:     MRec:      Ctry: mnu
Desc: a   Time: 030  Tech: l   DtSt: s   Dates: 1977,
  1 040      XXX ‡c XXX
  2 007      v ‡b f ‡d c ‡e b ‡f a ‡g h ‡h o ‡i u
  3 090      HQ76.25 ‡b .O8 1977
  4 049      XXXX
  5 245 00   Out of the closet ‡h [videorecording] / ‡c a presentation of the
Public Affairs Unit, WCCO Television News ; produced and written by Jim
Hayden.
  6 260      ‡c [1977].
  7 300      1 videocassette (30 min.) : ‡b sd. col. ; ‡c 1/2 in.
  8 490 1    Moore on Sunday
  9 500      Title from narration.
 10 500      Broadcast on WCCO-TV Oct. 23, 1977; taped with permission.
Transferred to VHS from 3/4 in. tape in 1990.
 11 520      Commentary on the oppression of gays, role of Anita Bryant, and
Minneapolis reaction.
 12 650  0   Gays ‡x Civil rights.
 13 650  0   Gay liberation movement ‡z United States.
 14 600 1    Bryant, Anita.
 15 700 1    Hayden, Jim.
 16 700 1    Moore, Dave, ‡d 1924-1998
 17 710 2    WCCO-TV (Television station : Minneapolis, Minn.).
 18 650  0   WCCO Television News. ‡b Public Affairs Unit.
 19 830  0   Moore on Sunday (Television program).
```

Comments

General: OCLC guidelines for local videorecordings are in section 3.7 of *Bibliographic Formats and Standards.* The date is the only information to appear in field 260 for off-air recordings.

Cataloging: The title of this program did not appear in the title and credits frames; it was announced.

Example 29. Power, Politics & Current Issues in Rehabilition

Transcription of title and credits frames:

Power, Politics & Current Issues in Rehabilitation
Workshop
Presented by Rehabilitation Counseling Department
Mankato State University
Staff: Dr. Robert Hopper, Department Chairman
Dr. Richard Ugland, Project Director
Dr. Ward Thayer, Workshop Director

```
Type: g    ELvl: I   Srce: d   Audn: f   Ctrl:      Lang: eng
BLvl: m    TMat: v   GPub:     AccM:     MRec:      Ctry: xx
Desc: a    Time: 101 Tech: l   DtSt: s   Dates: 1990,
 1 040     XXX ‡c XXX
 2 007     v ‡b f ‡d b ‡e d ‡f a ‡g h ‡h o ‡i u
 3 090     HD7255 ‡b .P6 1977
 4 049     XXXX
 5 700 1   Humphrey, Hubert H. ‡q (Hubert Horatio), ‡d 1911-1978.
 6 245 10  Power, politics & current issues in rehabilitation ‡h
[videorecording] : ‡b workshop / ‡c presented by Rehabilitation Counseling
Department, Mankato State University.
 7 246 3   Power, politics, and current issues in rehabilitation
 8 260     ‡c [1977].
 9 300     1 videoreel (60 min.) : ‡b sd., b&w ; ‡c 1/2 in.
10 508     Workshop director, Ward Thayer ; project director, Richard Ugland
; department chair, Robert Hopper.
11 520     Senator Hubert H. Humphrey speaks at a workshop held July 6, 1977,
at Mankato State University, on the use of politics and the applications of
power in advancing the program, objectives, and goals of handicapped and
disabled persons.
12 650  0  Handicapped ‡x Rehabilitation.
13 700 1   Thayer, Ward.
14 700 1   Ugland, Richard.
15 700 1   Hopper, Robert.
16 710 2   Mankato State University. ‡b Rehabilitation Counseling Dept.
```

Comments

General: This unpublished item is cataloged according to the OCLC guidelines for local videorecordings.

Example 30. The Age of Steam

Transcription of title and credits frames:

The Age of Steam
Written, Produced and Directed by
William A. McGinley
Special Assistance by
Thomas E. Harmening
and
George H. Collins
Produced In Association With
Indiana University
Department
of
Radio and Television
1968

```
Type: g   ELvl: I   Srce: d   Audn: e   Ctrl:      Lang: eng
BLvl: m   TMat: v   GPub:     AccM:     MRec:      Ctry: xx
Desc: a   Time: 030 Tech: 1   DtSt: s   Dates: 1968,
 1 040      XXX ǂc XXX
 2 007      v ǂb f ǂd b ǂe n ǂf a ǂg h ǂh r ǂi u
 3 090      TJ615 ǂb .M4 1968
 4 049      XXXX
 5 100 1    McGinley, William A., ǂd 1943-
 6 245 14   The age of steam ǂh [videorecording] / ǂc written, produced, and
directed by William A. McGinley ; special assistance by Thomas E. Harmening
and George H Collins.
 7 260      ǂc 1968.
 8 300      1 videocassette (30 min.) : ǂb sd., b&w ; ǂc 3/4 in.
 9 500      Produced in association with Indiana University Department of
Radio and Television.
10 502      Thesis (M.A.)--Indiana University, 1968.
11 520      Brief historical study of the steam locomotive from its inception
to its replacement by the diesel.
12 650  0   Locomotives.
13 650  0   Railroads.
14 700 1    Harmening, Thomas E.
15 700 1    Collins, George H.
16 710 2    Indiana University. ǂb Dept. of Radio and Television.
```

Comments

General: This item is a video thesis. Directions for cataloging locally produced materials are given in OCLC *Bibliographic Formats and Standards*, section 3.7.

DVD
Digital Video Discs

A DVD disc looks like a CD-ROM or a music CD. They are all the same size (4 3/4 in. in diameter) and are all shiny optical discs with label information on one side. However, the DVD discs cannot be played in a music CD player, a videodisc player, or a CD-ROM drive. They need their own DVD player connected to a television set.

DVD stands for digital video disc/disk or digital versatile disc/disk. There is no standardization in the literature or advertising either on the wording or spelling of the full phrase, but DVD is a registered trademark with the letters "DVD" over an elongated oval containing the word "video." The digital technology allows up to 133 minutes of video and sound to be stored on one side of a DVD disc. The picture and sound quality are supposed to be much superior to that of a viceo cassette.

Cataloging Considerations

I suggest the following approach to cataloging any DVD. At present this technology is being used for movies and copies of titles previously available on videocassette. Descriptive information would be the same as for the videocassette with the following exceptions:

```
300      1 videodisc (___ min.) : ‡b sd., col. ; ‡c 4 3/4 in.
538      DVD player required; has Dolby surround sound.
```

An additional difference might be in languages found on the item because the large storage capacity of this technology permits a number of sound tracks to be included. The disc I have ("Jumanji") carries the information:

Languages: English, Spanish, French
Subtitles: Spanish, Korean

These languages would be listed in a note and coded in MARC field 041. The "Jumanji" package also carries the symbol for closed-captioning, so both a note and subject heading would be needed for that aspect.

The "Jumanji" package has other information as well. It says "NTSC" and "Deluxe widescreen presentation" and "Presented in the original theatrical aspect ratio, approx. 1.85:1" It includes symbols/trademarks for closed-captioning, color, PG (for the parental guidance rating), Dolby digital, Dolby surround, surround sound, and two other symbols that I don't recognize. One of these is a number 1 on what appears to be a globe with latitude and longitude lines; the whole enclosed in a square with rounded corners. The other is an oval enclosing what appears to be a film reel superimposed over longitudinal lines and an equator; there is a trademark symbol on this one. I'd appreciate help identifying these.

A TRISTAR PICTURE ©1995 TRISTAR PICTURES, INC. ALL RIGHTS RESERVED.

Symbols and trademarks on one DVD

GRAPHIC MATERIALS

AACR 2 Chapter 8

Graphic materials of all kinds, whether opaque or intended to be projected or viewed, are cataloged using rules of AACR 2 chapter 8. Examples for many types of graphic materials are included here. Those materials intended to be projected so as to create the illusion of movement are cataloged by the rules of AACR 2 chapter 7.

Special Rules for Cataloging Graphic Materials

In this section the special rules for cataloging graphic materials will be discussed. For rules and/or areas not discussed here, see chapter 2 of this book. Parts of some of the rules are given; the user is referred to the rules themselves for complete text and examples. All of the Library of Congress rule interpretations are included.

For cataloging original art works and historical collections, refer also to: *Graphic Materials: Rules for Describing Original Items and Historical Collections*, compiled by Elisabeth W. Betz (Washington, D.C.: Library of Congress, 1982).

Chief Source of Information

8.0B1. The chief source of information for graphic materials is the item itself including any labels that are permanently affixed to the item or a container that is an integral part of the item. If the item being described consists of two or more separate physical parts, treat a container that is the unifying element as the chief source of information if it furnishes a collective title and the items themselves and their labels do not....

The chief source of information for a filmstrip is the title and credits frames of the filmstrip. For a set of filmstrips, one would look at all the title and credits frames, and compare that information to the information on the container for the set. If the box/container for the set carries a collective title that does *not* appear on the title and credits frames of the filmstrips, the container is chosen as the chief source of information.

The chief source of information for a set of slides is the title and credits slides and the information on the slide mounts. If a container furnishes a collective title not found on the individual slides or their mounts, the container is used as the chief source of information.

The chief source of information for a set of transparencies is any title/credit transparency and the transparency mounts. Transparencies are less likely to have title/credit information on the film itself. This information is more likely to be on the transparency mounts or on the container.

Title and Statement of Responsibility Area
MARC field 245

There are no problems of title that are unique to these materials. The GMDs used for materials cataloged by rules of this chapter are listed in the extent of item section on the next page.

LCRI 8.1F1. This rule is merely a reference to chapter 1. If there is a corporate body responsible overall for the work, usually record in the note area the names of persons responsible for only a segment of the work. Contributors who are considered to be of major importance to the item always may be recorded in the statement of responsibility. (*CSB* 11)

LCRI 8.1F1. When deciding whether to give names in the statement of responsibility or in a note, generally give the names in the statement of responsibility when the person or body has some degree of overall responsibility; use the note area for others who are responsible for only one segment or one aspect of the work. Be liberal about making exceptions to the general policy when the person's or body's responsibility is important in relation to the content of the work, i.e., give such important people and bodies in the statement of responsibility even though they may have only partial responsibility. Normally the Library of Congress considers producers, directors, and writers (or, in the case of slides and transparencies, authors, editors, and compilers) as having some degree of overall responsibility and gives them in the statement of responsibility. (*CSB* 13)

Publication, Distribution, Etc., Area
MARC field 260

LCRI 8.4F2. Give a date of original production differing from the dates of publication/ distribution or copyright, etc., in the note area (see 8.7B9). Apply the provision if the difference is greater than two years. When dealing with different media, see 8.7B7. (*CSB* 33)

Physical Description Area
MARC field 300

Extent of item (MARC field 300 ǂa)

A long list of terms is given for use as specific material designations. At the end of the rule is the option to substitute or add a term more specific than those listed. It would be useful to have the word "Poster" available as a GMD. The various specific material designations would be apportioned among the GMDs as follows:

Activity card	**Flash card**	**Technical drawing**
Activity card	Flash card	Technical drawing
Art original	**Picture**	**Transparency**
Art original	Photograph	Transparency
Art reproduction	Picture	
Art print	Postcard	
Art reproduction	Radiograph	
Chart	Study print	
Chart	**Slide**	
Flip chart	Slide	
Wall chart	Stereograph	
Filmstrip		
Filmslip		
Filmstrip		

Other physical details (MARC field 300 ǂb)

Directions are given in AACR2 for describing all types of graphic material. Rule 8.5C1e refers to filmstrips where the sound is integral; this means the sound is on the film or is packaged with the filmstrip in a permanent container. Rule 8.5C1h refers to slides with integral sound; these slides are individually packaged in cassettes with sound, or have sound on the film in some way.

There is no provision in area 5 for including the information that captions are on the frames of a filmstrip. This information is given in a note (MARC field 546).

Dimensions (MARC field 300 ǂc)

Directions are given for measuring all types of graphic materials. Note that in rule 8.5D4 we are directed to *exclude* the mount in measuring for transparencies and for art works and their reproductions.

Accompanying material (MARC field 300 ǂe)

We are directed to record the number and name of accompanying material; physical description of that material is optional, but when done is in parentheses following the name of the material.

If the sound is on the item, it is mentioned under other physical details; if it is on a separate physical item, it is mentioned as accompanying material.

Notes Area
MARC fields 5XX

Notes permitted in this chapter are:

8.7B1. Nature or artistic form
8.7B2. Language
8.7B3. Source of title proper
8.7B4. Variations in title
8.7B5. Parallel titles and other title information
8.7B6a. Statements of responsibility
8.7B6b. Donor, source, etc., and previous owners
8.7B7. Edition and history
8.7B9. Publication, distribution, etc.
8.7B10. Physical description
8.7B11. Accompanying material
8.7B12. Series
8.7B13. Dissertations
8.7B14. Audience
8.7B16. Other formats
8.7B17. Summary
8.7B18. Contents
8.7B19. Numbers
8.7B20. Copy being described, library's holdings, and restrictions on use
8.7B21. "With" notes
8.7B22. Notes relating to the original

Explanation of notes

Each of the notes will be explained in the following section and examples of their use given.
Notes may be combined.

```
500      Designed and copyright by Richard Miller; to be assembled
into model of human skull.
```

8.7B1. *Nature or artistic form* (MARC field 500)

To be used to name or explain the form of the item as necessary.

```
500      Original watercolor.
```

8.7B2. *Language* (MARC field 546)

To be used to name the language or languages of the item cataloged if not obvious from other information given.

```
546      Captions in French.
546      Description in German.
```

8.7B3. *Source of title proper* (MARC field 500)

To be used if the title proper is taken from other than the chief source of information.

```
500      Title from publisher's catalog.
500      Title supplied by cataloger.
```

8.7B4. *Variations in title* (MARC field 246 or 500)

To be used to note any title appearing on the item that differs significantly from the title proper. Field 246 is used if the title applies to the entire item.

```
246 1    ‡i Title on container: ‡a Surveillance
```
   (*Title proper:* Make the case with surveillance)

8.7B5. *Parallel titles and other title information* (MARC field 246 or 500)

To be used for parallel titles and important other title information not recorded in the title and statement of responsibility area.

```
246 1    ‡i English title: ‡a Maintaining workers' interest
```
   (*Title proper:* Conserve el interés de sus empleados)

8.7B6. *Statements of responsibility* (MARC fields 500, 508)

To be used to record important information not recorded in the statement of responsibility area.

> **LCRI 8.7B6.** For audiovisual items, generally list persons (other than producers, directors, and writers) who have contributed to the artistic and technical production of a work in a credits note (see 8.1F1). Give the following persons in the order in which they are listed below. Preface each name or group of names with the appropriate term(s) of function:
>
>> photographer(s); camera; cameraman/men; cinematographer
>> animator(s)
>> artist(s); illustrator(s); graphics
>> film editor(s); photo editor(s); editor(s)
>> narrator(s); voice(s)
>> music
>> consultant(s); adviser(s)

Do not include the following persons:

> assistants or associates
> production supervisors or coordinators
> project or executive editors
> technical advisers or consultants
> audio or sound engineers
> writers of discussion, program, or teacher's guides
> other persons making only a minor or purely technical contribution

(*CSB* 22)

In response to a question referring to the fact that a "Credits:" note is not authorized in chapter 8, Richard Thaxter stated:

> LC's rule interpretation 8.7B6 was intended to show that we will continue to use formally captioned "Credits:" notes for filmstrips, slide sets, etc. Chapter 8 encompasses a wide range of materials, most of which would never have a "Credits:" note.
> One of the advantages of the integrated structure of AACR 2 is that *one can usually borrow from one chapter when a provision is lacking in another* ... The list of persons to include and the order in which they should go (RI 8.7B6) is neither prescriptive nor exhaustive ... If more than three persons perform the same function only the first will be listed, marks of omission and the phrase "et al." will be used (Verna Urbanski. "LC Answers Questions on 508 "Credits" RI." Online Audiovisual Catalogers. *Newsletter*, 3 (Sept. 1983): 9).

This LCRI is intended as guidelines for general cases. When cataloging photographs by a famous photographer, or reproductions of those photos, the photographer's name should go in the statement of responsibility rather than in a note if that name appears in a prominent position in the chief source of information.

8.7B6. Donor, source, etc., and previous owners (MARC field 561)

To be used for information about the donor, source, and previous owners of an original graphic item.

> 561   Donated in 1989 by Aileen Marcy.

8.7B7. Edition and history (MARC field 500)

To be used for information about earlier editions or the history of the item being cataloged.

> **LCRI 8.7B7.** When an item is known to have an original master in a different medium and the production or release date of the master is more than two years earlier than that of the item being cataloged, give an edition/history note:
>
> > Originally issued as filmstrip in [year]
>
> Make a similar note when an item is known to have been previously produced or issued (more than two years earlier) in a different medium, but the original medium is unknown.
>
> > Previously issued as slide set in [year]
>
> If the date of production or release of an original master or an earlier medium is unknown or if the difference between its production or release date and the production or release date of the item being cataloged is two years or less, indicate the availability of the other medium or media in a note according to 8.7B16.

```
Issued also as slide set and videorecording
Produced also as slide set
```

Note: The use of production versus release dates is left to the cataloger's judgment. Make the note that seems best to give information about either production or release of other formats on a case-by-case basis. (*CSB* 15)

8.7B9. Publication, distribution, etc. (MARC field 500)

To be used for important information not recorded in the publication, distribution, etc., area.

LCRI 8.7B9. When a foreign firm, etc., is given in the source as emanator or originator, do not assume that the item was either made or released in that country if not so stated. Instead use the note:

```
A foreign filmstrip (Yugoslavia)
A foreign slide set (Yugoslavia)
```

For a U.S. emanator and a foreign producer, or a foreign emanator and a U.S. producer, do not make the note. (*CSB* 13)

8.7B10. Physical description (MARC field 500)

To be used for any important information not given in area 5, the physical description area.

```
500      Transparencies and duplicating masters perforated for
removal.
```

8.7B11. Accompanying material (MARC field 500)

To be used for any important information not given in the accompanying material part of area 5.

```
500      Guide includes bibliography.
```

8.7B12. Series (MARC field 500)

To be used for any important information not recorded in the series area.

```
500      Series on container: America and world power.
```

8.7B13. Dissertations (MARC field 502)

To be used for the standard dissertation note when applicable.

```
502      Thesis (M.S.)--Iowa State University, 1979.
```

8.7B14. Audience (MARC field 521)

To be used to record the intended audience of a work; use this note only if the information is stated on the item. Do not attempt to judge the audience for an item. A blank first indicator generates the display constant "Audience:".

```
521      Construction management personnel.
```

8.7B16. Other formats (MARC field 530)

To be used to list other formats in which the work is available.

```
530      Issued also as slide set.
```

8.7B17. Summary (MARC field 520)

To be used for a brief objective summary of the content of the item.

```
520      Summary: Illustrates simple random sampling and some of
its applications.
```

8.7B18. Contents (MARC fields 505, 500, 504)

To be used for a formal (MARC field 505) or informal (MARC field 500) listing of the contents of the item. Number of frames may be added. Playing time may also be added after each title.

```
505 0    Careers (80 fr.) -- …
505 0    What's your point? (55 fr., 13 min., 2 sec.) -- …
505 0    Residential architecture, tools (15 min., 10 sec.) -- …
```

The following examples show both formal and informal contents notes.

```
505 0    Pottery painters at work -- Silversmith at work --
Building with adobe bricks -- Drying sisal -- Printing textiles
-- Fishermen at work -- Refining petroleum -- Port of Veracruz.
504      Bibliography in guide, p. 70-77.
```

8.7B19. Numbers (MARC field 500)

To be used to list any important number appearing on the item other than those to be recorded in area 8. Most numbers appearing on an item can be recorded in field 020, 024, 028 or 037.

```
500      "S 1967"
037      No. 789 ǂb Ideal School Supply Co.
```

8.7B20. Copy being described, library's holdings, and restrictions on use (MARC fields 506, 590, 500)

To be used for any notes applicable only to the particular copy of the item being described. Also used (MARC 590) for local library restrictions on the material being described or for information of use only to patrons of the local library.

```
590      Use restricted to Film 404 class.
```

8.7B21. "With" notes (MARC field 501)

To be used for "with" notes.

```
501      With: Sneetches.
```

8.7B22. Notes relating to original (MARC field 534)

To be used for information about the original of a reproduced art work.

```
534      ‡p Original: ‡c National Gallery of Art.
```

Example 31. Selecting Leisure Activities

Title frame of filmstrip

SELECTING LEISURE ACTIVITIES

Produced by MULTI-MEDIA PRODUCTIONS, INC.
Stanford, CA 94305   Copyright 1979
All Rights Reserved Throughout The World

Credits frame of filmstrip

Written and Photographed by

John Loughary, Theresa Ripley,
and Vanesa Tsang
of UNITED LEARNING CORPORATION

```
Type: g    ELvl: I    Srce: d    Audn: d    Ctrl:        Lang: eng
BLvl: m    TMat: f    GPub:      AccM:      MRec:        Ctry: cau
Desc: a    Time: nnn  Tech: n    DtSt: s    Dates: 1979,
 1 040     XXX ǂc XXX
 2 007     g ǂb o ǂd c ǂe j ǂf b ǂg f ǂh f
 3 090     BJ1498 ǂb .S4 1979
 4 049     XXXX
 5 245 00  Selecting leisure activities ǂh [filmstrip] / ǂc written and
photographed by John Loughary, Theresa Ripley, and Vanesa Tsang.
 6 260     Stanford, CA : ǂb Multi-Media Productions, ǂc 1979.
 7 300     1 filmstrip (61 fr.) : ǂb col. ; ǂc 35 mm. + ǂe 1 sound cassette
(20 min., analog) + 1 program script + 1 teacher's manual.
 8 520     Discusses 15 satisfactions of leisure activities as well as
conditions to be considered such as time, costs, physical needs, skills, and
aptitude.
 9 650  0  Leisure.
10 650  0  Recreation.
11 700  1  Loughary, John William, ǂd 1930-
12 700  1  Ripley, Theresa M.
13 700  1  Tsang, Vanesa.
14 710  2  Multi-Media Productions.
```

Comments

General: While filmstrips were the most common form of audiovisual material that I handled for many years, they are now almost obsolete. I kept one example in this book for those who may still have some in your collections.

Cataloging: While this package of material contains four items, it is not a kit, as the filmstrip is considered the dominant form of media, with the recorded narration treated as accompanying material.

The title and credits frames of the filmstrip contained the most complete information about the item, so they were treated as the chief source of information. Those title and credits frames would be the chief source if no other material were included.

Processing: Each item in the box needs a call number label. The barcode, on the outside of the box, has the name of our library on it.

Example 32. Make the Case With Surveillance

Contents and container

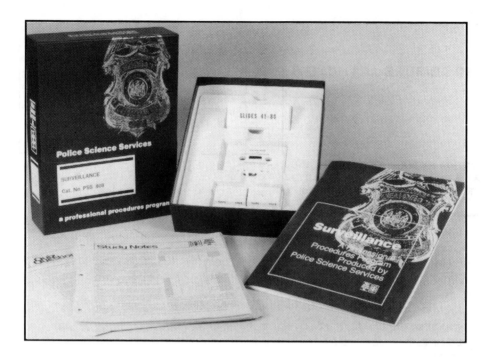

Title slide

Make the case with
Surveillance
Copyright © 1976 by Police Science Services, Inc.

Last slide

**Produced for
United Learning
by
Police Science Services**

© 1976 Police Science Services, Inc.
All Rights Reserved

Example 32. Make the Case With Surveillance

```
Type: g   ELvl: I   Srce: d   Audn: f   Ctrl:       Lang: eng
BLvl: m   TMat: s   GPub:     AccM:     MRec:       Ctry: ilu
Desc: a   Time: nnn Tech: n   DtSt: s   Dates: 1976,
 1 040      XXX ǂc XXX
 2 007      g ǂb s ǂd c ǂe j ǂf b ǂg f ǂh j ǂi c
 3 090      HV8080.P2 ǂb M3 1976
 4 049      XXXX
 5 245 00   Make the case with surveillance ǂh [slide] / ǂc produced for
United Learning by Police Science Services.
 6 246 30   Surveillance
 7 260      Niles, Ill. : ǂb Police Science Services, ǂc c1976.
 8 300      80 slides : ǂb col. + ǂe 1 sound cassette + 1 instructor's
guide + 1 set study notes + 1 set quiz questions.
 9 520      Foot, vehicular, and fixed surveillance are detailed in this
program. Planning, working with non-surveillance officers, avoiding
detection, and evasion are covered, as are environment blending,
qualification for assignments, equipment, briefings, routine problems,
leapfrogging, the perimeter-box technique, and reporting. Safety precautions
are emphasized.
10 650  0   Police patrol ǂx Surveillance operations.
11 650  0   Criminal investigation.
12 650  0   Police training.
13 710  2   Police Science Services, inc.
14 710  2   United Learning (Firm)
```

Comments

General: This is another type of material now obsolete or almost so. Slide sets have been converted by publishers to video; the next step is to CD-ROM.

Cataloging: This example presents us with a title problem. We have the title "Surveillance" on the set everywhere except the title screen of the filmstrip, where the title "Make the case with surveillance" appears. The second title is fuller, and we are told to prefer fuller titles when they can be found. So I'll go with that fuller title for the title proper, and use the short form of the title in an added entry.

Access: I have included the narrowest possible subject heading as well as two that are broader. Users might think only in general terms while searching for this type of material.

MARC coding/tagging: Time is coded "nnn" for visual materials other than film or video. At one time other information was sometimes supplied in this field, so you may still see old records for slides or filmstrips with information about the number of slides or frames in this part of the fixed fields.

Processing: Every single slide and every piece of paper need some identification so it can be matched up with the rest of the set when it gets mislaid. Slides were a particular problem, as the last slide tended to remain in the projector.

Example 33. Women Who Dare

Biographical information on back of card

HARRIET TUBMAN
(American, c. 1820-1913)

Harriet Tubman was the best-known "conductor" on the Underground Railroad, a network of abolitionists who spirited blacks to freedom. A fugitive slave herself, Tubman made some nineteen return trips to rescue as many as three hundred slaves from bondage. Her courage and shrewdness were widely known and all the more remarkable given the blackouts she suffered throughout her life as a result of being struck on the head with a two-pound weight by an overseer. During the Civil War she served as a nurse, spy, and scout for groups of raiders penetrating Confederate lines. In her later years Tubman worked for black education and social betterment, woman suffrage, and other causes.

Photograph by H. B. Lindsley
Prints and Photographs Division • Library of Congress
KNOWLEDGE CARDS™
Published by Pomegranate Publications
Box 6099, Rohnert Park, California 94927
PRINTED IN KOREA

Box and deck

Example 33. Women Who Dare

```
Type: k   ELvl: I   Scrce: d  Audn: f   Ctrl:       Lang: eng
BLvl: m   TMat: i   GPub:      AccM:     MRec:       Ctry: cau
Desc: a   Time: nnn Tech: n   DtSt: s   Dates: 199u,
```

```
 1 040      XXX ‡c XXX
 2 007      k ‡b i ‡d b ‡e c
 3 020      0876544871
 4 090      HQ1123 ‡b .W6 1990
 5 049      XXXX
 6 245 00   Women who dare ‡h [picture] / ‡c Prints and Photographs Division,
Library of Congress.
 7 260      Rohnert Park, CA : ‡b Pomegranate Publications, ‡c [199-?].
 8 300      48 photographs : ‡b b&w ; ‡c 11 x 9 cm.
 9 440  0   Knowledge cards
10 500      Photographs selected from the Prints and Photographs Division,
Library of Congress.
11 520      Pictures of 48 women (mostly American) who made lasting
contributions in their respective fields of literature, medicine, sports,
performing arts, politics, and women's rights. Back of each card contains
brief biographical information about the woman pictured.
12 650  0   Women ‡x Portraits.
13 650  0   Women ‡x Biography.
13 710  2   Pomegranate Publications.
14 710  2   Library of Congress. ‡b Prints and Photographs Division.
```

Comments

   General: These cards could be considered to be flash cards.

   Cataloging: You might want to list some of the names (those of local interest) in a partial contents note or list all of the names in a contents note that could be subfielded. The exent of your cataloging would depend on the depth of your collection in this area, and on the needs of your patrons.

   Processing: Each card would need a call number and/or some type of library identification. Because the box is so small, you might want to put them in a larger container so they would not get lost on a shelf.

Example 34. Composition of the Earth

Cover of book

Title and contents page

Earth Science Series

COMPOSITION OF THE EARTH

written by Virginia Powers Leftwich
illustrated by Larry Weaver

CONTENTS

Page
*   1. Atomic Theory
  1A. Atomic Theory
*   2. Subatomic Particles
  2A. Atomic Structure
*   3. Atomic Models
*   4. Periodic Table of the Elements
  4A. Periodic Table of the Elements
  4B. Atomic Models
*   5. Distribution of the Elements
  5A. Distribution of the Elements
*   6. Chemical Bonding
  6A. Atomic Bonding
  6B. Atomic Bonding
*   7. The Six Crystal Systems
*   8. The Inner Structure of Crystals
  8A. Six Crystal Systems
*   9. Berzelian System of Major Mineral Classes
  9A. Minerals
*   10. Genetic Classification of Rocks
  10A. Genetic Classification of Rocks
*   11. Rock Cycle
  11A. The Rock Cycle
*   12. Model of the Earth
  12A. The Earth's Structure
  13—16. Unit Test
    Composition of the Earth

Indicates full color transparency.

Example 34. Composition of the Earth

```
Type: g   ELvl: I   Srce: d   Audn: d   Ctrl:       Lang: eng
BLvl: m   TMat: t   GPub:     AccM:     MRec:       Ctry: mou
Desc: a   Time: nnn Tech: n   DtSt: s   Dates: 1971,
 1 040      XXX ǂc XXX
 2 007      g ǂb t ǂd c ǂe j ǂh z
 3 090      QE509 ǂb .L4 1971
 4 049      XXXX
 5 100 1    Leftwich, Virginia Powers.
 6 245 10   Composition of the earth ǂh [transparency] / ǂc written by
Virginia Powers Leftwich ; illustrated by Larry Weaver.
 7 260      St. Louis, Mo. : ǂb Milliken, ǂc c1971.
 8 300      12 transparencies : ǂb col. ; ǂc 21 x 28 cm. + ǂe 16 duplicating
pages + 1 teacher's guide (12 p. ; 28 cm.).
 9 440 0    Earth science series
10 500      "A Milliken full-color transparency-duplicating book"--Cover.
11 500      Transparencies and duplicating masters are perforated for
removal.
12 505 00   ǂg Transparencies: 1. ǂt Atomic theory ǂg -- 2. ǂt Subatomic
particles ǂg -- 3. ǂt Atomic models ǂg -- 4. ǂt Periodic table of the
elements ǂg -- 5. ǂt Distribution of the elements ǂg -- 6. ǂt Chemical
bonding ǂg -- 7. The ǂt six crystal systems ǂg -- 8. The ǂt inner structure of
the crystals ǂg -- 9. ǂt Berzelian system of major mineral classes ǂg -- 10.
ǂt Genetic classification of rocks ǂg -- 11. ǂt Rock cycle ǂg -- 12. ǂt Model
of the earth.
13 650  0   Earth ǂx Internal structure.
14 700 1    Weaver, Larry.
15 710 2    Milliken Publishing Company.
```

Comments

General: This was one of those problem things—it came in as a book. But the heavy, colored, plastic sheets (perforated for removal) were obviously transparencies, and just as obviously had to be removed to be used. The rest of the material remained bound into the book for our collection, though the duplicating masters were also perforated. They, however, could be copied while bound.

Access and MARC coding/tagging: The contents note in this bibliographic record is only for the transparencies; compare it to the contents information for the book, shown with this example, and you will see the transparency titles do not always match the unit titles. I added codes to this contents note so the titles of the transparencies could be searched, and so those titles would also be term-searchable.

Processing: This would have to be packaged in a box once the transparencies and/or duplicating masters were removed for use.

Example 35. Environmental Values Action Cards

Activity cards

The EVA cards are intended to be used as idea banks for teachers, and it is suggested that teachers explore many ways of introducing them to students. The cards may be used with individual children or with groups. It is important to note that each card contains a metaphor plus activities that extend it. In this way the cards should encourage children to explore their own values and become more aware of themselves. The cards also encourage means of expression that are significantly different from those normally used in the classroom.

Extra special thanks to Marc Wanveg, Minneapolis Schools, who did the photography and supervised the art work for this project.

Richard C. Clark
Project Director

Example 35. Environmental Values Action Cards

```
Type: k    ELvl: I    Srce: d    Audn: c    Ctrl:       Lang: eng
BLvl: m    TMat: o    GPub: s    AccM:      MRec:       Ctry: mnu
Desc: a    Time: nnn Tech: n    DtSt: s    Dates: 1976,
 1 040       XXX ǂc XXX
 2 007       K ǂb o ǂd b ǂe c
 3 090       BF408 ǂb .E5 1976
 4 049       XXXX
 5 245 00  Environmental values action cards ǂh [activity card] / ǂc Richard
C. Clark, project director.
 6 260       [Saint Paul, Minn.] : ǂb Minnesota Dept. of Education, ǂc 1976.
 7 300       50 activity cards : ǂb b&w ; ǂc 21 x 21 cm.
 8 520       Each card has a picture on the front; on the back each has a
title, suggested activities, and questions to extend meanings and
implications. Intended to help children explore their values, become aware of
themselves, and express their ideas creatively.
 9 650  0  Creative thinking.
10 650  0  Self-perception.
11 650  0  Social values.
12 700  1  Clark, Richard C.
13 710  1  Minnesota. ǂb Dept. of Education.
```

Comments

Cataloging: These are typical activity cards. The GMD "activity card" became available for use after the *1993 Amendments* were published.

Processing: These would need to be packaged in some kind of box.

Example 36. Mexico, Crafts and Industries

Set of study prints

From back of study print

From the SVE *Picture-Story Study Print* Set
MEXICO, CRAFTS AND INDUSTRIES—SP 145
(Series: Mexico, Central America, and the West Indies Today)

Consultant: Carroll J. Schwartz, Ph.D.
  Assistant Professor of Geography
  Northeastern Illinois State College
  Chicago, Illinois

SINGER
EDUCATION & TRAINING PRODUCTS

Produced and
Distributed by
SVE SOCIETY FOR VISUAL EDUCATION INC.
        1345 DIVERSEY PARKWAY   CHICAGO, ILL. 60614

Example 36. Mexico, Crafts and Industries

```
Type: k   ELvl: I   Srce: d   Audn: c   Ctrl:      Lang: eng
BLvl: m   TMat: i   GPub:     AccM:     MRec:      Ctry: ilu
Desc: a   Time: nnn Tech: n   DtSt: s   Dates: 1968,
```

```
 1 040      XXX ǂc XXX
 2 007      k ǂb f ǂd c ǂe c
 3 043      n-mx---
 4 090      F1210 ǂb .M4 1968
 5 049      XXXX
 6 245 00   Mexico, crafts & industries ǂh [picture] / ǂc produced by Society
for Visual Education ; consultant, Carroll J. Schwartz.
 7 246 3    Mexico, crafts and industries
 8 260      Chicago, Ill. : ǂb SVE, ǂc c1968.
 9 300      8 study prints : ǂb col. ; ǂc 33 x 46 cm.
10 440 0    Mexico, Central America, and the West Indies today
11 500      Notes, research questions, enrichment activities, key words, maps,
picture, and list of related filmstrips on back of each study print.
12 505 00  ǂt Pottery painters at work -- ǂt Silversmith at work -- ǂt
Building with adobe bricks -- ǂt Drying sisal -- ǂt Printing textiles -- ǂt
Fishermen at work -- ǂt Refining petroleum -- ǂt Port of Veracruz.
13 651  0   Mexico ǂx Industries ǂx Pictorial works.
14 700 1    Schwartz, Carroll J.
15 710 2    Society for Visual Education.
```

Comments

General: Study prints are similar to activity cards, but are much bigger and have lots of activities for both individuals and classes or groups. They are usually printed on heavy card stock.

Cataloging: One could name the consultant in the statement of responsibility, or in a note, or ignore him.

Access: I used an enhanced field 505 to increase access to these titles and words.

MARC coding/tagging: The second subject heading subdivision is a genre term, so it could be coded as subfield "ǂv" when that coding is implemented.

Processing: These things come in a heavy plastic "portfolio" and don't fit on a shelf very well. If you have lots of them, you could set up a special shelving area or use a cabinet with large drawers.

Example 37. The Black Cat

Full view of poster

Copyright information from lower left edge of poster

Example 37. The Black Cat

```
Type: k    ELvl: I   Srce: d   Audn: e   Ctrl:       Lang: eng
BLvl: m    TMat: i   GPub:     AccM:     MRec:       Ctry: cau
Desc: a    Time: nnn Tech: n   DtSt: s   Dates: 1976,
 1 040      XXX ǂc XXX
 2 007      k ǂb z ǂd c ǂe o
 3 090      PN1995.9.H6 ǂb C3 1976
 4 049      XXXX
 5 245 00   Carl Laemmle presents Karloff and Bela Lugosi in Edgar Allan Poe's
the black cat ǂh [picture].
 6 246 30   Edgar Allan Poe's The black cat
 7 246 30   Black cat
 8 260      Corte Madera, Calif. : ǂb Portal Publications, ǂc c1976.
 9 300      1 poster : ǂb col. ; ǂc 74 x 48 cm.
10 500      Reproduction of poster for 1934 movie by Universal Pictures.
11 650    0 Horror films ǂx Pictorial works.
12 650    0 Film posters.
13 700 12   Poe, Edgar Allan, ǂd 1809-1849. ǂt Black cat.
14 700 1    Laemmle, Carl, ǂd 1867-1939.
15 700 1    Karloff, Boris, ǂd 1887-1969.
16 700 1    Lugosi, Bela, ǂd 1882-1956.
17 710 2    Universal Pictures Company.
18 710 2    Portal Publications Ltd.
19 730 4    The black cat (Motion picture)
```

Comments

Cataloging: The title of this is somewhat of a problem. One can use the wording on the poster itself as a title, or create and bracket a title. If using the second option, one would need to make a note and title added entry for the words on the poster.

I don't like the GMD "picture" for this, but that is as close as we can get from the list of GMDs. It is a poster.

MARC coding/tagging: In the 007, one must use a code for the specific material designation. "Poster" is not on the list, so I used "z" for "other." This is a reproduction of some artwork.

Example 38. Common Loon

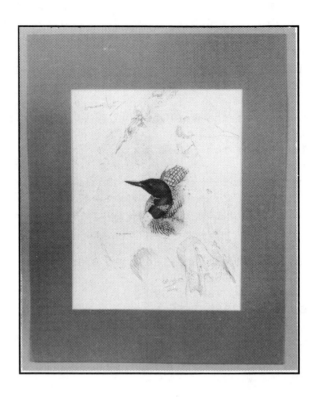

```
QL       Loates, Martin Glen, 1945-
696          Common loon [art reproduction] / M.G. Loates.
.G33     -- Kenyon, Minn. : Nature Incentives, U.S.A.,
L6       [198-?].
1980         1 art reproduction : col. ; 36 x 31 cm. in mat
         51 x 41 cm.

             Watercolor of loon head with sketches of loon.
             Sketch in lower right labeled: Tail and wing
         movement diving.

             1. Loons.  I. Nature Incentives, U.S.A. (Firm :
         Kenyon, Minn.) II.  Title.
```

Example 38. Common Loon

```
Type: k   ELvl: I   Srce: d   Audn: f   Ctrl:       Lang: eng
BLvl: m   TMat: c   GPub:     AccM:     MRec:       Ctry: mnu
Desc: a   Time: nnn Tech: n   DtSt: s   Dates: 198u,
 1 040      XXX ǂc XXX
 2 007      k ǂb f ǂd c ǂe o
 3 090      QL696.G33 ǂb L6 1980
 4 049      XXXX
 5 100 1    Loates, Martin Glen, ǂd 1945-
 6 245 10   Common loon ǂh [art reproduction] / ǂc M.G. Loates.
 7 260      Kenyon, Minn. : ǂb Nature Incentives, U.S.A., ǂc [198-?].
 8 300      1 art reproduction : ǂb col. ; ǂc 36 x 31 cm. in mat 51 x 41 cm.
 9 500      Watercolor of loon head with sketches of loon.
10 500      Sketch in lower right labeled: Tail and wing movement diving.
11 650  0   Loons ǂx Pictorial works.
12 710 2    Nature Incentives, U.S.A. (Firm : Kenyon, Minn.)
```

Comments

General: This item is an art reproduction and the next is an art original.
Cataloging: This item is published, so it has the usual information present in the bibliographic record.

Example 39.   Common Loons

```
QL        Danbom, Carroll D.
696           Common loons [art original] / C. Danbom. --
.G33      1982.
D3            1 art original : pastel on paper ; visible
1982      image 32 x 43 cm. in frame 50 x 60 cm.


              Signed on back: Common loons, a pastel by
          Carroll D. Danbom.


              1. Loons.  I. Title.
```

Example 39. Common Loons

```
Type: k    ELvl: I    Srce: d    Audn: f    Ctrl:       Lang: eng
BLvl: m    TMat: a    GPub:      AccM:      MRec:       Ctry: xxu
Desc: a    Time: nnn  Tech: n    DtSt: s    Dates: 1982,
 1 040     XXX ‡c XXX
 2 007     k ‡b e ‡d c ‡e o
 3 090     QL696.G33 ‡b D3 1982
 4 049     XXXX
 5 100 1   Danbom, Carroll D.
 6 245 10  Common loons ‡h [art original] / ‡c C. Danbom.
 7 260     ‡c 1982.
 8 300     1 art original : ‡b pastel on paper ; ‡c visible image 32 x 43 cm.
in frame 50 x 60 cm.
 9 500     Signed on back: Common loons, a pastel by Carroll D. Danbom.
10 650   0 Loons ‡x Pictorial works.
```

Comments

   General: This item is an art original.
   Cataloging: This item is not published, so it has only the date in field 260. *Graphic Materials* was helpful in preparing the physical description.

How would you catalog this item?

This poster used red, white, and blue books to give the impression of a flag. Below the quotation it says "Congressman William S. Moorhead, Chairman, Foreign Operations and Congressional Information Subcommittee, U.S. House of Representatives. Author, 1974 Freedom of Information Act Amendments."

Along left margin of poster: "United States Historical Documents Institute, Inc. — Carrollton Press Inc. — Washington, D.C. — ©1975 — William W. Buchanan"

COMPUTER FILES

AACR 2 Chapter 9

Special Rules for Cataloging Computer Files

Computer files are cataloged using rules found in AACR 2 chapter 9 and Amendments 1993. For rules and/or areas not discussed in this chapter, see chapter 2 of this book. Other publications that may be useful when cataloging computer files are:

• *Cataloging Computer Files*, by Nancy B. Olson. (Lake Crystal, Minn.: Soldier Creek Press, 1992)

• *Cataloging Internet Resources: A Manual and Practical Guide,* Nancy B. Olson, editor. 2nd ed. (Dublin, Ohio: OCLC, 1997).

• *Guidelines for Bibliographic Description of Interactive Multimedia.* (Chicago, Ill.: ALA, 1994).
    Developed by an ALA committee chaired by Laurel Jizba.

• *Draft Interim Guidelines for Cataloging Resources* (LC, 1998). http://lcweb.loc.gov/catdir/cpso

I have chosen to divide this chapter into three parts and include all the general discussion of computer files in part 1 while reserving specific discussion of cataloging Internet resources for part 2, and interactive multimedia for part 3.

Watch for Further Developments

The cardinal principle of bibliographic description, according to AACR 2 rule 0.24, is to base the description on the physical form of the item in hand or being cataloged. So a disc/disk that goes into a computer would be a computer file, as would anything cataloged from the Internet.

OCLC, in *Technical Bulletin* number 212 (Jan. 1996), announced that, as part of format integration, OCLC users would follow the Library of Congress in entering digital cartographic materials (both atlases and maps) on the maps format rather than the computer files format (see example 44). Fields 006 and 007 for computer files may be used, and the description follows the rules of the computer files chapter together with the maps chapter. MARBI approved this use in proposal 95-9 in June 1995.

In June 1997, the computer file format was limited by approval of MARBI proposal 97-3R to "computer software, numeric data, games, computer-oriented multimedia, and online systems and services". All other types of computer files will use the type code appropriate to the **content** of the file. Field 007 will be mandatory, to be used for computer file characteristics. This change will take place after LC publishes the *USMARC Bibliographic Update* number 3, and the bibliographic utilities implement it.

In January 1998 there will be further discussion of these concepts.

Chief Source of Information

The chief source of information for computer files is the title screen(s). If there is no title screen, or if the cataloger does not have access to the equipment needed to use the computer file and one is cataloging a physical item, information is to be taken from the physical carrier and its labels, the documentation, or the container. If one is cataloging an item available online, take information from whatever source is available, whether title screen, home page, Web site, or the file itself. Prefer the source with the most complete information.

A note is **always** made stating the source of the title proper.

Title and Statement of Responsibility Area
MARC field 245

There are no title proper problems unique to computer software.

The GMD for this chapter is "computer file", though there is a proposal going forward to Joint Steering Committee to change this to "electronic resource" to match the GMD in the newly revised ISBD (ER), *International Standard Bibliographic Description for Electronic Resources.*

Edition Area
MARC field 250

Where a statement of change in the content of a computer file is indicated, generally accept the statement as an edition statement. It might be called an *edition, issue, version, release, level, update,* or some other term, or it might be a date.

One must be careful when cataloging computer files to differentiate between a new version of the file and the version of the operating system needed to run that file. Both might be expressed as "version 3.3" or some other number. The term that refers to the operating system generally will be prefaced by the letters "DOS" or "CP/M" or some combination of numbers and letters, frequently including the letters "OS" for operating system. A statement referring to the version of the software may be recorded as an edition statement; a statement referring to the version of the operating system needed to run that software is included in the system requirements note.

File Characteristics Area
MARC field 256

This area **must** be used when a file is available only by remote access, according to AACR 2. LC decided not to use this area in their cataloging, so I usually omit it. CONSER participants have been told to omit this area. The revision of the ISBD (CF) and its change to ISBD (ER) will also bring about change to this area by adding a list of useful terms and phrases.

Designation

One of the following terms is used when the information is readily available:

> Computer data
> Computer program(s)
> Computer data and program(s)

Number of records, statements, etc.

For computer data, the number of files and the number of records and/or bytes may be added.

```
256      Computer data (1 file : 90 records)
256      Computer data (300 records, 3000 bytes)
```

For computer programs, the number of files and the number of program statements and/or bytes may be given.

```
256     Computer program (1 file : 94 statements)
```

Publication, Distribution, Etc., Area
MARC field 260

There are no unique problems with computer software in this area of bibliographic description.

Physical Description Area
MARC field 300

If a computer file is available only by remote access, there is no area 5 in the bibliographic record.

Extent of item

Terms used as specific material designations include:

computer cartridge
computer cassette
computer optical disc
computer disk
computer reel

A magnetic carrier is called a computer disk (spelled with a "k"), while an optical carrier is spelled with a "c," as in computer optical disc. (JSC, 1995)

More specific terms may be used:

computer chip cartridge
computer tape cartridge
computer tape reel

If none of these terms is appropriate, use the exact term needed.

All discs/disks are counted. If one or more are for backup, they are included in the extent and described in a note.

Other physical details

The presence of sound is indicated by "sd."
A display in two or more colors is indicated by "col."

```
300     1 computer disk : sd.
300     3 computer disks : col.
300     2 computer disks : sd., col.
```

Dimensions

The diameter of a computer disk is given to the next higher ¼ inch.

```
300        1 computer disk : ǂb sd., col. ; ǂc 5 1/4 in.
300        2 computer disks ; ǂc 3 1/2 in.
300        1 computer optical disc : ǂb sd., col. ; ǂc 4 3/4 in.
```

The length of the side of a cartridge that is inserted into the machine is measured to the next higher ¼ inch.
The length and height of the face of a cassette are measured to the next higher ⅛ inch.
No dimension is given for reels.
For other carriers, measurements are given, rounded, in centimeters.

Notes Area
MARC fields 5XX

Types of notes:

9.7B1.   Nature and scope and systems requirements
9.7B2.   Language and script
9.7B3.   Source of title proper
9.7B4.   Variations in title
9.7B5.   Parallel titles and other title information
9.7B6.   Statements of responsibility
9.7B7.   Edition and history
9.7B8.   File characteristics
9.7B9.   Publication, distribution, etc.
9.7B10. Physical description
9.7B11. Accompanying material
9.7B12. Series
9.7B13. Dissertations
9.7B14. Audience
9.7B16. Other formats
9.7B17. Summary
9.7B18. Contents
9.7B19. Numbers
9.7B20. Copy being described, library's holdings, and restrictions on use
9.7B21. "With" notes

9.7Bl. Nature and scope and system requirements

This note is divided into three parts.

9.7B1a. Nature and scope (MARC fields 516, 500)

To be used to name or explain the nature of the item as necessary.

```
500        An educational game for two or more players.
500        Role-playing game.
516        Summary statistics.
```

9.7B1b. System requirements (MARC field 538)

The systems requirement note gives information concerning the computer system on which the computer file will run. The characteristics are given in the following order:

make and model of the computer(s) on which the file is designed to run
the amount of memory required
the name of the operating system
the software requirements, including the programming language
the kind and characteristics of any required or recommended peripherals

The type of computer needed to use the item must be named. Any special equipment needed to use the item also must be described in this note.

```
538        System requirements: Apple II or higher; printer.
538        System requirements: IBM PC or compatible.
```

9.7B1c. Mode of access (MARC field 538)

If the file is available only by remote access, the mode of access **must** be specified here.

```
538        Available through Internet.
```

9.7B2. Language and script (MARC field 546)

To be used if the information is given and not recorded elsewhere.

```
546        Language of text: German.
```

9.7B3. Source of title proper (MARC field 500)

This note must be used to give the source from which the title proper was taken.

```
500        Title from title screens.
500        Title from container.
500        Title supplied by cataloger.
500        Title from disc label.
```

9.7B4. Variations in title (MARC fields 246, 500)

To be used to note any title appearing on other than the chief source of information that differs significantly from the title proper. If the title applies to the entire item, MARC field 246 is used.

```
246 1    ǂi Title on disk label: ǂa Genetics
         (Title proper: Elementary genetics)
```

9.7B5. Parallel titles and other title information (MARC fields 246, 500)

To be used for parallel titles and other title information that were not recorded in the title and statement of responsibility area; give only if considered important. If the title applies to the entire item it may be recorded in field 246.

```
246 1    ǂi Title on guide: ǂa Getting ready to read and add
         (Title proper: Préparation à la lecture et à l'addition)
```

9.7B6. Statements of responsibility (MARC field 500)

To be used to record the information not given in the chief source of information, or not given prominently there, concerning programmers, system designers, etc.

```
500        James Bach, Scott Bailey, programmers.
```

9.7B7. Edition and history (MARC field 500)

To be used for information about earlier editions.

```
500      First ed. called: Step by step.
```
(Title proper: New step by step)

9.7B8. File characteristics (MARC field 516)

To be used for important file characteristics not included in area 3.

```
516      File size unknown.
```

9.7B9. Publication, distribution, etc. (MARC field 500)

Any detail not given in the publication, distribution, etc., area, but considered important, would be given in this note.

```
500      "Published in the U.K. for the Schools Council by
Longman"--T.p. of guide.
```

9.7B10. Physical description (MARC fields 500, 538)

To be used for any important information not given in area 5.

```
500      One disk is backup.
500      Stereo. sound.
```

9.7B11. Accompanying material (MARC fields 500, 556)

To be used for any important details concerning accompanying material not given in area 5.

```
500      User's manual includes 5-lesson tutorial.
556      Documentation may be printed out from file.
```

9.7B12. Series (MARC field 500)

To be used for any important information not given in area 6.

```
500      Issued also as part 3 of Tax management series.
```

9.7B13. Dissertations (MARC field 502)

To be used for the standard dissertation note when applicable.

```
502      Thesis (M.S.)--Mankato State College, 1972.
```

9.7B14. Audience (MARC field 521)

To be used to note the intended audience or intellectual level if the information is given on the item or in its documentation. If no indicator, the display constant "Audience:" is supplied.

```
521 8    For children 3 to 8 years old.
```

9.7B16. Other formats (MARC field 530)

To be used to list other formats in which the work is available.

```
530     Issued also on disk for IBM-PC.
```

9.7B17. Summary (MARC field 520)

To be used for a brief objective summary of the content of the software unless the information is obvious from the rest of the bibliographic description. Indicator "8" is used if one does not want the display constant "Summary:".

```
520 8   Simulation for one to three players of presidential
campaigning from Labor Day to election night; players decide how
to allocate campaign funds. Includes six historical scenarios,
hypothetical scenarios, and minute-by-minute election returns.
```

9.7B18. Contents (MARC fields 505, 500)

To be used to list the contents of the item, either formally (field 505) or informally (field 500).

```
500     Includes nine versions of the game.
505 0   ABC time -- Letter game -- Spelling zoo.
```

9.7B19. Numbers (MARC field 500)

Give any numbers on the item, other than an ISBN (recorded in field 020) or UPC (field 024), in field 037 if they seem to be manufacturer stock numbers. Record them in this note if they seem important and don't fit elsewhere. The numbers should be quoted.

```
500     "No. 1881"
020     0965145603
024 1   605961104158
037     TUM4744AE ǂb MECC
```

9.7B20. Copy being described, library's holdings, and restrictions on use (MARC field 590)

To be used for notes that apply only to the copy being cataloged. To provide information of importance to patrons of the library cataloging the item.

```
590     On Reserve in the ERC.
590     Use restricted to Sociology 454 class.
```

9.7B21. "With" notes (MARC field 501)

To be used for "with" notes.

```
501     With: Hypercard.
```

Access Points

For those of us using a MARC-based online system, access to computer make and model is available through field 753 in the MARC format, which provides an added entry for machine and model number, programming language, and operating system. The Library of Congress stopped using this access in 1996, as the trend is toward computer files that can be used on any type of computer.

Many catalogers are confused by wording, qualifiers, and MARC coding of headings for names of computer programs.

The first headings for computer programs were subject headings coded in field 650. Some of these had qualifiers, but they did not all use the same qualifier.

Now all headings for computer software are established as name headings, coded in field 630. If a qualifier is used, it is always "(Computer file)."

```
630 00  Microsoft Excel (Computer file)
630 00  Microsoft Excel for Windows
```

The authority files carry many earlier headings; LC revises these headings only as/if they are needed for use.

A qualifier is added only if there is a conflict with another work with the same title proper and entered under title. For a fuller explanation, see LCRI 25.5B, section on computer file headings.

Processing Material for Circulation

Paper clips on date due cards or on package inserts are not recommended because they can become entangled with disk covers and scratch disk surfaces. Sometimes paper clips have become magnetized from magnetic holders. These can cause problems with data on magnetic disks. Labels put on the front or back of a magnetic disk can peel back, as can write-protect tabs, catching in disk drives.

Automated check-out devices can be harmful to magnetic computer materials, as can theft-protection systems. Here are examples of two notices you might want to put on software packages.

DO NOT SENSITIZE or De-SENSITIZE
═══════════════════════════════════

Beware of Computer Viruses!
Check Disk with Anti-Virus Software Before Using

Optical discs are not affected by any magnetic fields including those created by tattle-tape devices. They are, however, not as sturdy as thought when they were first developed. They can easily be scratched or broken. Nothing should be marked on any optical disc, as the chemical components of marker fluid can migrate through the plastic and cause loss of data.

No labels of any type should be applied to any surface of an optical disc. Labels have adhesive, so there is a potential chemical migration problem. Labels can affect the balance of the optical disc as it spins in the play-back device. These discs spin very fast and it takes very little added weight to affect this, causing distortion of the data. Labels can loosen and get stuck inside a play-back device. The only safe marking for an optical disc is to write with a Sharpie-type pen on the clear inner ring of the disc.

Copyright Restrictions

By law, the following notice must be displayed on all computer software that is circulated by a library or media center. Commercial labels are available from Soldier Creek Press as well as from some regular library supply catalogs.

Enhanced CDs

Enhanced CDs are sound recordings with one or more tracks that are computer files. The manufacturers call these "enhanced CDs" and usually include warning information such as "Do not play track one on CD player." The computer track may work on an IBM PC or a Macintosh, or on any or all of several other configurations. Indication the CD includes a computer track might be clearly printed on the container, hidden in some fine print, or it might be stated on a slip of paper inserted in the container.

If you have one of these to catalog, I'd suggest cataloging it as a sound recording if most of the CD is music. You should add MARC fields 006 and 007 for the computer track(s) thus permitting searching by either sound recording or computer formats. You would need MARC field 538 for the system requirements note for the computer portion, and a note saying it is an enhanced CD. I'd want that "enhanced" information in a searchable field — in my system that would include MARC fields 505, 520, and/or 590. It could be given in the opening statement of a summary note. You would want to place a prominent warning label on the container when processing such material for circulation — some correspondents have indicated playing the computer track on a sound system could damage the system.

Example 40. Reader Rabbit

Box and disks

Example 40. Reader Rabbit

```
Type: m    ELvl: I    Srce: d    Audn: b    Ctrl:      Lang: eng
BLvl: m    File: g    GPub:                 MRec:      Ctry: cau
Desc: a                          DtSt: s    Dates: 1991,
 1 040      XXX ǂc XXX
 2 007      c ǂb j ǂd c ǂe a ǂf a
 3 090      LB1525.55 ǂb .R4 1991
 4 049      XXXX
 5 245 00   Reader rabbit ǂh [computer file].
 6 246 1    ǂi Title on container: ǂa Talking reader rabbit
 7 250      V[ersion] 3.0.
 8 260      Fremont, CA : ǂb The Learning Company, ǂc [1991].
 9 300      2 computer disks : ǂb sd., col. ; ǂc 3 1/2 in. + ǂe 1 user's guide.
10 538      System requirements: Macintosh Plus or Macintosh SE, SE/30,
Macintosh II, IIx, IIcx; 1MB; System 6.0 or later; hard disk.
11 500      Title from title screen.
12 500      Created and designed by Leslie Grimm.
13 521 1    Ages 3-7.
14 520      Four animated games help beginning readers develop early reading
skills, increase vocabulary, improve spelling, develop spatial awareness, and
sharpen memory and concentration skills.
15 650  0   Reading games.
16 650  0   Spelling games.
17 650  0   Computer games.
18 700 1    Grimm, Leslie.
19 710 2    Learning Company.
```

Comments

General: This is an educational game package for beginning readers.

MARC coding/tagging: In field 521, the indicator "1" supplies a display constant "Interest age level:"

In the fixed field, "Lang" used to be "N/A" for computer files, with field 041 used to indicate the language was English (or whatever). This coding is no longer used. These items are coded for language just as is done with books or videos or anything else.

Field 007 was added to the computer file format during the last phase of format integration. Earlier bibliographic records do not have this field.

Processing: Packaging for the material sold in computer stores is not designed for circulation in a library. The material is often flimsy, and a single disk may be packaged in a large box. Library supply catalogs show a variety of packaging for computer files. We use packages that have clear plastic sleeves on the outside that will hold the cut up box sections. We are able to retain the attractive designs from the original package together with all the information about the product.

Example 41. The Oregon Trail

Facsimile of disc label

Container and contents

Example 41. The Oregon Trail

```
Type: m   ELvl: I   Srce: d   Audn: d   Ctrl:      Lang: eng
BLvl: m   File: g   GPub:               MRec:      Ctry: mnu
Desc: a                       DtSt: s   Dates: 1994,
```

```
 1 040      XXX ‡c XXX
 2 020      0792908856
 3 007      c ‡b o ‡d c ‡e g ‡f a
 4 090      F880 ‡b .O7 1994
 5 049      XXXX
 6 245 04   The Oregon Trail ‡h [computer file].
 7 250      Version 1.0.1 for Windows or Macintosh.
 8 260      Minneapolis, Minn. : ‡b MECC, ‡c [1994].
 9 300      1 computer optical disc : ‡b sd., col. ; ‡c 4 3/4 in. + ‡e 1
insert.
10 538      System requirements for Macintosh: Macintosh; 4 MB memory;
hard disk; System 7.
11 538      System requirements for Windows: IBM or compatible 386 or higher
computer; Microsoft Windows 3.1 (running in 256-color video model); 4 MB
memory required; Windows-compatible sound card required for music and sound.
12 500      Title from disc label.
13 500      Includes online manual.
14 521      Ages 10-Adult.
15 520      An educational simulation game designed to develop social
studies skills as students travel by covered wagon on an 1848 journey from
Independence, Mo., to the Willamette Valley of Oregon, learning about the
perils of the trip and making life or death decisions.
16 505 2    Also includes demonstration versions of Amazon Trail, Yukon Trail,
and Oregon Trail II.
17 651  0   Oregon Trail.
18 650  0   Frontier and pioneer life ‡x Simulation methods.
19 650  0   Simulation games in education.
20 710 2    Minnesota Educational Computing Corporation.
```

Comments

General: This is a very popular educational game developed by MECC as one of its first educational software programs. Many versions have been published. Note that this CD-ROM is for both Macintosh and Windows computers. This is becoming common practice for these materials.

Cataloging: The audience note is given exactly as stated on the package.

MARC coding/tagging: In field 521, there is no indicator, so the constant "Audience" would be generated.

Processing: This needs to be repackaged in a binder or box with an outside plastic sleeve to hold the front, back, and spine of the original box.

Example 42a. The Manhole (1988 ed.)

Disc and container of the 1988 ed.

Title and credit screens

Cyan presents

World Design
Robyn Miller

Illustrations
Robyn Miller

Scripting and Editing
Rand Miller

Theme music composed and conducted by
Russell Lieblich

Sound effects ...

Voice characterizations ...

Technical production ...

Example 42a. The Manhole (1988 ed.)

Title and credit screens (continued)

CD-ROM scripting ...

Produced by
Sherry Whiteley

Distributed by
MEDIAGENIC

© 1988 Activision

The Manhole

```
Type: m    ELvl: I    Srce: d   Audn: c   Ctrl:      Lang: eng
BLvl: m    File: g    GPub:                MRec:      Ctry: cau
Desc: a                         DtSt: s    Dates: 1988,
 1 040     XXX ǂc XXX
 2 007     c ǂb o ǂd c ǂe g ǂf a
 3 090     GV1469.2 ǂb .M3 1988
 4 049     XXXX
 5 245 04  The manhole ǂh [computer file] / ǂc [developed by Robyn Miller and
Rand Miller] ; produced by Sherry Whiteley.
 6 260     Menlo Park, CA : ǂb Activision : ǂb Distributed by Mediagenic,
ǂc c1988.
 7 300     1 computer optical disc : ǂb sd., col. ; ǂc 4 3/4 in.
 8 500     "A fantasy exploration for children of all ages."
 9 538     System requirements: Macintosh Plus, SE, or II; 1 megabyte of
memory; Hypercard version 1.2.1 or higher; SCSI hard drive.
10 500     Title from title screens.
11 650  0  Fantasy games.
12 650  0  Computer games.
13 700  1  Miller, Robyn.
14 700  1  Miller, Rand.
15 710  2  Mediagenic (Firm)
16 710  2  Activision (Firm)
17 710  2  Cyan, Inc.
```

Comments

General: Here we have two editions of the same program.

Cataloging: When this runs, it shows a file labeled "credits." The credits are transcribed here. The "developed by" phrase was on the package rather than in the credits frames. I chose to bracket it into the statement of responsibility with similar information rather than separate it as a note.

I quoted the description from the container rather than attempting to construct a summary.

Example 42b. The Manhole (1994 ed.)

Photo of package 1994 ed.

```
Type: m    ELvl: I    Srce: d    Audn: c    Ctrl:       Lang: eng
BLvl: m    File: g    GPub:                 MRec:       Ctry: wau
Desc: a                          DtSt: s    Dates: 1994,
 1 040       XXX ǂc XXX
 2 020       1885040016
 3 007       c ǂb o ǂd c ǂe g ǂf a
 4 090       GV1469.22 ǂb .M3 1994
 5 049       XXXX
 6 245 00    Cyan presents The manhole ǂh [computer file].
 7 246 30    Manhole
 8 250       CD-ROM masterpiece ed.
 9 260       Spokane, WA : ǂb Cyan, ǂc 1994.
10 300       1 computer optical disc : ǂb sd., col. ; ǂc 4 3/4 in. + ǂe 1 user's
guide + 1 poster (35 x 24 cm.).
11 538       System requirements: Macintosh; 4MB; system 7.0.1 or higher.
12 500       Title from disc label.
13 500       Stereo. sound. Soundtrack can be played on audio CD player (begin
at track 2). Music by Chris Brandkamp.
14 520       A fantasy adventure approach to education. Teaches letters and
their sounds, numbers, and vocabulary.
15 650  0    Computer adventure games.
16 650  0    Educational games.
17 650  0    Fantasy games.
18 700  1    Brandkamp, Chris.
19 710  2    Cyan, Inc.
```

Comments

   General: The information on the package of this edition made it clear that this game has an educational purpose. That was not mentioned on the earlier edition.
   Cataloging: This is one of the "problem" titles. It must be transcribed as it appears. I made an added entry for the "real" title.
   Notice that "stereo." cannot be used in the physical description area. Rather than make a separate note, I combined that information with related information.

Example 42b. The Manhole (1994 ed.)

Text from the back of the package 1994 ed.

I N 1988 YOU MET MR. RABBIT
AND A HOST OF HIS FRIENDS IN THE WORLD OF
THE MANHOLE.

Your friends are still here, but they've done some remodeling…

PREPARE FOR A GRAND ADVENTURE in the
world of *The Manhole CD-ROM Masterpiece Edition.* A
world of epic wonder and whimsical magic. A fantastic
world where every character comes alive and every new
hallway leads to another wild dream.

JUST POINT-AND-CLICK. Soon you may find
yourself shooting down a winding waterway with Rejan
Elephant. Click again and you're climbing to the top of the
rook tower to greet Molly Rhinocerous. Click on Mr. Rabbit's dresser drawer and moments
later you're flipping through the pages of his noisy ABC book. Or you're suddenly
transported to dine with that esteemed soul-cat,
Mr. Dragon.

So let the child in your home, or the child in
your heart, become the main character in a
journey through an unforgettable land. A land
where imaginations run wild and creativity is as
close as the next wonderful doorway.

THIS CRITICALLY-ACCLAIMED, AWARD-WINNING WORLD IS BACK,
meticulously recreated in lush color. Every note of music has been delicately rewritten and every
character has been expertly redrawn with the attention to the detail, richness, warmth and humor
that was and is *The Manhole.*

For more information about Cyan's
products, write to us at PO Box 28096,
Spokane, WA 99228, USA.

The Manhole CD-ROM Masterpiece Edition, Myst, and
Cosmic Osmo are trademarks of Cyan, Inc. *Spelunx* is a
trademark of Cyan, Inc. and Brøderbund, Inc.
Macintosh is a registered trademark of Apple Computer,
Inc. Cyan is a registered trademark. © 1993 by Cyan,
Inc. All rights reserved. Box design by Cyan.

Example 43. Adobe PageMaker

With this example we show the title screens for versions 1.1, 2.0a, 3.0, 4.0, and 6.0 to show how this has changed.

PageMaker
PageMaker
Aldus PageMaker
Aldus PageMaker 4.0
Adobe PageMaker 6.0

Version 1.1 title screen

Version 2.0a title screen

Example 43. Adobe PageMaker

Version 3.0 title screen

Version 4.0 title screen

Example 43. Adobe PageMaker

Version 6.0 title screen

Example 43. Adobe PageMaker

```
Type: m    ELvl: I    Srce: d    Audn: f    Ctrl:       Lang: eng
BLvl: m    File: c    GPub:                 MRec:       Ctry: cau
Desc: a                          DtSt: s    Dates: 1995,
 1 040      XXX ǂc XXX
 2 007      c ǂo ǂd c ǂe g
 3 090      Z286.D47 ǂb P3 1995
 4 049      XXXX
 5 245 00   Adobe PageMaker 6.0 ǂh [computer file].
 6 246 30   PageMaker
 7 250      Version 6.0/Deluxe CD-ROM ed.
 8 260      Mountain View, CA : ǂb Adobe Systems, ǂc c1995.
 9 300      2 computer optical discs : ǂb col. ; ǂc 4 3/4 in. + ǂe 1 user
manual (x, 445 p.) + 1 getting started manual (iv, 19 p.) + 1 print publishing
guide (79 p.) + 1 quick reference card + 1 enhancement pack.
10 500      Second disc is Type on call CD-ROM, version 4.0, with 220 fonts.
11 500      Title from title screen.
12 500      Enhancement pack changes version to 6.0.1.
13 538      System requirements: Macintosh with 68030 processor (or
later model) with 10 MB RAM, or Power Macintosh with 12 MB RAM; 20 to 40 MB
hard disk space for installation; system software version 7.1 or higher
(Macintosh) or 7.1.2 or higher (Power Macintosh).
14 520      A desktop publishing package allowing the user to integrate text
and graphics and to control the appearance of documents.
15 650  0   Desktop publishing.
16 710  2   Adobe Systems.
```

Comments

General: This example shows the use of the embedded capital letter, a technique used with many titles of computer software. It is transcribed as it appears.

Cataloging: The edition statement was given with a slash "Version 6.0/Deluxe CD-ROM ed." I transcribed it as given.

Example 44. Ely, MN and Two Harbors, MN

Facsimile of disc label

Facsimile of container

MINNESOTA, WI, MI   47091
Digital Raster Graphic (DRG) Data   1-Degree Cell

[map of Minnesota
showing area covered
by this CD-ROM]

This CD-ROM contains DRG's of the following
USGS standard series quadrangles:

1:24,000-scale: All the quadrangles comprising the Ely
and Two Harbors 1:100,000-scale quadrangles.
(area shown at left)
1:100,000-scale: Ely, MN
(West half of 250K) **Two Harbors, MN-WI**
1:250,000-scale: Two Harbors, MN-WI-MI

US GeoData
U.S. Department of the Interior
U.S. Geological Survey
800 USA MAPS
http://www.usgs.gov/

**Minimum configuration to run MS-DOS
menu system & viewers:**
• **IBM compatible PC with 80386 or higher**
• **Microsoft Windows 3.1**
• **Microsoft compatible pointing device (mouse)**
• **16 MB of hard drive space**
• **4 MB of RAM (8 MB recommended)**

Starting MS-DOS menu system:
Set active drive to CD-ROM reader and enter **DRG**

Text files are in ASCII
Image files are in TIFF - *PackBits compressed*

U|S
G|S

Edition 1   Mastered 6/96

[UPC symbol]

U.S. Geological Survey

Example 44. Ely, MN and Two Harbors, MN

```
Type: e   ELvl: I   Srce: d   Relf: ag   Ctrl:        Lang: eng
BLvl: m   SpFm:     GPub: f   Prme:      MRec:        Ctry: vau
CrTp: a   Indx: 0   Proj: bh  DtSt: s    Dates: 1996,
Desc: a
 1 040     XXX ‡c XXX
 2 006     [m    m f   ]
 3 007     c ‡b o ‡d c ‡e g
 4 020     0607847190
 5 034 0   a ‡d W0920000 ‡e W0910000 ‡f N0480000 ‡g N0470000
 6 052     4141
 7 052     4121
 8 086 0   I 19.128:47091
 9 090     G4142.C2 1996 ‡b .G4 no.47091
10 049     XXXX
11 110 2   Geological Survey (U.S.)
12 245 10  Ely, MN, and Two Harbors, MN ‡h [computer file] : ‡b Two Harbors,
MN : 47091, digital raster graphic data : DRG / ‡c U.S. Geological Survey.
13 246 30  Two Harbors, MN
14 246 30  Ely, MN
15 246 30  DRG
16 246 30  47091, digital raster graphic data
17 250     Ed. 1.
18 255     Scales differ ; ‡b universal transverse Mercator proj. ‡c (W 92°--W
91°/N 48°--N 47°).
19 260     [Reston, Va.] : ‡b The Survey ; ‡a [Denver, Colo. : ‡b USGS
Branch of Distribution, ‡c 1996]
20 300     1 computer optical disc : ‡b col. ; ‡c 4 3/4 in.
21 538     System requirements: IBM compatible PC 80386 or higher; 4 MB of
RAM (8 MB recommended); 16 MB of hard drive space; Microsoft Windows 3.1
(optional); Microsoft Extensions 2.0 or later.
22 538     System requirements for DOS-based Aerial View Lite viewing
software: graphics card that displays 256 colors with resolution of at least
640 x 480; mouse with mouse driver loaded; minimum of 4 MB of RAM (more is
recommended).
23 538     System requirements for Windows-based Arc View Version viewing
software: 387 math co-processor or emulator; 15 MB of disc space; 8 MB of free
memory; Microsoft Windows 3.0 through 3.11.
24 500     Title from disc label.
25 500     "TIFF PackBits compressed"--Disc label.
26 500     "Mastered 6/96"--Disc label.
27 500     "47091 1-degree cell"--Container insert.
28 520     Contains 1:100,000-scale and the associated 1:24,00-scale
quadrangles for Ely, MN, and Two Harbors, MN, and 1:250,000-scale quadrangle
for Two Harbors, MN.
29 651 0   Minnesota ‡x Maps ‡x Databases.
30 651 0   Wisconsin ‡x Maps ‡x Databases.
```

Example 44. Ely, MN and Two Harbors, MN

Comments

   General: While this is a computer file, the map people consider the map aspect to be of more importance than the fact that its physical form is a computer file. So it is cataloged on the map workform, with fields 006 and 007 for the map characteristics.
   Cataloging: I have edited this only slightly from the way GPO cataloged it on OCLC.
   Access: Because the most prominent information on the disc is "DRG" I added this to field 245 and made an added entry for it. There are many of these to cover the state of Minnesota and our patrons refer to them as "DRG discs."

Chapter 8, Part 2

INTERNET RESOURCES

Special Rules for Cataloging Internet Resources

Internet resources are cataloged according to *Cataloging Internet Resources: A Manual and Practical Guide*, Nancy B. Olson, editor, 2nd ed. (Dublin, Ohio: OCLC, 1997). These guidelines, developed as part of an OCLC-U.S. Dept. of Education project under the direction of Erik Jul, are based on AACR 2 (1988 revision), the *Amendments 1993*, the Library of Congress rule interpretations, and the *ISBD(ER): International Standard Bibliographic Description for Electronic Resources* (revised in 1997; much of the work done by John Byrum and Ann Sandberg-Fox), and are for use by OCLC participants and may be used by anyone else who wishes to do so.

This chapter will concentrate on those aspects of cataloging that are different from those presented in the previous chapter on cataloging computer files. For rules and/or areas not discussed here or in chapter 8, see chapter 2 of this book.

Internet resources and other computer files are often serial in nature. Serial and serial-like computer files are cataloged using a combination of rules from AACR 2 chapter 9 and chapter 12. Computer serials are cataloged on the computer workform with field 006 added for certain serial characteristics.

There are many Internet resources and computer files that do not fit the strict definition of a serial, but which change over time. The change may occur continuously, as with the OCLC database, or daily, weekly, monthly, or irregularly, as with some websites and home pages, but the changes are not indicated by a change in numeric or chronological designation. These items are cataloged as monographs, although that cataloging may include features, notes, and fixed and variable fields reserved for serials cataloging before format integration.

Chief Source of Information

The chief source of information for computer files available through the Internet is the title (or title and credits) screen(s) or similar display one sees when the file appears on your screen. If there is no title display, information may be available from a home page, a website, a "readme file" or other internal source.

Title and Statement of Responsibility Area
MARC fields 245, 246

There are no problems with title and statement of responsibility area that are unique to Internet resources; one will encounter the same types of problems as with other computer files, or other special materials.

Title added entries (variant titles, other forms of the title, part of the title, etc.) reflecting the entire work are entered in MARC field 246, while those that apply to a part of the work are entered as MARC field 740.

```
245 00  Autocat ǂh [computer file] : ǂb library cataloging and
authorities discussion group.
246 3   Library cataloging and authorities discussion group
```

General Material Designation

The only GMD now permitted for these materials is "computer file" although the ISBD(ER) has introduced the term "electronic resource" and there is movement to have this term accepted as a GMD.

```
245 00 Cataloging Internet resources ‡h [computer file] : ‡b a
manual and practical guide / ‡c Nancy B. Olson, editor.
```

Edition Area
MARC field 250

As with computer files, these materials tend to undergo revision and appear in multiple versions. Treat any statement or information that indicates the item being cataloged differs from an earlier version of the item as an edition statement.

File Characteristics Area
MARC field 256

This area is required for cataloging of all files available only by remote access, although LC is not now using it nor do CONSER participants.

The ISBD(ER) introduces an expanded list of terms to be used in the file characteristics area, and the OCLC guidelines recommend their use. The list is as follows:

Computer data
    Computer numeric data
        Computer census data
        Computer survey data
    Computer text data
        Computer bibliographic database
        Computer journal(s)
        Computer newsletter(s)
        Computer document(s)
            (e.g. letters, articles)
    Computer pictorial data
        Computer image(s)
    Computer representational data
        Computer map(s)
    Computer sound data
Computer programs
    Computer utility program(s)
Computer application program(s)
    Computer CAD program(s)
    Computer database program(s)
    Computer spreadsheet program(s)
    Computer word processor program(s)
    Computer desktop publishing program(s)
    Computer game(s)
Computer system program(s)
    Computer operating system program(s)
    Computer programming language(s)
    Computer retrieval program(s)

Computer data and program(s)
Computer interactive multimedia
Computer online service
(e.g. bulletin boards, discussion groups)

[terms from the above lists may be combined]

Publication, Distribution, Etc., Area
MARC field 260

Information available through the Internet is considered to be published, so the usual parts of this area are to be supplied. If information is not available, the cataloger is to supply place of publication, making assumptions as necessary; name of publisher (or *s.n.* if no information available), and some kind of date, either exact or assumed.

```
260     [Dublin, Ohio] : ‡b OCLC Online Computer Library Center,
‡c c1995.
260     [Buffalo, N.Y. : ‡b State University of New York at
Buffalo, ‡c 1995-
```

Physical Description Area
MARC field 300

Do **not** use the physical description area when cataloging Internet resources. Information about color or sound is to be recorded in a physical description note (9.7B10).

Series Area
MARC fields 4XX

Series information is treated as for any other type of material.

Notes Area
MARC fields 5XX

Order of notes

According to AACR 2, notes are to be entered in order by rule number. CONSER participants, however, are directed to enter notes in order by MARC tag, and some online catalogs order notes by MARC tag rather than as input. Rule numbers arrange information in notes in the same order as the bibliographic description itself: title, other title information, statement of responsibility, etc. It is frustrating to arrange notes carefully so as to follow the rules, and perhaps to display the one note first that seems most important (as permitted in the rules), then have your online system ignore that order.

Only those notes that have special uses with Internet resource cataloging or differ significantly from the notes used for computer files in the previous chapter will be discussed here.

9.7B1a. Nature and scope (MARC fields 516, 500)

If the nature and/or scope of the item can be described briefly, that information is given here. If a lenghthier description is needed, the summary and/or contents note is used for all this information.

```
516      Home page.
```

9.7B1b. System requirements (MARC field 538)

This note is **required** for any computer file cataloged without a physical item in hand. Use of the mode of access note fills this requirement.

This note is used to specify any specific program or type of program and/or equipment that is needed to use the resource being cataloged.

9.7B1c. Mode of access (MARC field 538)

Detailed information for obtaining the resource being cataloged is coded in MARC field 856. In this field you may be brief

```
538      Available through Internet.
```

or you may include more detailed information, depending on local needs and local decisions. The Joint Steering Committee in 1996 rejected a proposal to require the Internet address in this note.

```
538      Available through the Internet from OCLC.
538      Internet (http://www.ncs.usace.army.mil)
```

9.7B3. Source of title proper (MARC field 500)

This note is **required** when cataloging any type of computer file.

```
500      Title from title screen.
500      Title from home page.
500      Title from header file.
```

12.7B23. Item described (MARC field 500)

This note is used when the description is based on other than the first issue. It contains information to identify whatever is used as the basis for the bibliographic description.

For Internet resources, when the screen used as the basis for the description contains a date that represents the latest update of this information, this note could be expressed as the following:

```
500      Description based on Web site update: 6 June 1997.
```

If there is information that leads you to believe the file is updated at some interval, but no dates are given, you might use

```
500      Description based on home page as of June 28, 1997.
```

Electronic Location and Access
MARC field 856

Field 856 was developed to include a "button-pushable" address that could be used to link directly to the resource being cataloged; click on the address and have the resource appear! When we first talked about this at OCLC not so many years ago, some of us laughed at the very idea. Now we are using it.

Rather than reproduce the many pages of the OCLC format document that explain all the indicators and subfields of this field, I refer you to that document. When the field was first developed, there was no World Wide Web, nor were there URLs—so field 856 looks more complicated than it actually is in use.

For a document with an URL, the field appears as shown below:

```
856  7  ‡u http://www.oclc.org/oclc/man/9256cat/toc.htm ‡2 http
```

A MARBI proposal was approved in June 1997 to use indicator "4" for URLs and drop the subfield 2 for these. This will be implemented by OCLC and other systems after it is published in an LC update to the USMARC format. The example shown above will then appear as:

```
856  4  ‡u http://www.oclc.org/oclc/man/9256cat/toc.htm
```

The only difficulty with this is handling addresses longer than one line. Glenn Patton at OCLC suggests the best solution is to let the URL wrap from one line to the next; this would not create any blank spaces in the critical field. However, your local system may not like this. If it doesn't, consult with your systems people.

The Library of Congress Network Development and MARC Standards Office maintains the "Guidelines for the Use of Field 856" at http://www.loc.gov/marc/856guide.html

Local decisions need to be made about whether to catalog Internet resources or not. If it is decided that they should be cataloged, then decisions need to be made about classification and holdings. Do you want to assign a classification number to something that won't go on a shelf? Or might you want to use a class number for collection evaluation and/or development? Will you attach a "virtual barcode" so you can list holdings? What will your online catalog display to the patron for location and call number?

Some suggestions:

```
Electronic resource available through Internet
Online access through Internet
```

Main Entry for Internet Resources

Main entry for an Internet resource is chosen just as for any other type of material. It is quite likely that some will qualify for corporate main entry.

Example 45. Cataloging Internet Resources

Title screen as displayed on Internet

Cataloging Internet Resources

A Manual and Practical Guide

Nancy B. Olson, Editor

Copyright 1995 OCLC Online Computer Library Center, Inc.

OCLC encourages the dissemination of this electronic document and expressly grants rights to copy this document provided this copyright statement and all attributions are retained.

Published in the United States

ISBN 1-55653-189-3

Example 45. Cataloging Internet Resources

```
Type: m    ELvl: I    Srce: d   Audn:       Ctrl:       Lang: eng
BLvl: m    File: d    GPub:                 MRec:       Ctry: ohu
Desc: a                         DtSt: s    Dates: 1995,
 1 040      XXX ǂc XXX
 2 006      [a       b 000 0 ]
 3 007      c ǂb r ǂd a ǂe n
 4 020      ǂz 1556531893
 5 090      Z695.1.I6 ǂb C38 1995
 6 049      XXXX
 7 245 00   Cataloging Internet resources ǂh [computer file] : ǂb a manual and
practical guide / ǂc Nancy B. Olson, editor.
 8 256      Computer document.
 9 260      [Dublin, Ohio] : ǂb OCLC Online Computer Library Center, Inc.,
ǂc c1995.
10 538      Available through the Internet from OCLC.
11 500      Title from title screen.
12 650   0  Cataloging of computer files.
13 650   0  Internet (Computer network)
14 700 1    Olson, Nancy B.
15 710 2    OCLC.
16 856 1    ǂu ftp://ftp.rsch.oclc.org/pub/internet~cataloging~project/
Manual.txt
17 856 7    ǂu http://www.oclc.org/oclc/man/9256cat/toc.htm ǂ2 http
```

Comments

General: This example shows the cataloging of a single document available only through the Internet.

Cataloging: This cataloging includes the required fields 256 and 538 as well as the required note about source of title.

MARC coding/tagging: In the fixed fields "File" is coded "d" for document. The 020 begins with subfield ǂz for an invalid ISBN, because this ISBN was assigned for the print version that was never printed.

Example 46. Mankato State University Library [home page] as displayed on Internet

Ceramic artwork at MSU Library

Mankato
STATE UNIVERSITY
Library

WebPals (Web access to **PALS** catalog / databases)

Guides
(Using the MSU Library)

Catalogs
(WebPals & other databases)

Collections
(Gov Docs, ERC, ...)

Virtual Library
(Electronic Resources,
Britannica Online,
NEW InfoTrack SearchBank)

Services
AskRef (E-mail Reference)

News
(Announcements, Hours,
Maps, Newsletter, Policies)

Library Staff Directory
(Phones, E-mail, Home Pages)

What's New

Comments

Memorial Library
Mankato State University
MSU #19 - PO Box 8419
Mankato, MN 56002-8419 (USA)
(507) 389-5952 or 389-5953
FAX: (507) 389-5155

MSU
Home Page

Revised: February 5 1996 (jr)
URL: http://www.lib.mankato.msus.edu/

Example 46. Mankato State University Library [home page]

```
Type: m    ELvl: I    Srce: d    Audn: f    Ctrl:       Lang: eng
BLvl: m    File: j    GPub:                 MRec:       Ctry: mnu
Desc: a                          DtSt: m    Dates: 1996,9999
 1 040      XXX ǂc XXX
 2 007      c ǂb r ǂd c ǂe n
 3 090      Z664.M3 ǂb M3
 4 049      XXXX
 5 245 00  Mankato State University Library ǂh [computer file] : ǂb [home
page].
 6 256      Computer online service.
 7 260      Mankato, MN : ǂb Memorial Library, Mankato State University,
 8 310      Updated frequently.
 9 516      Home page.
10 538      Available through Internet.
11 500      Title from first screen.
12 520      Provides access to WebPals (Web access to PALS catalog and
databases), guides to using the library, as well as information about
services, library news, staff directory, and a virtual library of electronic
resources.
13 500      Description based on: Feb. 5, 1996.
14 610 20  Mankato State University. ǂb Library Services and Information
Technology.
15 710 2   Mankato State University. ǂb Library Services and Information
Technology.
16 856 7    ǂu http://www.lib.mankato.msus.edu/ ǂ2 http
```

Comments

General: This example shows cataloging of a home page with color display. Color is coded in subfield ǂd of field 007. If desired, the word "color" could be used somewhere in the summary.

Cataloging: I did not have the first appearance of this home page for cataloging, but it did begin in 1996.

MARC coding/tagging: In the fixed fields, "File" is coded "j" for an online system or service.

Example 47. OLAC Web Page

First screen

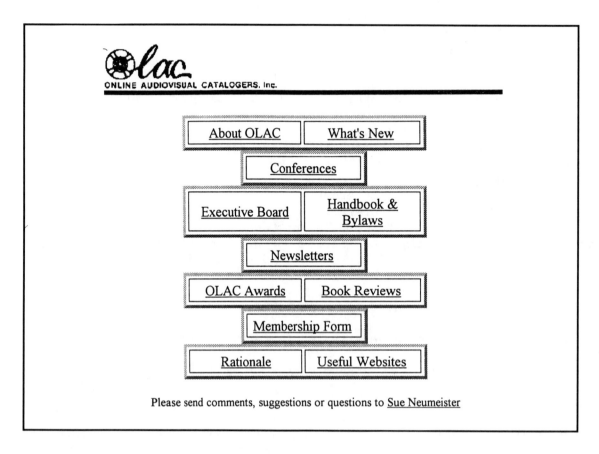

ONLINE AUDIOVISUAL CATALOGERS, Inc.

About OLAC | What's New

Conferences

Executive Board | Handbook & Bylaws

Newsletters

OLAC Awards | Book Reviews

Membership Form

Rationale | Useful Websites

Please send comments, suggestions or questions to Sue Neumeister

"About" screen

Welcome to the OnLine Audiovisual Catalogers Web Page!

In 1980, OLAC was founded to establish and maintain a group that could speak for catalogers of audiovisual materials. OLAC provides a means for exchange of information, continuing education, and communication among catalogers of audiovisual materials and with the Library of Congress. While maintaining a voice with the bibliographic utilities that speak for catalogers of audiovisual materials, OLAC works toward common understanding of AV cataloging practices and standards.

Example 47. OLAC Web Page

```
Type: m    ELvl: I    Srce: d    Audn:       Ctrl:      Lang: eng
BLvl: m    File: j    GPub: s               MRec:      Ctry: nyu
Desc: a                         DtSt: m    Dates: 1995,9999
 1 040      XXX ǂc XXX
 2 007      c ǂd r ǂd a ǂe n
 3 090      Z695.66 ǂb .O4
 4 049      XXXX
 5 245 00   OLAC ǂh [computer file] : ǂb OnLine Audiovisual Catalogers, Inc.
 6 246 1    ǂi On "about" screen: ǂa OnLine Audiovisual Catalogers web page
 7 256      Computer online service.
 8 260      [Buffalo, N.Y. : ǂb State University of New York at Buffalo, ǂc
1995-
 9 310      Updated frequently
10 516      Home page.
11 538      Access through Internet.
12 500      Title from first screen.
13 500      Web site coordinator: Sue Neumeister (neumeist@acsu.buffalo.edu).
14 520      OLAC provides a means of exchange of information, continuing
education, and communication among catalogers of audiovisual materials and
with the Library of Congress. While maintaining a voice with the bibliographic
utilities that speak for catalogers of audiovisual materials, OLAC works
towards common understanding of AV cataloging practices and standards.
15 505 10   ǂt Book reviews -- ǂt Conferences -- ǂt Executive board, past
presidents and liaisons -- ǂt OLAC handbook and by-laws -- ǂt Membership form
-- ǂt Newsletters -- ǂt OLAC awards -- ǂt Rationale for cataloging nonprint
collections.
16 610 20   On-Line Audiovisual Catalogers, Inc.
17 650  0   Cataloging of nonbook materials.
18 700 1    Neumeister, Susan M.
19 856 7    ǂu http://ublib.buffalo.edu/libraries/units/cts/olac/ ǂ2 http
```

Comments

General: This example shows the cataloging of another home page. It does not have corporate main entry because, while it is about a corporate body, it does not "emanate" from that corporate body.

Cataloging: In line 8 there is no closing bracket. When the serial ceases and the closing date is supplied, it would be followed by a closing bracket.

Access: In line 16, the name of the organization appears as it is in the LC authority file. The hyphen was dropped several years ago, but the authority file has not been changed.

Example 48. Autocat

```
Type: m    ELvl: I    Srce: d    Audn: f    Ctrl:       Lang: eng
BLvl: m    File: j    GPub:                 MRec:       Ctry: nyu
Desc: a                          DtSt: m    Dates: 1990,9999
 1 040        XXX ǂc XXX
 2 007        c ǂb r ǂd a ǂe n
 3 090        Z693 ǂb .A8
 4 049        XXXX
 5 245 00     Autocat ǂh [computer file] : ǂb library cataloging and authorities
discussion group.
 6 246 30     Library cataloging and authorities discussion group
 7 256        Computer online service.
 8 260        [Buffalo, N.Y. : ǂb State University of New York at Buffalo, ǂc
1990-
 9 310        Continuously updated
 9 516        Online discussion list.
10 538        Mode of access: Internet e-mail; host: acsu.cc.buffalo.edu.
Subscribe via e-mail message to (Bitnet) listserv@ubvm or (Internet)
listserv@acsu.buffalo.edu, with message: subscribe autocat [firstname
lastname].
11 538        Also available as a Usenet newsgroup: bit.listserv.autocat.
12 500        Title from header file.
13 500        Founded Oct. 1990 by Nancy Keane at the University of Vermont;
transferred Apr. 26, 1993, to the University at Buffalo.
14 500        Listowners: Nancy Keane, Oct. 1990-1992; Brenda Hutchins, 1992-
Apr. 26, 1993; Judith Hopkins and Douglas Winship, Apr. 26, 1993-
15 500        Archived.
16 650   0    Cataloging.
15 650   0    Authority files (Cataloging)
17 700 1      Keane, Nancy.
18 700 1      Hutchins, Brenda.
19 700 1      Hopkins, Judith.
20 700 1      Winship, Douglas.
21 856 0      ubvm.cc.buffalo.edu ǂa ubvm.bitnet ǂf Autocat ǂh Listserv ǂi
subscribe ǂm Judith Hopkins (ulcjh@ubvm.cc.buffalo.edu) ǂm Douglas Winship
(winship@tenet.edu) ǂn State University of New York at Buffalo, Buffalo, N.Y.
22 856 7      ǂu news:bit.listserv.autocat ǂ2 news
```

Comments

General: Here's the bibliographic record for the electronic discussion list Autocat, slightly edited from the form in which it appears on OCLC.

MARC coding/tagging: Notice field 256 in which we can now use the descriptive phrase "Computer online service" for this list.

INTERACTIVE MULTIMEDIA

Throughout this discussion of cataloging interactive multimedia, only parts of the bibliographic record that differ in their cataloging from those discussed in chapter 8 on computer files will be covered. For rules and/or areas not discussed in this chapter or in chapter 8, see chapter 2 of this book.

Special Rules for Cataloging Interactive Multimedia

Earliest examples of interactive multimedia usually had computer files on computer disks and audio/video aspects on videodiscs or other separate media. The combination of physical items of different types with content of different types of audio and visual media presented a unique cataloging challenge. The *Guidelines for Bibliographic Description of Interactive Multimedia* (Chicago, Il.: ALA, 1994) were developed over a period of several years to answer this challenge.

Interactive multimedia may be considered a separate category of material, or a special kind of computer file. While most titles now are produced with everything on one physical item, the presence of computer files **and** two or more types of audio and/or visual media, regardless of number of physical items, is one of the required characteristics of interactive multimedia.

There are several tests an item must meet to be considered interactive multimedia. The first is mentioned above; "multimedia" must contain more than one type of media—audio with maps, still photographs with film clips and audio, music and images of paintings with narration, etc.

The item must be interactive. This may be hard to decide. Do not accept advertising as a basis for this decision—I have seen ads that claim a sound recording with a book is interactive, and it is (you interact with your child while reading it), but it is not interactive multimedia as defined by the ALA *Guidelines.*

The interactivity must be computer-controlled and must involve the ability to randomly access the information contained. If the computer program is written in such a way that it progresses in a linear fashion, it is not interactive, even though one may make all kinds of detours while on the linear path. The packages that involve reading a book while investigating words, concepts, or parts of the illustrations, are linear in design—there is an end to the story. Games are designed to entice the player to come to some end to the adventure involved, though there may be many paths to that end. Packages that allow the user to make notes, bookmarks, etc., are not interactive—the user is performing some action, but the program does not do anything in return, other than save some information.

Using an encyclopedia or dictionary involves random access. When that reference tool is computer-controlled and includes photos, film clips, maps, excerpts from speeches, and animated drawings, the item is interactive multimedia.

At the highest level of interactivity, the user may take various bits of information, images, etc., and move them into a word processing package to create a lecture for a class or other new work.

Interactive multimedia may be available through the Internet or other remote access. If such items are to be cataloged, use the *Guidelines* in combination with those for cataloging Internet resources.

The *Guidelines* are clear in their directions; when in doubt about whether an item is interactive multimedia, do **not** catalog it as such.

Chief Source of Information

The chief source of information is the entire work. If the title appears in several places, and differs from place to place (as often happens with nonprint materials), choose the fullest (or most descriptive) form that applies to the work as a whole, and state the source of the title in a required note.

Remember that the relative size and type of various bits of information, and the relative position of those bits of information, are significant when deciding what the title is, and what, if any, other information is significant for transcribing the title and statement of responsibility.

Title and Statement of Responsibility Area
MARC fields 245, 246

As stated above, the source of the information chosen to be included in the title and statement of responsibility area must be named in a note.

General Material Designation

The general material designation "interactive multimedia" may be used for this material when cataloging according to the *Guidelines*.

```
245 00  Civil War ǂh [interactive multimedia] : ǂb America's epic
struggle.
```

Edition Area
MARC field 250

When there is an edition statement, the source of that information must be specified in a note; it may be combined with the note about the source of title information.

```
250      Upgraded version.
500      Title and ed. statement from container.

250      3rd ed., Macintosh version.
500      Title from disc label; ed. statements from package.
```

Publication, Distribution, Etc., Area
MARC field 260

```
260      Farnham, Surrey, England : ǂb Media Design Interactive :
ǂb Distributed by Sony Electronic Pub. Co., ǂc c1993.
```

The *Guidelines* give clear information about choosing the date of publication; this guidance may be used with other types of media as well. We are directed to "use the latest date, wherever it can be located" as date of publication. Obviously the package will not have been published earlier than this latest date, regardless of whatever other dates are carried by other items in the package. Other dates may be mentioned in notes if important—these may include the date a video was produced, the date of a guide, and/or the date the computer software was written.

If the date chosen is one of several carried on the package and is not clearly the publication date (it may be a copyright date, for example), I would bracket it as an assumed date of publication. The following example has a copyright date of 1993 and the date 1994 on the material.

```
260      Portland, OR : ǂb Creative Multimedia, ǂc [1994].
```

Physical Description Area
MARC field 300

The *Guidelines* establish the specific material designation of "computer optical disc" as a briefer form of the phrase used in AACR2 chapter 9, "computer laser optical disc."

```
300      1 computer optical disc : ǂb sd., col. ; ǂc 4 3/4 in. + ǂe
1 booklet.
```

For multiple physical items we may choose to use multiple physical description statements (field 300 is repeatable). This technique is useful when each item needs additional physical information.

No physical description area is used when cataloging an Internet resource. If an item has stereo sound or other special sound characteristics, that information is given in a note rather than in this area.

Notes Area
MARC fields 5XX

9.7B1a. Nature and scope (MARC fields 516, 500)

If a summary is not to be used, a brief phrase or sentence must appear here to tell the user what this item is or does.

```
500      Interactive dictionary with illustrations.
```

9.7B1b. System requirements (MARC field 538)

The system requirements note is required for any computer-controlled item and contains the same kinds of information as stated in the earlier chapter on cataloging computer files.

If there are two or more physical items needing different types of equipment, one may use multiple system requirements notes or combine requirements into one note.

```
538      System requirements for MPC/Windows: 386 DX or higher (486
recommended); double-speed CD-ROM drive; 8 MB RAM; sound card;
SVGA monitor.
538      System requirements for Macintosh: Mac LCIII or higher
(040 processor recommended); double-speed CD-ROM drive; 8 MB RAM;
13 in. monitor or larger.
538      System requirements for Macintosh; 4 MB memory; system
6.07 or better (compatible with system 7.0).
```

9.7B3. Source of title proper (MARC field 500)

A note giving the source of the title proper is **required** according to the *Guidelines*; this follows the procedure established for the cataloging of computer files. If there is edition information, the source of this information must also be stated. These can be combined into one note.

```
500      Title from disc label; ed. statement from title screen.
```

9.7B17. Summary (MARC field 520)

Summary notes are always important with non-book materials because we can give patrons enough information about the item through this note to let them decide if they are interested enough in it to check it out (assuming, of course, they have already read the system requirements note and know they can run the item).

520   Interactive database includes answers to over 2300 of the most commonly asked medical questions, 300 color medical illustrations, data on 1,600 prescription drugs, animated guide to first aid, and an anatomy section with full-motion video, illustrations, and text.

520   Interactive access to 3,000 photographs and drawings, over 100 maps (many animated), biographical entries for most Union and Confederate generals, coverage of every major battle, complete chronology of the war, two hours of narration, and over 1,000 pages of text including many first-hand accounts. Photos and text can be cut and pasted into your own documents.

Example 49. Ludwig van Beethoven Symphony no. 9

Facsimile of disc label

Example 49. Ludwig van Beethoven Symphony no. 9

Disc and user's guide

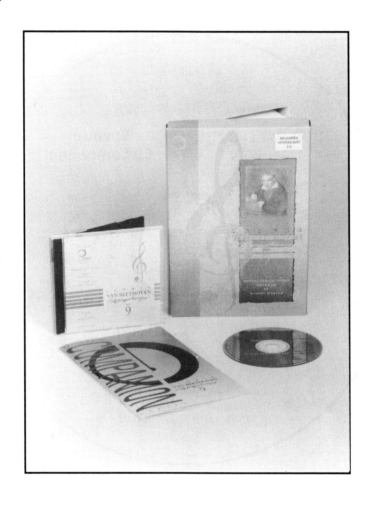

Example 49. Ludwig van Beethoven Symphony no. 9

From container

Example 49. Ludwig van Beethoven Symphony no. 9

```
Type: m   ELvl: I   Srce: d   Audn: f   Ctrl:      Lang: eng
BLvl: m   File: i   GPub:                MRec:      Ctry: cau
Desc: a                        DtSt: s   Dates: 1991,
 1 040       XXX ǂc XXX
 2 007       c ǂb a ǂd a ǂe g ǂf a
 3 020       1559400463
 4 090       MT130.B43 ǂb L8 1991
 5 049       XXXX
 6 245 00    Ludwig van Beethoven Symphony no. 9 ǂh [interactive multimedia] /
ǂc program by Robert Winter ; program design by Robert Winter & Robert Stein.
 7 250       Upgraded version.
 8 260       Santa Monica, Calif. : ǂb Voyager Company, ǂc c1991.
 9 300       1 computer optical disc : ǂb sd. ; ǂc 4 3/4 in. + ǂe 1 user's guide
([20] p. ; 12 cm.).
10 440 0     CD companion series
11 500       "A Hypercard/CD audio program by Robert Winter."--Container.
12 538       System requirements: Macintosh Plus, SE, or Mac II; System and
Finder version 6.0.5 or higher; HyperCard software version 2.0 or higher;
Audio CD access; foreign file access; earphones or speakers.
13 546       Disc includes English, French, German and Italian versions of
the program; words to final movement by Schiller.
14 500       Title and ed. statement from container.
15 511 0     Joan Sutherland, soprano ; Marilyn Horne, contralto ; James King,
tenor ; Martti Talvela, bass ; Vienna State Opera Chorus ; Vienna Philharmonic
; Hans Schmidt-Isserstedt, conductor.
16 500       Original sound recordings copyright 1966, 1988, by Decca.
17 520       Interactive program allows user to examine the music itself along
with the historical and personal setting in which it was created. Features
include detailed real-time commentary on the entire work and explanation of
music showing excerpts from the score. Also includes a game that tests the
user on information provided in other parts of the program.
18 600 10    Beethoven, Ludwig van, ǂd 1770-1827. ǂt Symphonies, ǂn no. 9, op.
125, ǂr D minor ǂx Analysis, appreciation.
19 600 10    Schiller, Friedrich, ǂd 1759-1805 ǂx Musical settings.
20 650 0     Symphonies.
21 650 0     Music appreciation.
22 650 0     Musical analysis.
23 700 1     Winter, Robert, ǂd 1945-
24 700 1     Stein, Robert.
25 700 1     Sutherland, Joan, ǂd 1926-
26 700 1     Horne, Marilyn.
27 700 1     King, James, ǂd 1925-
28 700 1     Talvela, Martti.
29 700 2     Schmidt-Isserstedt, Hans, ǂd 1900-1973.
30 700 1     Schiller, Friedrich, ǂd 1759-1805.
31 700 12    Beethoven, Ludwig van, ǂd 1770-1827. ǂt Symphonies, ǂn no. 9, op.
125, ǂr D minor.
32 710 2     Konzertvereinigung Wiener Staatsopernchor.
33 710 2     Wiener Philharmoniker.
34 710 2     Voyager Company.
```

Example 49. Ludwig van Beethoven Symphony no. 9

Comments

General: The first version of this title had the computer files on 2 computer disks (magnetic) that accompanied the sound recording CD. Before interactive multimedia guidelines were developed, I would have cataloged the package as a sound recording accompanied by 2 computer disks.

Developments in technology now allow the computer files and the sound recording to be contained on the same physical item. A user may listen to the music as with any CD by skipping the first track that contains the computer programs.

While Beethoven wrote the symphony being analyzed in this interactive multimedia title, he is not responsible for this computer resource, so is not used as main entry, nor does he appear in the statement of responsibility that is based on the information appearing in the chief source of information.

Cataloging: This bibliographic record combines rules from AACR 2 chapter 6 on sound recordings with the rules from chapter 9 on computer files.

I consider this to be interactive multimedia because it uses computer technology with several types of media to provide interactive random access to any part of the work.

Access: All the standard added entries for the musical work are used together with subject headings for the analysis and appreciation of the music.

MARC coding/tagging: In the fixed fields "File" is coded "i" for interactive multimedia.

Example 50. London

Instruction booklet

LONDON
THE MULTIMEDIA TOUR

Use of this computer software indicates acceptance of Media Design Interactive's terms & conditions of use and warranty disclaimer.

Installation

Copy the "QuickTime™" extension (version 1.5) from the CD-ROM into the system folder and restart.

System 6.0.7 users copy the following extensions from the CD-ROM folder "System 6.0.7 Extras" into the system folder: "32-Bit Quickdraw" & "FS6Patch" and restart.

Using London

After the opening sequence (which you can skip by clicking the mouse) you will see the contents page. You can choose one of three sections:

Introduction- The obvious place to start: this section gives you an overview, and tells you how to use London.

Tours - Choose an area of London to explore: West, West End, or City, or explore the unique Sights and Sounds of London.

A-Z - A full listing of the places to visit in London. When you choose a place to visit, you will be shown a slide show of the area (see below). Icons show the availability of video and information pages. The number shows the number of pictures in the slideshow.

Tours

West, West End, and City - Once you have chosen a tour, you will be presented with a list of places to visit. 'Introduction' will give you an overview of the area. Use the left and right buttons to see more of the list.

When you choose a place to visit, you will be shown a slide show of the area (see below).

Sights and Sounds - This section is divided into three pages.

The first page contains three slide shows of London. Click on a picture to see a slide show.

The second page shows six video clips. Click on a picture to see a video.

The third page has ten CD-Audio tracks typical of London. Click on a picture to listen to the sound.

Slideshows

Once you have chosen a place to visit, you will see a slide of the area. To control the slide show, press the space bar. Then the left and right arrows on your keyboard will move through the pictures. Press space again to resume the slide show. At any time, a mouse click will take you to the end of the slide show.

Once you are past the slide show, you will see left and right buttons to take you to the next or previous place. If available, you can choose to see a video clip, or see further information about the place.

The Guardsman

Whenever you see a guardsman in the bottom right of the screen, clicking on him will take you back to the previous page of choices.

Bookmark

Up to 100 bookmarks can be defined and will be added to the Bookmark menu in alphabetical order. You can save your list of bookmarks at any time to reload at a future date - your current position and any search criteria and results will also be saved.

About Media Design Interactive

Established in 1990, Media Design Interactive develops, distributes and internationally markets innovative multimedia publications for Macintosh, PC, Acorn and Sony EB platforms. Media Design Interactive's multimedia products appeal to a wide cross section of users including those in education, entertainment and business. The company's portfolio includes: **Dinosaurs! The Multimedia Encyclopedia** - The Ultimate Guide to the Most Exciting Creatures that ever walked the Earth! **Creepy Crawlies** - The Definitive Multimedia Guide to the Creatures we Love to Hate. **Dictionary of the Living World** - The Eddy award winning multimedia database of life on Earth; the first commercial CD ROM product to feature full motion video clips. **LifeSaver** - a revolutionary First Aid course which combines full motion QuickTime video sequences with color illustrations and digitized narration. **Grooves** - a collection of quality music clips for use in multimedia presentations. **Image Warehouse** - The Best Collection of Royalty Free Clip Art, Backgrounds, Textures and graphics resources EVER! Watch out for many great new titles from MDI including **Cute'n'Cuddlies, 1992 World News & Space.**

Warranty disclaimer regarding
Media Design Interactive Software

Media Design Interactive limited makes no warranties, express or implied, including without limitation the implied warranties of merchantability and fitness for a particular purpose regarding this software. Media design interactive do not warrant guarantee or make any representations regarding the use or the results of the use of this software in terms of its correctness, accuracy, reliability, currentness or otherwise. The entire risk as to the results and performance of the Media Design Interactive software is assumed by you.

In no event will Media Design Interactive, its directors, officers, employees or agents be liable to you for any consequential, incidental or indirect damages (including damages for loss of business profits, business interruption, loss of business information, personal injury or death) arising out of the use or inability to use this software even if media design interactive have been advised of the possibility of such damages.

Please, Please, Please...

Return your registration form... Thank you.

All parts Copyright © Media Design Interactive 1993.
All rights reserved
Apple, Macintosh and QuickTime are Trademarks of Apple Computer.

MEDIA DESIGN INTERACTIVE
The Old Hop Kiln, 1 Long Garden Walk
Farnham, Surrey, GU9 7HP. England
Tel: 0252 737630 Fax: 0252 710948
International +44 252 737630 AppleLink: MEDIA.DESIGN

Example 50. London

Facsimile of disc label

Bottom of the back of the box

- **Over 50 minutes of video**

- **20 minutes of digitally recorded CD audio**

- **Over 460 colour photographs**

- **Uses MDI's award winning human interface.**

- **Fully narrated chapter introductions.**

- **Three guided tours to London's main areas of interest.**

[logos for Media Design Interactive, Sony Electronic Publishing, and QuickTime]

QuickTime
Macintosh Version
Requires color Macintosh with minimum 4Mb memory, 13" monitor, system version 6.0.7 or greater and compatible CD-ROM drive. Fully compatible with System 7.0.
Macintosh and QuickTime are trademarks of Apple Computer.

Example 50. London

```
Type: m    ELvl: I    Srce: d    Audn: g    Ctrl:       Lang: eng
BLvl: m    File: i    GPub:                 MRec:       Ctry: enk
Desc: a                          DtSt: s    Dates: 1993,
 1 040      XXX ǂc XXX
 2 020      1874421803
 3 024 1    758411100801
 4 007      c ǂb o ǂd c ǂe g ǂf a
 5 043      e-uk-en
 6 090      DA684.25 ǂb .L6 1993
 7 049      XXXX
 8 245 00   London, the multimedia tour ǂh [interactive multimedia].
 9 246 30   London
10 250      Macintosh version, Version 1.0.
11 260      Farnham, Surrey, England : ǂb Media Design Interactive : ǂb
Distributed by Sony Electronic Pub. Co., ǂc c1993.
12 300      1 computer optical disc : ǂb sd., col. ; ǂc 4 3/4 in. + ǂe 1 user's
guide.
13 538      System requirements: Macintosh; 4 MB memory; System 6.0.7 or
greater (compatible with System 7.0).
14 500      Title from package and disc label; ed. statements from package
label.
15 520      Interactive multimedia tour of London featuring video (50 min.),
slide shows (460 col. photos), and historical information (20 min. digital
stereo. recordings) about London's major tourist attractions.
16 651  0   London (England) ǂx Description and travel.
17 710 2    Media Design Interactive (Firm)
18 710 2    Sony Electronic Publishing Company.
```

Comments

Cataloging: While the title on the title screen was London, a fuller form of the title appeared everywhere else. We are to use a fuller form of the title when one is available.

I combined information about the contents with description in the summary. We cannot put the word "stereo." in field 300 unless we are cataloging sound recordings.

Example 51. The Family Doctor

Container and contents

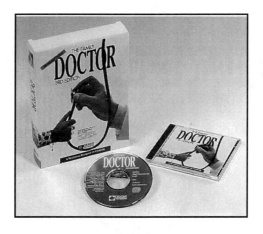

```
Type: m    ELvl: I    Srce: d    Audn: g    Ctrl:      Lang: eng
BLvl: m    File: i    GPub:                 MRec:      Ctry: oru
Desc: a                          DtSt: s    Dates: 1994,
 1 040      XXX ǂc XXX
 2 020      1880428210
 3 007      c ǂb o ǂd c ǂe g
 4 090      RC81 ǂb .F3 1994
 5 049      XXXX
 6 245 04   The family doctor ǂh [interactive multimedia] / ǂc edited by Allan
H. Bruckheim.
 7 246 30   Doctor
 8 250      3rd ed., Macintosh version.
 9 260      Portland, OR : ǂb Creative Multimedia, ǂc [1994].
10 300      1 computer optical disc : ǂb sd., col. ; ǂc 4 3/4 in. + ǂe 1
booklet.
11 538      System requirements: Macintosh; 2.5 MB free RAM; System 6.07 or
greater; color display with 32-bit QuickDraw; printer.
12 500      Title from disc label; ed. statements from package.
13 520      Interactive database includes answers to over 2,300 of the most
commonly asked medical questions. Also includes 300 color medical
illustrations, data on more than 1,600 prescription drugs, animated guide to
first aid, and an anatomy section with full-motion video, illustrations, and
text.
14 650  0   Medicine, Popular.
15 700  1   Bruckheim, Allan H.
16 710  2   Creative Multimedia Corporation.
```

Comments

Comments: This is interactive because it uses computer capabilities to randomly access information that is available in a variety of media.

Cataloging: Many packages of computer software and interactive multimedia contain multiple edition statements. We may combine them as shown here and in the previous example.

Processing: This is another example of the type of material that needs to be repackaged for circulation. It came in a big flimsy box with one CD-ROM and a little booklet.

Example 52. Civil War

Computer disc

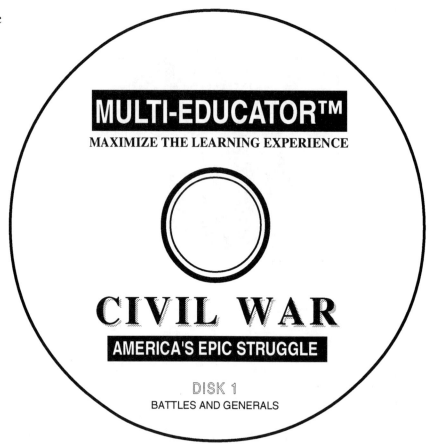

Container and contents

Example 52. Civil War

```
Type: m    ELvl: I    Srce: d    Audn: g    Ctrl:        Lang: eng
BLvl: m    File: i    GPub:                 MRec:        Ctry: nyu
Desc: a                          DtSt: s    Dates: 1995,
 1 040      XXX ǂc XXX
 2 007      c ǂb o ǂd c ǂe g ǂf a
 3 090      E468 ǂb .C4 1995
 4 049      XXXX
 5 245 00   Civil War ǂh [interactive multimedia] : ǂb America's epic struggle.
 6 246 30   America's epic struggle
 7 260      New Rochelle, N.Y. : ǂb MultiEducator, ǂc c1995.
 8 300      2 computer optical discs : ǂh sd., col. ; ǂc 4 3/4 in. + ǂe 1
user's manual (15 p. : ill. ; 22 cm.)
 9 538      Systems requirements for MPC/Windows: 386 DX or higher (486
recommended); double-speed CD-ROM drive; 8 MB RAM; sound card; SVGA monitor.
10 538      Systems requirements for Macintosh: Mac LCIII or higher (040
processor recommended); double-speed CD-ROM drive; 8 MB RAM; 13 in. monitor or
larger.
11 500      Title from disc label.
12 520      Interactive access to 3,000 photographs and drawings, over 100 maps
(many animated), biographical entries for most Union and Confederate generals,
coverage of every major battle, complete chronology of the war, two hours of
narration, and over 1,000 pages of text including many first-hand accounts.
Photos and text may be cut and pasted into your own documents.
13 505 0    Disk 1. Battles and generals -- Disk 2. Navy and photo archives.
14 651  0   United States ǂx History ǂx Civil War, 1861-1865.
15 710 2    MultiEducator, Inc.
```

Comments

General: This interactive title allows the user to cut and paste information into a word processing program to create new materials. This capability is typical of the more advanced items of interactive multimedia.

Example 53. The New Family Bible

Facsimile of disc label

THE NEW
FAMILY BIBLE
FROM THE GARDEN TO THE PROMISED LAND

For MPC and
Macintosh

COMPACT
disc
DATA STORAGE

TIME WARNER INTERACTIVE GROUP
© 1993 Time Warner Interactive Group. International rights secured.
Not for broadcast transmission. All rights reserved. Do not duplicate.
Not available for separate rental

14004

Example 53. The New Family Bible

```
Type: m    ELvl: I    Srce: d    Audn: g    Ctrl:       Lang: eng
BLvl: m    File: i    GPub:                 MRec:       Ctry: cau
Desc: a                          DtSt: s    Dates: 1993,
 1 040     XXX ǂc XXX
 2 007     c ǂb o ǂd c ǂe g ǂf a
 3 090     BS191.5.A1 1993 ǂb .N4
 4 049     XXXX
 5 130 0   Bible. ǂp O.T. ǂl English. ǂs New Revised Standard. ǂk Selections.
ǂf 1993.
 6 245 14  The new family Bible ǂh [interactive multimedia] : ǂb from the
garden to the promised land.
 7 260     Burbank, CA : ǂb Time Warner Interactive Group, ǂc c1993.
 8 300     1 computer optical disc : ǂb sd., col. ; ǂc 4 3/4 in. + ǂe 1 user's
guide (7 p.).
 9 538     System requirements for Multimedia PC: PC with 386SX/16
microprocessor or higher; 4MB RAM; DOS; Windows 3.0 with multimedia
extensions, or Windows 3.1; VGA graphics capabilities; MPC-compatible sound
card; mouse or compatible pointer; CD-ROM drive with 150KB/sec. transfer rate.
10 538     System requirements for Macintosh computer: Macintosh II series
or greater; 4MB RAM; System 6.0.7 or later; thirteen-inch color monitor; CD-
ROM drive.
11 500     Title from disc label.
12 520     Multimedia presentation of the New Revised Standard version of
the Bible from Genesis to Malachi. Includes a thirty-minute narrated overview
of Biblical events, maps, family trees, and a pronunciation guide in English
and Hebrew, all of which are interactively accessible. Translation of the
original Hebrew and Aramaic is searchable by book, chapter, and verse.
13 630 00  Bible. ǂp O.T.
14 710 2   Time Warner Interactive Group.
```

Comments

General: This item is interactive, contains several types of media, and uses computer technology. So it is cataloged as interactive multimedia.

Cataloging: It is easier to use repeated 538 fields than to try to combine all this information into one clearly stated note.

Access: This needs the uniform title main entry for Bible, as well as a subject heading in uniform title form.

How would you catalog (and handle) this record?

This sound sheet appears in the August 1965 issue of *National Geographic*, inserted between pages 198 and 199. To be played, you carefully removed the item along the perforated inner edge and put it on the turntable. It played at 33 1/3 rpm. Directions on the label said to tape a dime to the record to make it heavy enough to be stable on the turntable. Information on the label includes:

The Funeral of
Sir Winston Churchill
January 30, 1965
with excerpts from his speeches
Narrator
David Brinkley

Chapter 9

THREE-DIMENSIONAL ARTEFACTS AND REALIA

AACR 2 Chapter 10

This chapter covers the cataloging of all types of three-dimensional materials including models, dioramas, games, sculptures, machines, clothing, toys, puppets, and exhibits. It also covers naturally occurring objects ("realia") such as rocks, minerals, shells, and mounted microscopic specimens.

These materials are covered by the rules found in AACR 2 chapter 10.

Special Rules for Cataloging Three-Dimensional Artefacts and Realia

In this section the special rules for cataloging three-dimensional artefacts and realia will be discussed. For rules and/ or areas not discussed here, see chapter 2 of this book. Parts of some of the rules are given; the user is referred to the rules themselves for complete text and examples.

Chief Source of Information

The chief source of information for all materials covered in this chapter is the item itself, together with any accompanying material.

Title and Statement of Responsibility Area
MARC field 245

Frequently the cataloger will have to supply a title for materials cataloged by this chapter. In such a case, the title is to be bracketed and a note citing the source of the title is to be supplied.

The general material designations used for materials in this chapter are:

art original
art reproduction
diorama
game
microscope slide
model
realia
toy

The GMD "toy" was added in the 1988 revision of AACR 2.

Publication, Distribution, Etc., Area
MARC field 260

Naturally occurring objects

No date is given or implied in area 4. For example, if one were cataloging ash from the 1980 eruption of Mount Saint Helens, one would give the date of the volcanic eruption in a note rather than in area 4.

A naturally occurring object, such as a rock, will not have any information in this area because it is not published or distributed and there is no date of publication. "S.l." and "s.n." are not used because we do not want to imply an unknown publisher for natural objects. If, however, a naturally occurring object is commercially packaged and distributed, the package will have a publisher and/or distributor.

Manufactured objects

Material cataloged according to AACR 2 chapter 10 might have been manufactured rather than published. If so, the material will have place of manufacture, name of manufacturer, and date of manufacture.

```
260      ‡e (Place of manufacture : ‡f Name of manufacturer, ‡g
Date of manufacture)
260      [United States : ‡b s.n., ‡c 186-]
```

Material may be manufactured by one company and distributed by a different company. If the distributor and the manufacturer are both known, include the distributor in the usual way in area 4, bracketing in the words "distributed by" or "distributor" if that function is not clear, and use the information about the manufacture of the item as shown above.

An item may have a date of manufacturing and a date of distribution. If both are known or given on the item, both may be used. If only one date is known, decide whether it is the date of manufacture or the date of distribution (or both) and place it accordingly.

```
260      Place of distribution : ‡b Name of distributor, ‡c Date
of distribution ‡e (Place of manufacture : ‡f Name of
manufacturer, ‡g Date of manufacture)
```

Hand-made items

Hand-made three-dimensional items may be cataloged by the rules in AACR 2 chapter 10. The name of the person who made the item would go in the statement of responsibility if given on the item.

If the person or body who made the item is named in the statement of responsibility, that name is not repeated in the name of manufacturer area. If the place where the item was made is given in the title proper or other title information, that place is not to be repeated as place of manufacture.

"Artefacts not intended primarily for communication"

This phrase is used in 10.4C2 through 10.4F2. I have wondered what was intended when the phrase was written. My cannon ball is an artifact, and definitely communicates something about the horrors of the Civil War.

Ben Tucker explains: "I remember rather clearly the discussion that went into the formulation of the rule. The words 'not intended for communication' mean nothing more than 'not published,' or 'not issued in an edition.' Another term that might have served is 'not commercially available in multiple copies.' 'Artefacts' means man-made or man-manipulated." (Ben R. Tucker, LC, letter to the author, 17 Dec. 1984).

Physical Description Area
MARC field 300

Extent of item (MARC field 300 ǂa)

The number of physical units is given followed by the specific name of the item or the names of the parts.

Added to this, when appropriate, are the number and name of pieces. The phrase "various pieces" may be used. A note may be used to give further details.

Other physical details (MARC field 300 ǂb)

The material or materials of which the item is made is given next, if appropriate. This is followed by "col." or "b&w" or the name(s) of the color(s) if in one or two colors.

Dimensions (MARC field 300 ǂc)

The dimensions are given in centimeters, rounded up to the next whole centimeter. Dimensions of a three-dimensional object are given in height times width times depth. Only one dimension is given if appropriate; to this should be added a word to indicate which dimension is given.

If the object is in a container, the container is named and its dimensions given, either as the only dimensions, or after the dimensions of the object.

Accompanying material (MARC field 300 ǂe)

The name of any accompanying material is recorded. Physical description of the accompanying material is optional.

Notes Area
MARC fields 5XX

Notes permitted in this chapter are:

10.7B1.   Nature of the item
10.7B3.   Source of title proper
10.7B4.   Variations in title
10.7B5.   Parallel titles and other title information
10.7B6.   Statements of responsibility
10.7B7.   Edition and history
10.7B9.   Publication, distribution, etc.
10.7B10. Physical description
10.7B11. Accompanying material
10.7B12. Series
10.7B14. Audience
10.7B17. Summary
10.7B18. Contents
10.7B19. Numbers
10.7B20. Copy being described, library's holdings, and restrictions on use
10.7B21. "With" notes

10.7B1. Nature of the item (MARC field 500)

To be used to name or explain the form of the item as necessary.

```
500      Electronic game.
```

10.7B3. Source of title proper (MARC field 500)

To be used if the title proper is taken from other than the chief source of information.

```
500      Title supplied by cataloger.
```

10.7B4. Variations in title (MARC fields 246, 500)

To be used to record any title appearing on the item that differs significantly from the title proper. Field 246 is used if the title refers to the whole item.

```
246 1    ‡i Title in guide: ‡a Pac Man
```
(*Title proper:* Tomytronic Pac Man)

10.7B5. Parallel titles and other title information (MARC field 500)

To be used for parallel titles and important other title information not recorded in the title and statement of responsibility area.

```
500      Subtitle on manual: Implementing institutional self-
evaluation.
```

10.7B6. Statements of responsibility (MARC field 500)

To be used to record important information not recorded in the statement of responsibility area.

```
500      Crocheted by Betty Robbin.
```

10.7B7. Edition and history (MARC field 500)

To be used for information about earlier editions or the history of the item being cataloged.

```
500      Assembled from: The human skull. London : Fisher-Miller,
1980.
```

10.7B9. Publication, distribution, etc. (MARC field 500)

To be used for important information not recorded in the publication, distribution, etc., area.

```
500      Distributed by R. Dakin, San Francisco.
```

10.7B10. Physical description (MARC field 500)

To be used for any important information not given in area 5, the physical description area.
If the phrase "various pieces" was used in the physical description area, a more complete description may be given here.

```
500      Signed in pencil on base.
500      Includes 1,000 red wooden beads, 1,000 black plastic
beads, 20 red shoestrings, 20 black shoestrings, 20 pattern
boards.
```

10.7B11. Accompanying material (MARC field 500)

To be used for any important information not given in the accompanying material element of area 5.

```
500      Teacher's guide has directions for making artifacts and
for the educational simulation; includes pages for reproduction.
```

Libraries in the United States are to use American spellings such as "artifact" in descriptions.

10.7B12. Series (MARC field 500)

To be used for any important information not recorded in the series area.

```
500      Previously issued as part of series: Introduction to the
crime laboratory.
```

1.7B14. Audience (MARC field 521)

To be used to record the intended audience of a work. Use this note only if the information is stated on the item. Do not attempt to judge the audience for an item. The first indicator of field 521 must be blank to generate the display constant "Audience:" .

```
521      Grade 2.
```

10.7B17. Summary (MARC field 520)

To be used for a brief objective summary of the content of the item.

```
520      Game for two to four players in which players try to
accumulate wealth through buying and developing property, gaining
power, and acquiring connections.
```

10.7B18. Contents (MARC fields 505, 500)

To be used for a formal (MARC field 505) or informal (MARC field 500) listing of the contents of the item.

```
505 0    Contents: A. Checked (grade 2) -- B. Striped (grade 3) --
C. Polka-dot (grade 4) -- D. Plaid (grade 5).
```

10.7B19. Numbers (MARC field 500)

To be used to list any important number appearing on the item other than those to be recorded for area 8 in field 020 for an ISBN, or in field 024 for a UPC, or field 037 for manufacturer number.

```
500      "24/125"
```

10.7B20. Copy being described, library's holdings, and restrictions on use (MARC fields 500, 506, 590)

To be used for any notes applicable only to the particular copy of the item being described (MARC field 500 if general, field 506 if restrictions). Also used for local library restrictions (MARC field 590) on the material being described or for information of use only to patrons of the local library.

```
590      Library's copy signed by artist.
590      For library use only.
```

10.7B21. "With" notes (MARC field 501)

To be used for "with" notes.

```
501      With: Geodes from Keokuk, Iowa.
```

How would you catalog this?

This object is hand made from clay in Mexico. There is no writing on it. The tree has a serpent climbing the trunk, and there are apples hanging from it. The item, 26 cm. high, is designed to hold two candles.

Example 54. Minnesota Trivia

Game board and pieces

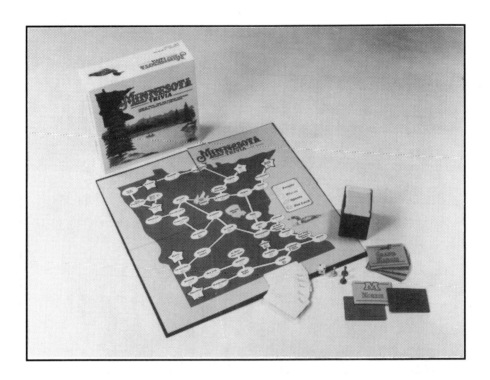

```
Type: r   ELvl: I   Srce: d   Audn: g   Ctrl:      Lang: eng
BLvl: m   TMat: g   GPub:     AccM:     MRec:      Ctry: mnu
Desc: a   Time: nnn Tech: n   DtSt: s   Dates: 1984,
 1 040     XXX ǂc XXX
 2 090     F606.5 ǂb .M4 1984
 3 049     XXXX
 4 245 00  Minnesota trivia ǂh [game].
 5 260     Minnetonka, MN. : ǂb Minnesota Trivia, ǂc c1984.
 6 300     1 game ; ǂc in box 27 cm. x 27 cm. x 9 cm.
 7 500     Includes 1 game board, 4 markers, 1 die, 500 question/answer
cards, 2 card boxes, 28 scoring cards, 1 rule sheet.
 8 520     Game for two or more players or teams in which players must
correctly answer Minnesota-related questions on people, places, sports, or
"pot-luck" to move from city to city on the board.
 9 650  0  Board games.
10 650  0  Educational games.
11 651  0  Minnesota ǂx History ǂx Games.
12 710  2  Minnesota Trivia, Inc.
```

Comments

> **General:** This is a game patterned after Trivial Pursuit, except the questions are all about Minnesota.
> **Cataloging:** In area 5 one could choose to list all the pieces, use "various pieces," or use "1 game."
> **Access:** This could be classified with Minnesota history, as I have done, or with trivia games in class GV.
> **Processing:** Each piece would need some kind of label or marking.

Example 55. Monopoly

Game board and pieces

Example 55. Monopoly

```
Type: r   ELvl: I   Srce: d   Audn: g   Ctrl:      Lang: eng
BLvl: m   TMat: g   GPub:     AccM:     MRec:      Ctry: mau
Desc: a   Time: nnn Tech: n   DtSt: s   Dates: 1985,
 1 040     XXX ǂc XXX
 2 090     GV1469.M65 ǂb M6 1985
 3 049     XXXX
 4 245 00  Monopoly ǂh [game].
 5 250     Deluxe anniversary ed.
 6 260     Beverly, MA : ǂb Parker Brothers, ǂc c1985.
 7 300     1 game (various pieces) ; ǂc in container, 26 x 51 x 7 cm.
 8 500     "Parker Brothers real estate trading game" for 2 to 8 players.
 9 500     Includes game board, play money, 2 dice, 11 gold-colored metal
playing pieces, red wooden hotels, green wooden houses, title deed cards,
chance and community chest cards, rule book.
10 500     Rule book includes illustrated 50-year history of the game.
11 520     "The object of the game is to become the wealthiest player through
buying, renting, and selling property."
12 650  0  Monopoly (Game)
13 650  0  Board games.
14 710  2  Parker Brothers, inc.
```

Comments

General: This version of Monopoly was issued to celebrate the 50th anniversary of the game. The pieces are gold colored, and the special booklet includes an illustrated history of the game. I have been collecting versions/editions of this game and now have about 30.

Cataloging: We would need to use a uniform title main entry for this if we had more than one version in our catalog. It would be

```
130 00  Monopoly (Game : Deluxe anniversary ed.)
```

In line 8 I have combined the nature and form note information with audience information, rather than make two shorter notes.

We do not need to cite the source of quotes if they come from anywhere on the item because the chief source of information for these materials is the entire item.

Sometimes it is easier and clearer to quote information from the item than to try to write a clear summary.

Access: The game of Monopoly has its own number in the classification for games.

MARC coding/tagging: The qualifier in the 650 does not have a subfield code .

Example 56. Speedy Andrew's Repair Shop

The finished model

From cover of container of kit

Example 56. Speedy Andrew's Repair Shop

```
Type: r   ELvl: I   Srce: d   Audn: f   Ctrl:        Lang: eng
BLvl: m   TMat: q   GPub:     AccM:     MRec:        Ctry: xxu
Desc: a   Time: nnn Tech: n   DtSt: s   Dates: 1979,
 1 040       XXX ǂc XXX
 2 090       TL153 ǂb .O4 1979
 3 049       XXXX
 4 100 1     Olson, Andrew A., ǂd 1960-
 5 245 10    Speedy Andrew's repair shop ǂh [model].
 6 260       ǂc [1979].
 7 300       1 model : ǂb plastic, col. ; ǂc 10 x 16 x 14 cm.
 8 500       Assembled by Andrew A. Olson from 76-piece Tyco-kit manufactured
in West Germany by Pola.
 9 520       Model of automobile repair shop of the 1920-1930 time period.
10 650  0    Service stations.
```

Comments

General: The cataloging of the original kit is given as the last example in this book. This is the model made from that kit.

Cataloging: I treated this assembled model as an unpublished work. The title is taken from the sign above the door. It has the apostrophe before the "s" while the package title has the apostrophe after the "s."

I could have combined both notes into one.

Example 57: Geode

Two halves of a geode

```
Type: r    ELvl: I    Srce: d    Audn: g    Ctrl:      Lang: N/A
BLvl: m    TMat: r    GPub:      AccM:      MRec:      Ctry: xx
Desc: a    Time: nnn  Tech: n    DtSt: n    Dates: uuuu,uuuu
 1 040     XXX ǂc XXX
 2 090     QE471.15.G4 ǂb G4
 3 049     XXXX
 4 245 00  [Geode] ǂh [realia].
 5 300     1 geode (2 halves) : ǂb white and tan ; ǂc 4 x 5 x 4 cm.
 6 500     Title supplied by cataloger.
 7 500     Geode, from Keokuk, Iowa, contains calcite crystals. Collected in
1965.
 8 650  0  Geodes.
```

Comments

General: This is true "realia." It is a real, naturally occurring, item. Many of us have been asked to add material such as this to our collections.

A geode is a rock, usually round, that was originally a cavity within a bed of rock deep within the earth. As water-borne minerals moved through it over time, mineral crystals formed on the inner surface of the cavity. In some places these nodules were exposed by weathering and could be picked up and cracked open.

Cataloging: For naturally occurring material that is not commercially packaged and/or distributed, there is no area 4. Not even the date is assumed. We can, through notes, explain where, when, and how the material was acquired.

We are required to make the note shown in line 6.

MARC coding/tagging: There is no coding for language, country, or dates in the fixed fields for realia that is not commercially packaged and/or distributed.

Processing: I painted a spot on the outside of each half with white model paint, then lettered on the call number with a fine brush.

Example 58. Golden Adventure Kit of Rocks and Minerals

Box of rocks

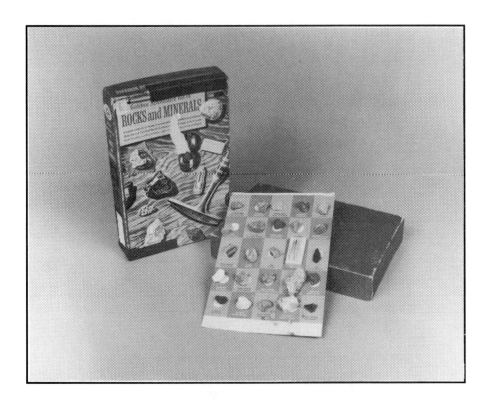

```
Type: r   ELvl: I   Srce: d   Audn: d   Ctrl:      Lang: eng
BLvl: m   TMat: r   GPub:     AccM:     MRec:      Ctry: xxu
Desc: a   Time: nnn Tech: n   DtSt: s   Dates: 1957,
 1 040      XXX ǂc XXX
 2 090      QE432.2 ǂb .G6 1957
 3 049      XXXX
 4 245 00   Golden adventure kit of rocks and minerals ǂh [realia].
 5 246 30   Rocks and minerals
 6 260      [United States] : ǂb Golden Press, ǂc c1957.
 7 300      24 rock specimens ; ǂc 2 x 3 cm. each. in box (31 x 21 x 5 cm.) +
ǂe 1 streak plate.
 8 500      Rocks mounted on labeled cardboard.
 9 650  0   Rocks.
10 650  0   Mineralogy.
11 710  2   Golden Press.
```

Comments

   General: These naturally occurring objects are commercially published, so we have a normal area 4.

   Cataloging: There is no indication as to where this is published. We assume it is in the United States. We are not allowed to abbreviate "United States" in the place of publication when it stands alone.

   Processing: The rock specimens are glued to the box, so they would not need to be individually labeled.

Example 59. Frog Hand Puppet

Frog hand puppet with Insect finger puppet

Tag on puppet

NANCY RENFRO STUDIOS
1117 W. 9th STREET
AUSTIN, TEXAS 78703
(512) 472-2140

Example 59. Frog Hand Puppet

```
Type: r    ELvl: I    Srce: d   Audn: b   Ctrl:       Lang: eng
BLvl: m    TMat: w    GPub:     AccM;     MRec:       Ctry: txu
Desc: a    Time: nnn  Tech: n   DtSt: s   Dates: 1979,
 1 040      XXX ǂc XXX
 2 090      PN1972 ǂb .F7 1979
 3 049      XXXX
 4 245 00   [Frog hand puppet] ǂh [toy].
 5 260      ǂc [1979?] ǂe (Austin, Tex. : ǂf Nancy Renfro Studios).
 6 300      2 puppets : ǂb fabric, col. ; ǂc 7-17 cm.
 7 500      Title supplied by cataloger.
 8 520      Yellow insect finger puppet (7 cm. long) attached by elastic to
green and pink frog hand puppet (17 cm. wide); designed to be used with story
or rhyme about a frog eating a fly.
 9 650   0  Hand puppets.
10 650   0  Frogs ǂx Games.
11 710 2    Nancy Renfro Studios.
```

Comments

Cataloging: The chief source of information for this item is the item itself with the attached paper tag.

We assume a date of distribution based on the date it was purchased. The place and name of manufacturer are used as shown.

MARC coding/tagging: Notice the coding and tagging of the place and name of manufacturer.

Processing: You could put a call number label on the back of the tag, if that didn't cover up important information, and if you were leaving the tag attached. I'm using plastic tags on metal chains (similar to key chains). I insert the chain through a hole and fasten it closed after threading a plastic tag onto it. The barcode is applied to one side of the tag and the call number label to the other.

I sew tattletape strips inside all puppets and soft dolls and toys.

Example 60. Cannon Ball

Cannon ball

```
Type; r    ELvl: I    Srce: d    Audn: f    Ctrl:       Lang: N/A
BLvl: m    TMat: r    GPub:      AccM:      MRec:       Ctry: xxu
Desc: a    Time: nnn  Tech: n    DtSt: s    Dates: 186u,
 1 040     XXX ǂc XXX
 2 043     n-us---
 3 045     w6w6
 4 090     E468.9 ǂb .C3 1860
 5 049     XXXX
 6 245 00  [Cannon ball] ǂh [realia].
 7 260     ǂe ([United States : ǂf s.n., ǂg 186-]).
 8 300     1 cannon ball : ǂb lead, gray ; ǂc 10 cm. in diam.
 9 500     "12-pounder" cannon ball used in the Civil War.
10 500     Title supplied by cataloger.
11 650  0  Ordnance.
12 651  0  United States ǂx History ǂy Civil War, 1861-1865.
```

Comments

   General: This is a real manufactured object with no information provided. From its size and material we know the type of cannon ball this is (I had to do some research on this one!). This type was used in the Civil War, and it was found in a yard (painted white in a flower border!) in a town that had a lot of Civil War veterans, so we assume it was from the Civil War. We assume it was made in the United States, but can make no assumptions about the name of the manufacturer.

   This is an artifact. The GMD "realia" is correct as it is a real object.

   MARC coding/tagging: Field 043 for geographic access and 045 for time period are both used here.

   Processing: This could have a class number and other identification painted on with model paint and a fine brush.

Example 61. Cow Pull Toy

Cow pull toy

```
Type: r   ELvl: I   Srce: d   Audn: b   Ctrl:      Lang: eng
BLvl: m   TMat: w   GPub:     AccM:     MRec:      Ctry: ohu
Desc: a   Time: nnn Tech: n   DtSt: s   Dates: 1982,
  1 040      XXX ǂc XXX
  2 090      GV1218.P8 ǂb H3 1982
  3 049      XXXX
  4 100 1    Hardy, Margaret.
  5 245 10   [Cow pull toy] ǂh [toy] / ǂc Margaret Hardy.
  6 260      ǂc 1982 ǂe (Trinway, Ohio).
  7 300      1 toy : ǂb wood, natural ; ǂc 26 x 34 x 16 cm.
  8 500      Wooden model of a cow mounted on wheeled base with string and
handle for child to pull.
  9 500      Title supplied by cataloger.
 10 500      Signed and dated on bottom of base.
 11 650  0   Wooden toys.
```

Comments

General: This hand-made toy is cataloged as shown. Because this toy is signed, we can use the name of the woman who made it in the statement of responsibility.

Although this item is handmade, Mrs. Hardy made these in quantity, so I did consider it to be "published."

Example 62. Nativity Set

Nativity set

```
Type: r    ELvl: I    Srce: d    Audn: g    Ctrl:      Lang: N/A
BLvl: m    TMat: d    GPub:      AccM:      MRec:      Ctry: xx
Desc: a    Time: nnn  Tech: n    DtSt: s    Dates: 1982,
 1 040     XXX ǂc XXX
 2 090     N8065 ǂb .R6 1982
 3 049     XXXX
 4 100 1   Robbin, Betty.
 5 245 10  [Nativity set] ǂh [diorama].
 6 260     ǂc [1982].
 7 300     12 figures : ǂb yarn, col. ; ǂc 3-28 cm. tall.
 8 500     Crocheted figures stuffed with batting; made by Betty Robbin,
Columbus, Ohio.
 9 500     Title supplied by cataloger.
10 650  0  Creches (Nativity scenes)
```

Comments

   General: This is as close as I could come to finding a "diorama." There is no information of any kind on the set, and it is unique. I got information about it when I bought the set from the woman who made it.
   Cataloging: I cataloged this as an unpublished item.
   MARC coding/tagging: "Lang" is coded "N/A" because there is no label or writing of any kind on any of the items.

Chapter 10

MICROFORMS

AACR 2 Chapter 11

This chapter emphasizes the cataloging of those microforms that are graphic materials. There are many sets of microforms available that are similar to sets of slides with captions; the example *Pottery Techniques* is of this type. There are also many sets of microforms in which most or all the frames are graphic materials such as drawings or paintings or photographs or X-rays. These materials are not reproductions of books; they are original publications in microform. They are cataloged by the rules given in AACR 2 chapter 11.

The LCRI for cataloging microform reproductions of books and documents has been added to this chapter with an example of this cataloging.

Special Rules for Cataloging Microforms

In this section the special rules for cataloging microforms will be discussed. For rules and/or areas not discussed here, see chapter 2 of this book. Parts of some of the rules are given; the user is referred to the rules themselves for complete text and examples.

Chief Source of Information

The chief source of information for a microform is the title frame(s). If there is no title frame on a microfiche, or if the information on that title frame is insufficient, the eye-readable information printed at the top of the microfiche is treated as the chief source of information. If that information includes a shortened title, and the accompanying materials or container provides a fuller form of the title, treat the accompanying materials or the container as the chief source of information.

Title and Statement of Responsibility Area
MARC field 245

There are no special problems in this area. The GMD used for this material is "microform".

Publication, Distribution, Etc., Area
MARC field 260

Information concerning the publisher and/or distributor of the microform is recorded here.

Physical Description Area
MARC field 300

Extent of item (MARC field 300 ǂa)

The number and name of the microform is given first. The plural of "microfiche" is "microfiches". The number of frames of a microfiche is added in parentheses if that number can be determined easily.

Other physical details (MARC field 300 ǂb)

If a microform is negative, this is indicated.
If the microform contains or consists of illustrations, this is indicated.
If the microform is colored, this is indicated, but black and white is not indicated.

```
300        2 microfiches : ǂb all col. ill.
300        1 microfiche : ǂb ill. (some col.)
```

Dimensions (MARC field 300 ǂc)

Dimensions are given in centimeters, height times width; for microfilm, only width is given. If microfiche is 10.5 x 14.8 cm., the standard dimensions, the dimensions are not given.

Accompanying material (MARC field 300 ǂe)

This is recorded as in all other chapters.

LC Rule Interpretation for Cataloging Microform Reproductions of Books and Documents

Chapter 11. Microforms. For microform reproductions of previously existing materials that are made for preservation purposes and for microform dissertations and other microform reproductions produced "on demand," Library of Congress policy is noted below.

1) Transcribe the bibliographic data appropriate to the original work being reproduced in the following areas:

title and statement of responsibility
edition
material (or type of publication) specific details
publication, distribution, etc.
physical description
series

2) Give in the title and statement of responsibility area the general material designation "[microform]" (cf. LCRI 1.1C).

3) Give in a single note (533 field) all other details relating to the reproduction and its publication/ availability. Include in the note the following bibliographic data in the order listed:

specific material designation of the microform
place and name of the agency responsible for the reproduction
date of the reproduction
physical description of the microform
series statement of the reproduction (if applicable)

LCRI *(cont.)*

Apply rules 1.4-1.6 for the formulation of the bibliographic data in the note. Enclose cataloger-supplied data in brackets. Omit the area divider (space-dash-space).

> 4) Consider the "agency responsible for the reproduction" to be the agency that selected the material to be filmed, arranged for filming, exercised control over production formats, has overall responsibility for quality, etc. If the agency is unknown, give "[s.n.]." Transcribe also the name of the agency from which to secure copies or the agency that made the microform if the agency is named in one of the prescribed sources for the publication, distribution, etc., area (11.0B2).

```
    Oslo 1947 [microform] : Fragen zur Vorbereitung einer
Welttagung christlicher Jugend. -- Stuttgart : Im Quellverlag
der Evangelischen Gesellschaft, 1947.
    64 p. ; 21 cm.

    Microfilm. Washington, D.C. : Library of Congress
Preservation Microfilming Program : Available from Library of
Congress Photoduplication Service, 1992. 1 microfilm reel; 35
mm.
```

Note: Items that are microreproductions of materials prepared or assembled specifically for bringing out an original edition in microform are cataloged according to chapter 11 of AACR 2.

(*CSB* 58)

Notes Area
MARC fields 5XX

Notes permitted in this chapter are:

11.7B1.   Nature, scope, or artistic or other form of an item
11.7B2.   Language
11.7B3.   Source of title proper
11.7B4.   Variations in title
11.7B5.   Parallel titles and other title information
11.7B6.   Statements of responsibility
11.7B7.   Edition and history
11.7B9.   Publication, distribution, etc.
11.7B10. Physical description:
                Reduction ratio
                Reader
                Film
                Other physical details
11.7B11. Accompanying material
11.7B12. Series
11.7B13. Dissertations
11.7B14. Audience
11.7B16. Other formats
11.7B17. Summary
11.7B18. Contents
11.7B19. Numbers

11.7B20. Copy being described, library's holdings, and restrictions on use
11.7B21. "With" notes
11.7B22. Notes relating to original

Explanation of notes

Each of the notes will be explained in the following section and examples of their use given.

11.7B1. Nature, scope, or artistic or other form of the item (MARC field 500)

To be used to name or explain the form of the item as necessary.

```
500      X-rays of Egyptian mummies.
```

11.7B2. Language (MARC field 546)

To be used to name the language or languages of the item cataloged if not obvious from other information given.

```
546      Abstracts in French, German, Italian, and English.
```

11.7B3. Source of title proper (MARC field 500)

To be used if the title proper is taken from other than the chief source of information.

```
500      Title from publisher's catalog.
500      Title supplied by cataloger.
```

11.7B4. Variations in title (MARC fields 246, 500)

To be used to note any title appearing on the item that differs significantly from the title proper. MARC field 246 is used if a title added entry is wanted.

```
500      Title of fiche 2: Powered flights.
```

11.7B5. Parallel titles and other title information (MARC field 500)

To be used for parallel titles and important other title information not recorded in the title and statement of responsibility area.

```
500      Subtitle on manual: A micropublication commemorating the
seventy-fifth anniversary of the first flight by the Wright
Brothers, December 17, 1903.
```

11.7B6. Statements of responsibility (MARC field 500)

To be used to record important information not recorded in the statement of responsibility area.

```
500      Exhibition organized by Peter Thompson.
```

11.7B7. Edition and history (MARC field 500)

To be used for information about earlier editions or the history of the item being cataloged.

```
500      Includes photographs of all works from the exhibition
Grant Wood in America.
```

11.7B9. Publication, distribution, etc. (MARC field 500)

To be used for important information not recorded in the publication, distribution, etc., area.

11.7B10. Physical description (MARC field 500)

Reduction ratio. Give the reduction ratio if it is outside the 16×-30× range. Use one of the following terms:

> *low reduction* for less than 16×
> *high reduction* for 31×-60×
> *very high reduction* for 61×-90×
> *ultra high reduction* for over 90×; for these, give also the specific ratio
> *reduction ratio varies*

Reader. Give the name of the reader on which a microform is to be used if it can only be used on that reader.

Film. Give details of the nature of the film used, if desired.

Other physical details. Make notes on any other physical information considered important.

Comments: To be used for any important information not given in area 5, the physical description area.

    500   Microfiche in pockets in binder.

11.7B11. Accompanying material (MARC field 500)

To be used for any important information not given in the accompanying material part of area 5.

    500   Introductory material also on first frames of microfiche.

11.7B12. Series (MARC field 500)

To be used for any important information not recorded in the series area.

    500   Some material previously issued in series: American
    architecture.

11.7B13. Dissertations (MARC field 502)

To be used for the standard dissertation note when applicable.

    502   Thesis (Ph. D.)--University of Iowa, 1966.

11.7B14. Audience (MARC field 521)

To be used to record the intended audience of a work; use this note only if the information is stated on the item. Do not attempt to judge the audience for an item. If no display constant is needed, use first indicator "8".

    521 8   For medical professionals only.

11.7B16. Other formats (MARC field 530)

To be used to list other formats in which the work is available. The Library of Congress lists all formats commercially available in this note.

```
530      Issued also as slides (b&w, col.), and as photographic
prints.
```

11.7B17. Summary (MARC field 520)

To be used for a brief objective summary of the content of the item.

```
520      Shows how to duplicate several Cherokee pots and bowls
using techniques developed by Cherokee potters.
```

11.7B18. Contents (MARC fields 505, 500)

To be used for a formal (MARC field 505) or informal (MARC field 500) listing of the contents of the item.

```
505 0    The White House -- The Octagon -- Treasury Building --
General Post Office -- Washington Monument.
```

11.7B19. Numbers (MARC field 500)

To be used to list any important number appearing on the item other than those to be recorded in area 8.

```
500      "LC-USZ62-66609"
```

11.7B20. Copy being described, library's holdings, and restrictions on use (MARC fields 500, 506, 590)

To be used for any notes applicable only to the particular copy of the item being described (MARC field 500 or field 506 if there are restrictions). Also used for local library restrictions (MARC field 590) on the material being described or for information of use only to patrons of the local library.

```
590      Library copy lacks fiche 4.
590      Some photograph frames have been removed from microfilm
reel.
```

11.7B21. "With" notes (MARC field 501)

To be used for "with" notes.

11.7B22. Notes relating to original (MARC field 534)

To be used for information on the original of a microform item.

```
534      ‡p Original negatives: ‡c Washington, D.C. ; Prints and
Photographs Division, Library of Congress.
```

How would you catalog this set?

THE BRITISH MUSEUM
REPLICA OF A CYLINDER SEAL IMPRESSION
1 AN AKKADIAN 'CONTEST SCENE'
A seal with a finely-modelled group showing a bull-man
and nude hero each holding a rampant bull by the horn
and tail. The forelegs of the bulls are engraved to make it
appear as if they touched the top of a stylized mountain,
on which stands a 'sacred tree'. It has been thought,
without much justification, that scenes of this type may
represent Gilgamesh, hero of a series of Sumerian epic
tales and of the famous Assyro-Babylonian *Epic of Gilgamesh*, and the bull-man his friend and fellow-adventurer,
Enkidu.
*Akkadian, about 2200 B.C. Greenstone. 3·8 cm high ×
2·3 cm diameter.*

THE BRITISH MUSEUM
REPLICA OF A CYLINDER SEAL IMPRESSION
2 THE SEAL OF A SCRIBE
A military figure, possibly the prince mentioned in the
inscription, wearing a flat cap and bearing an axe on his
left shoulder, is attended by three men led by a bowman
who wears shoes with turned-up toes. Behind the group
are two other attendants, bearing furniture and pro-
visions, depicted on a smaller scale beneath the inscription. This may be read either in Sumerian or in Akkadian:
 '(O) Ubil-Eshtar, brother of the king; KAL-KI, the
 scribe (is) thy servant' (Sumerian, or 'his servant',
 Akkadian).
The reading of the name of the scribe is uncertain.
*Akkadian, about 2200 B.C. Aragonite. 3·4 cm high ×
2·1 cm diameter.*

THE BRITISH MUSEUM
REPLICA OF A CYLINDER SEAL IMPRESSION
4 THE SEAL OF A GOVERNOR
A typical 'introduction scene'. A goddess introduces
Hashhamer, governor of the city Ishkun-Sin, to the
seated King Ur-Nammu, founder of the IIIrd Dynasty
of Ur (c. 2050 B.C.). Another goddess is in attendance.
The inscription, in Sumerian, reads:
 '(O) Ur-Nammu, mighty male, King of Ur—Hash-
 hamer, governor of Ishkun-Sin, (is) thy servant.
*Ur III period, 2050 B.C. Green schist. 5·4 cm high ×
3·2 cm diameter.*   (*Ref. No. 89126*)

THE BRITISH MUSEUM
REPLICA OF A CYLINDER SEAL IMPRESSION
3 AN EARLY 'CONTEST SCENE'
In this seal a nude hero, in the centre, holds a bull in each hand
while a bull-man, shown in profile, fights a rampant lion. Between
them is a bird with spread wings. To the right, the bull-man, here
full-faced, struggles with two lions to rescue an ibex shown between
the contestants. An ibex's head (above, right) is used as a space filler.
*Sumerian (Early-Dynastic II); about 2650 B.C. Aragonite. 4·2 cm
high × 3·6 cm diameter.*

THE BRITISH MUSEUM
CYLINDER SEAL IMPRESSION
5 SEAL OF THE SCRIBE ADDA
The sun-god, whose rays spring from his shoulder, holds
aloft his emblem, the saw, as he rises between two moun-
tains. Ea, god of the Sweet Underground Waters (indicated
by the flowing waters), steps over a rising bull and holds
a bird in his hand. His Janus-headed attendant, Usmu, stands
behind. On the mountain, to the left, stands a winged-goddess
of war, perhaps Ishtar, shown full-faced, carrying quivers on
her back and an object (a date-cluster?) in her hand. The tree
growing from the mountain is a symbol of fertility. Another
god, perhaps Ninurta, advances with a bow in hand, followed
by a roaring lion.
*Akkadian, about 2200 B.C. Green schist. 3·8 cm high ×
2·5 cm diameter.*

These items are mounted replicas of cylinder seal impressions. On the back of each mount is the descriptive
information reproduced above with the photograph.

Example 63. Pottery Techniques of Native North America

First of four sheets of microfiche

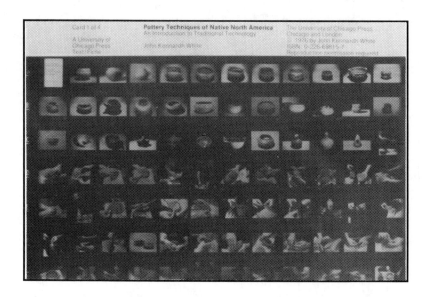

Facsimile of eye-readable data at top of microfiche

Card 1 of 4	Pottery Techniques of Native North America	The University of Chicago Press
	An Introduction to Traditional Technology	Chicago and London
A University of		© 1976 by John Kennardh White
Chicago Press	John Kennardh White	ISBN: 0-226-69815-7
Text/Fiche		Reproduction permission required

Example 63. Pottery Techniques of Native North America

```
Type: a    ELvl: I    Srce: d    Audn: f    Ctrl:        Lang: eng
BLvl: m    Form: b    Conf: 0    Biog:      MRec:        Ctry: ilu
           Cont:      GPub:      Fict: 0    Indx: 0
Desc: a    Ills: a    Fest: 0    DtSt: s    Dates: 1976,
```

```
 1 040      XXX ‡c XXX
 2 020      0226698157
 3 007      h ‡b e ‡d a ‡e m ‡f u--- ‡g c ‡h u ‡i c ‡j a
 4 043      n-us---
 5 090      E98.P8 ‡b W4 1976
 6 049      XXXX
 7 100 1    White, John Kennardh.
 8 245 10   Pottery techniques of native North America ‡h [microform] : ‡b an
introduction to traditional technology / ‡c John Kennardh White ; photographs
by Stewart J. MacLeod.
 9 260      Chicago : ‡b University of Chicago Press, ‡c c1976.
10 300      4 microfiches (336 fr.) : ‡b all col. ill. + ‡e 1 manual (vii, 52
p. : ill. ; 21 cm.).
11 440 2    A University of Chicago Press text/fiche
12 520      Using techniques developed by Cherokee craftworkers, shows how
to duplicate seven historic pots and bowls.
13 500      Bibliography: p. 51-52 of manual.
14 650 0    Indians of North America ‡x Pottery.
15 650 0    Pottery craft.
16 650 0    Cherokee Indians ‡x Pottery.
17 700 1    MacLeod, Stewart J.
```

Comments

General: This is an original publication in microform. It is not a microform reproduction of an existing work. It is similar to set of slides and can be viewed in a microfiche reader or projected with a microfiche projector. Now it would probably be done as a video.

Cataloging: The reduction ratio is 24 times, the standard reduction ratio, so nothing about reduction ratio is specified according to the rules.

The size is 11 by 15 cm., the standard size for microfiche, so that is not specified according to the rules.

Nothing in AACR 2 chapter 11 anticipated microfiche made up entirely of colored illustrations; I used "all col. ill." for the description.

The title frame is the chief source of information with the header being second choice. Information about the photographer did appear on the title frame.

MARC coding/tagging: Microforms use field 007 as do most types of audiovisual material.

Example 64. Water, Water, Everywhere

Facsimile of the top of first page

Water, Water, Everywhere
Minnesota Flooding 1993

Facsimile of the end of document

Department of
Natural Resources
Division of Waters

Printed on Recycled Paper
Contains 10% postconsumer waste

© 1994 State of Minnesota, Department of Natural Resources

Microfiche

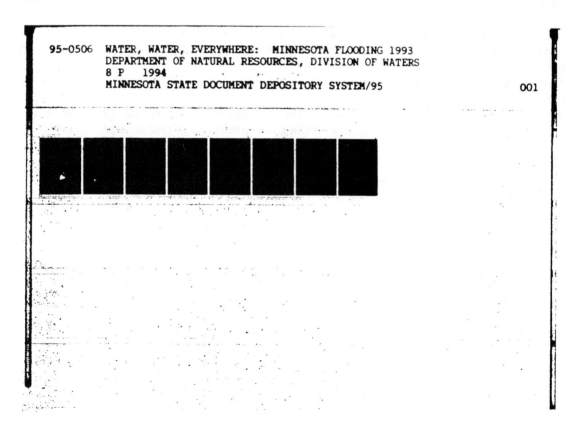

95-0506   WATER, WATER, EVERYWHERE: MINNESOTA FLOODING 1993
DEPARTMENT OF NATURAL RESOURCES, DIVISION OF WATERS
8 P   1994
MINNESOTA STATE DOCUMENT DEPOSITORY SYSTEM/95   001

Example 64. Water, Water, Everywhere

```
Type: a    ELvl: I    Srce: d    Audn: f    Ctrl:        Lang: eng
BLvl: m    Form: b    Conf: 0    Biog:      MRec:        Ctry: mnu
           Cont:      GPub: s    Fict: 0    Indx: 0
Desc: a    Ills: b    Fest: 0    DtSt: s    Dates: 1995,
  1 040       XXX ‡c XXX
  2 007       h ‡b e ‡d b ‡e m ‡f b--- ‡g b ‡h u ‡i u ‡j a
  3 043       n-us-mn
  4 090       GB1399.4.M6 ‡b W38 1994
  5 049       XXXX
  6 245 00    Water, water, everywhere ‡h [microform] : ‡b Minnesota flooding
1993.
  7 246 30    Minnesota flooding 1993
  8 260       [Saint Paul, Minn.] : ‡b Dept. of Natural Resources, Division of
Waters, ‡c [1994].
  9 300       8 p. : ‡b maps ; ‡c 28 cm.
 10 500       Caption title.
 11 533       Microfiche. ‡b St. Paul, Minn. : ‡c Minnesota State Document
Depository System, ‡d 1995. ‡e 1 microfiche : negative. ‡f Document number
95- 0506.
 12 650  0    Floods ‡z Minnesota.
 13 710  1    Minnesota. ‡b Division of Waters.
```

Comments

   General: This example shows the cataloging of a microform reproduction of a state document.
   Cataloging: This example is cataloged according to the LCRI for AACR 2 chapter 11. All information related to the fiche is given in field 533. Field 007 and subfield ‡h in the 245 are added to the cataloging for the document, and in the fixed fields "Form:" is coded "b" for microfiche.

How would you catalog this?

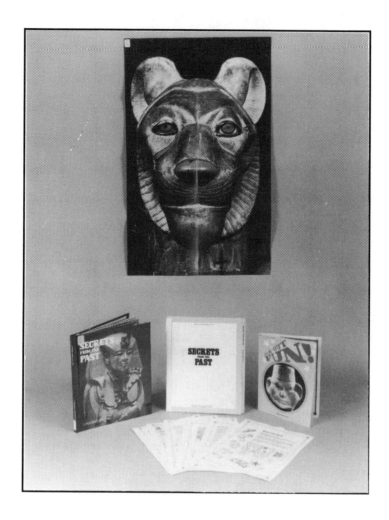

This package included a book, a poster, an activity booklet, and a set of duplicating masters. There was a game on the back of the poster.

Chapter 11

SERIALS (OTHER THAN PRINT)

AACR 2 Chapter 12

This chapter covers the cataloging of serials that are in media other than print. Serials are cataloged by the rules of AACR 2 chapter 12 together with the rules in the chapter for the type of material to which the serial belongs. Nonprint serials use the rules of chapter 12 together with the appropriate rules of the chapters that cover their types of media. Serials can be found on many types of audiovisual material. *SoftDisk Magazette, Microzine,* and *SoftSide DV Magazine* are serials on computer disks. *VideoJournal* is a serial on videocassette. *Getting It All Together* and *Young Fashion Forecast* are filmstrip serials. There are many serials on sound cassettes for doctors; *Pediatrics* and *Audiology* are only two of these. There are hundreds of online serials such as *Nucleic Acids Research.* Many serials are now available as computer files on CD-ROM, including *Pediatrics* and *American Family Physician,* and hundreds of government publications from GPO. *Verbum Interactive* is a multimedia serial on CD-ROM, with interactive columns and articles.

Special Rules for Cataloging Nonprint Serials

In this section the special rules for cataloging nonprint serials will be discussed. For rules and/or areas not discussed here, see chapter 2 of this book. Parts of some of the rules are given; the user is referred to the rules themselves for complete text and examples.

When a print serial changes to an electronic format, or to any type of nonprint format, a new bibliographic record is needed because of the format change.

Chief Source of Information

The basis for the description is the title page or title page substitute of the first issue of the serial. If the first issue is not available, we base our description on the first issue we have. The chief source of information for a printed serial is the title page; for an audiovisual serial we would use as chief source of information that title page substitute specified in the appropriate chapter. For a serial sound recording, the chief source of information would be the disc label(s) of the first issue.

The Library of Congress catalogs serials at augmented level one; other title information is omitted.

Title and Statement of Responsibility Area
MARC field 245

There are lengthy rule interpretations concerning titles of serials as well as concerning all other aspects of serials. Refer to these in the *Cataloging Service Bulletin* if there is any doubt as to what information belongs in which area of the bibliographic record.

For an audiovisual serial, the appropriate GMD is used.

Numeric and/or Alphabetic, Chronological, or Other Designation Area
MARC field 362

In the rules below, use standard abbreviations and numerals in place of words (see AACR 2 Appendixes B and C). This area is omitted if the description is based on other than the first issue.

> **12.3B1.** Give the numeric and/or alphabetic designation of the first issue of a serial as given in that issue....
>
> **12.3C1.** If the first issue of a serial is identified by a chronological designation, give it in the terms used in the item....
>
> **12.3F1.** In describing a completed serial, give the designation of the first issue followed by the designation of the last issue.

While this information is from area 3, field 362 follows fields 300, 310, and 321 in the MARC serials record.

Publication, Distribution, Etc., Area
MARC field 300

The information given in this area, as in the other areas, reflects the information given in the first issue of the serial.

> **12.4F1.** ... Give the date of publication even if it coincides, wholly or in part, with the date given as the chronological coverage.

Physical Description Area
MARC fields 5XX

> **12.5B1.** For a serial that is still in progress, give the relevant specific material designation preceded by three spaces....

Other parts of the physical description area are recorded as directed in the appropriate chapter.

Notes Area

The following notes are permitted in this chapter:

12.7B1. Frequency
12.7B2. Language
12.7B3. Source of title proper
12.7B4. Variations in title
12.7B5. Parallel titles and other title information
12.7B6. Statements of responsibility
12.7B7. Relationships with other serials
12.7B8. Numbering and chronological designation
12.7B9. Publication, distribution, etc.
12.7B10. Physical description
12.7B11. Accompanying material
12.7B12. Series
12.7B14. Audience
12.7B16. Other formats

12.7B17. Indexes
12.7B18. Contents
12.7B19. Numbers
12.7B20. Copy being described, library's holdings, and restrictions on use
12.7B21. "Issued with" notes
12.7B22. Item described

Explanation of notes

Each of the notes will be explained in the following section and examples of their use given. There is no summary note listed for this chapter. When we need one for audiovisual material, we borrow it from the chapter for the physical form of the material.

12.7B1. Frequency (MARC field 310 (current frequency), field 321 (former frequency))

To be used to give the frequency of the serial, or serial-like publication. USMARC convention is that this field does not end with a period.

        310   Weekly during the school year

12.7B2. Language (MARC field 546)

To be used to name the language or languages of the item cataloged if not obvious from other information given.

        546   Text in English and French.

12.7B3. Source of title proper (MARC field 500)

To be used if the title proper is taken from other than the chief source of information.

        500   Title from container.
        500   Title supplied by cataloger.

12.7B4. Variations in title (MARC field 246)

To be used to note any title appearing on the item that differs significantly from the title proper.

        246 1   ‡i Title on container: ‡a News lesson
                (*Title proper:* News program)

12.7B5. Parallel titles and other title information (MARC field 500)

To be used for parallel titles and important other title information not recorded in the title and statement of responsibility area.

        500   Subtitle on index: An audio journal for professionals.

12.7B6. Statements of responsibility (MARC fields 550, 500)

To be used to record important information not recorded in the statement of responsibility area.

        500   Editors: Larry J. Bradford, Frederick N. Martin.

12.7B7. Relationships with other titles (MARC fields 580, 78X)

To be used to note the relationship between the title being described and any title it continues or is continued by, or with which it has some relationship.

```
580      Continued by: Audiology (published in hard copy)
```

12.7B8. Numbering and chronological designation (MARC field 515)

To be used for notes on complex or irregular numbering, etc., not already specified.

```
515      Vol. 1, no. 3, numbered vol. 2, no. 3.
```

12.7B9. Publication, distribution, etc. (MARC field 500)

To be used for important information not recorded in the publication, distribution, etc. area.

```
500      Publisher varies.
```

12.7B10. Physical description (MARC field 500)

To be used for any important information not given in area 5, the physical description area.

```
500      Some issues on sound cassette, others on sound tape reel.
```

12.7B11. Accompanying material (MARC fields 500, 525 (supplement))

To be used for any important information not given in the accompanying material part of area 5.

```
500      Guide in braille.
525      Occasionally supplemented by posters.
```

12.7B12. Series (MARC field 500)

To be used for series information related to the original of a reproduction.

```
500      Some issues also part of: Math skills series.
```

12.7B14. Audience (MARC field 521)

To be used to record the intended audience of a work; use this note only if the information is stated on the item. Do not attempt to judge the audience for an item. First indicator "8" is used when no display constant is needed. To generate the display constant "Audience", a blank first indicator is needed.

```
521 8    Intended for health professionals working with the
hearing-impaired.
```

12.7B16. Other formats (MARC field 530)

To be used to list other formats in which the work is available. The Library of Congress lists all formats commercially available in this note.

```
530      Some numbers issued also on sound tape reels.
```

12.7B17. Indexes (MARC field 555)

To be used for notes on separately published indexes, and on cumulative indexes.

```
555     Printed index issued for each volume.
```

12.7B18. Contents (MARC field 505 (formal contents), field 500 (informal contents), field 504 (bibliography))

To be used for details of inserts, special items with their own titles, and serials within the serial being cataloged.

```
500     Poster included with first number of each semester.
```

12.7B19. Numbers (MARC field 500)

To be used to list any important number appearing on the item other than those to be recorded in fields 020, 024, 028, or 037.

12.7B20. Copy being described, library's holdings, and restrictions on use (MARC fields 500, 590)

To be used for any notes applicable only to the particular copy of the item being described. Also used for local library restrictions (MARC field 590) on the material being described or for information of use only to patrons of the local library.

```
590     Restricted for library use.
```

12.7B21. "Issued with" notes (MARC field 501)

To be used for a note listing other serials issued with the one being cataloged.

12.7B22. Item described (MARC field 500)

To be used if the description is not based on the first issue.

```
500     Description based on: Aug. 1982.
```

Example 65. News Program

Box of filmstrips

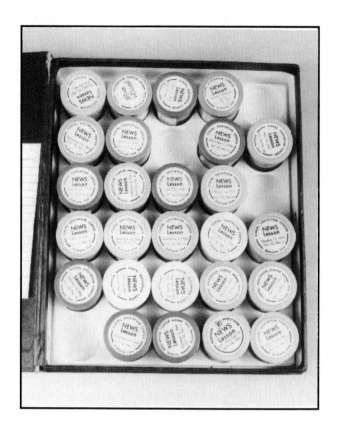

Example 65. News Program

```
Type: g   ELvl: I    Srce: d   Audn: c   Ctrl:       Lang: eng
BLvl: s   TMat: f    GPub:     AccM:     MRec:       Ctry: iau
Desc: a   Time: nnn  Tech: n   DtSt: d   Dates: 1950,196u
 1 040     XXX ǂc XXX
 2 007     g ǂb o ǂd b ǂe j ǂh f
 3 006     [s n   0]
 4 090     D421 ǂb .N4
 5 049     XXXX
 6 245 00  News program ǂh [filmstrip].
 7 246 3   ǂi Title on container: ǂa News lesson
 8 260     Dubuque, Ia. : ǂb Visual Education Center, ǂc 1950-
 9 300     filmstrips ; ǂb b&w ; ǂc 35 mm. + ǂe teacher's guides + semester
quizzes.
10 310     Weekly during the school year.
11 362 0   Vol. 1, no. 1 (Sept. 7, 1950)-
12 520     Pictures from the news of the week are presented with discussion
questions.
13 650  0  History ǂx Study and teaching.
14 650  0  Current events ǂx Periodicals.
15 710 2   Visual Education Center.
```

Comments

General: This is an example of an audiovisual serial. The filmstrips came weekly (during the school year) and had the traditional serial numbering on them. The serial ceased sometime in the 1960s. These were black & white filmstrips in metal cans.

Cataloging: Cataloging of these combines rules from chapter 12 with rules from chapter 8. We did have the first issue of this serial for cataloging, but did not have the last issues, and I could not find information about the date it ceased.

MARC coding/tagging: This is the kind of material that format integration was designed for. One bibliographic record contains both serial and audiovisual codes and it can be searched as either a serial or as an audiovisual title. Field 007 contains coding for additional audiovisual aspects, while field 006 contains coding for additional serial aspects.

Example 66. Audiology (sound recording)

Sound cassette

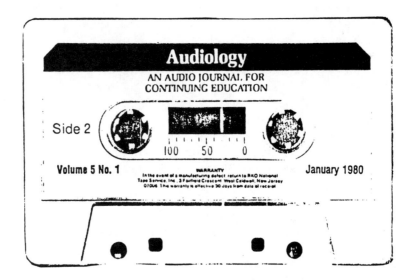

```
Type: i    ELvl: I    Srce: d    Audn: f    Ctrl:      Lang: eng
BLvl: s    Form:      Comp: nn   AccM:      MRec:      Ctry: nyu
Desc: a    FMus: n    LTxt: l    DtSt: d    Dates: 1976,1981
  1 040       XXX ǂc XXX
  2 006       [smr p 0 0]
  3 007       s ǂb s ǂd l ǂe m ǂf n ǂg j ǂh l ǂi b ǂn u
  4 022       0146-311X
  5 090       RF290 ǂb .A8
  6 049       XXXX
  7 130 0     Audiology (New York, N.Y. : 1976)
  8 245 10    Audiology ǂh [sound recording] : ǂb an audio journal for
continuing education.
  9 260       New York : ǂb Grune & Stratton, ǂc 1976-1981.
 10 300       7 v. (84 sound cassettes) : ǂb analog + ǂe 84 printed guides.
 11 310       Monthly
 12 362 0     Vol. 1 (Jan. 1976)-v. 7, no. 12 (Dec. 1981).
 13 500       Editor: L. J. Bradford.
 14 500       Each volume in a binder; printed contents list issued annually.
 15 580       Continued by: Audiology (New York, N.Y. : 1982), issued in paper
format.
 16 650  0    Audiology ǂx Periodicals.
 17 700 1     Bradford, Larry J.
 18 710 2     Grune & Stratton.
 19 785 10    ǂt Audiology (New York, N.Y. : 1982) ǂx 0146-311X ǂw
(OCoLC)8734006
```

Comments

   General: This pair of examples (66 and 67) show a periodical that was issued on sound cassette from 1976 through 1981, then changed to print but continued the volume numbering.
   Cataloging: The cataloging for this serial combines serial cataloging with sound recording cataloging.
   MARC coding/tagging: Field 007 provides additional information about the sound recording characteristics; field 006 provides additional information about serial characteristics.

Example 67. Audiology (paper)

```
Type: a   ELvl: I    Srce: d   GPub:      Ctrl:      Lang: eng
BLvl: s   Form:      Conf: 0   Freq: m    MRec:      Ctry: nyu
S/L:  0   Orig:      EntW:     Regl: r    ISSN: 1    Alph: a
Desc: a   SrTp: p    Cont:     DtSt: d    Dates: 1982,1984
 1 040       XXX ǂc XXX
 2 022  0    0146-311X
 3 090       RF290 ǂb .A82
 4 049       XXXX
 5 130  0    Audiology (New York, N.Y. : 1982)
 6 245 00    Audiology.
 7 260       New York : ǂb Grune & Stratton, ǂc 1982-1984.
 8 300       3 v. : ǂb ill. ; ǂc 28 cm.
 9 310       Monthly
10 362  0    Vol. 7, no. 1 (Jan. 1982)-v. 9, no. 12 (Dec. 1984).
11 500       Title from caption.
12 580       Continues: Audiology (New York, N.Y. : 1976), issued on 4-track
sound cassettes.
13 650  0    Audiology ǂx Periodicals.
14 780 10    ǂt Audiology (New York, N.Y. : 1976) ǂx 0146-311X ǂw
(OCoLC)8734013
```

Comments

   General: This is the bibliographic record for the paper serial that continued the same title on sound cassettes. Each record carries a linking entry referring to the other title.

Example 68. NOAA Weather Charts. Chart Series C, Tropical …

Front of container

NOAA WEATHER CHARTS

Chart Series C
Tropical Strip / Precipitation and Observed Weather Charts

VOLUME 3   NUMBER 4   APRIL 1996

SEP I I 1996

U.S. DEPARTMENT OF COMMERCE
National Oceanic and Atmospheric Administration
National Climatic Data Center
Asheville, North Carolina

Back of container

This CD-ROM contains the weather charts that are most commonly used by researchers and the general public. It is available on a monthly subscription basis, and serves as a continuation of NCDC's microfilm archive.

This product has been designed to run optimally in the MS-DOS/Windows operating environment. However, any computer platform that can play CD-ROMs and has software capable of displaying black and white graphic files in the ZSoft Version 5 PCX format should be able to display these charts. All "readme" files are plain ASCII text with 1" margins and can be read and printed in any environment that supports this format. Please refer to the "readme" files in the README.DIR directory for more information.

HARDWARE/SOFTWARE REQUIREMENTS
- MS-DOS version 3.3 or higher for PC platforms
- System 7.5 or higher for Macintosh platforms
- Graphics software capable of reading PCX files
- Printer capable of 300 DPI output for best results.

Example 68. NOAA Weather Charts. Chart Series C, Tropical ...

Disc

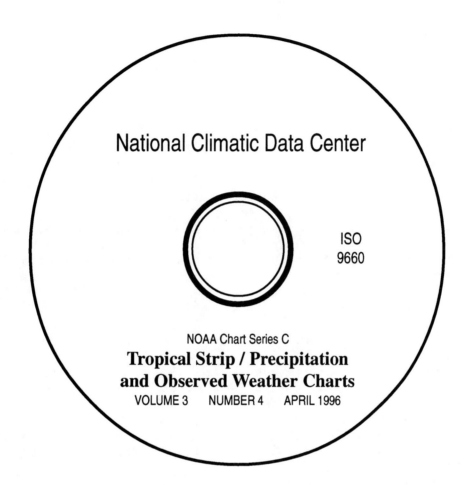

National Climatic Data Center

ISO
9660

NOAA Chart Series C
**Tropical Strip / Precipitation
and Observed Weather Charts**
VOLUME 3   NUMBER 4   APRIL 1996

Example 68. NOAA Weather Charts. Chart Series C, Tropical ...

```
Type: m    ELvl: I    Srce: d    Audn: f    Ctrl:       Lang: eng
BLvl: s    File: m    GPub: f               MRec:       Ctry: ncu
Desc: a                          DtSt: c    Dates: 1994,9999
```

```
 1 040       XXX ǂc XXX
 2 006       [smr    f0 0]
 3 007       c ǂb o ǂd a ǂe g ǂf u
 4 050 14    QC980 ǂb .N6 Series C
 5 049       XXXX
 6 245 00    NOAA weather charts. ǂn Chart series C, ǂp Tropical strip
precipitation and observed weather charts ǂh [computer file] / ǂc produced by
National Climatic Data Center.
 7 246 1     ǂi Title from disc label: ǂa NOAA. ǂn Chart series C, ǂp Tropical
strip/precipitation and observed weather charts
 8 246 1     ǂi Container spine title: ǂa Chart series C
 9 246 2     National Oceanic and Atmospheric Administration weather charts. ǂn
Chart series C, ǂp Tropical strip/precipitation and observed weather charts
10 246 2     Tropical strip precipitation and observed weather charts
11 246 30    Tropical strip/precipitation and observed weather charts
12 260       Asheville, N.C. : ǂb The Center,
13 300       computer optical discs ; ǂc 4 3/4 in.
14 310       Monthly
15 500       Description based on: Vol. 3, no. 3 (Mar. 1996); title from
container insert.
16 516       Written in ISO 9660 format.
17 538       System requirements for IBM: IBM PC or compatible; MS-DOS
version 3.3 or higher and graphics software capable of reading PCX files;
printer capable of 300 DPI output.
18 538       System requirements for Macintosh: Macintosh; System 7.5 or
higher and graphics software capable of reading PCX files; printer capable of
300 DPI output.
19 580       Continuation of NCDC's microfilm archive.
20 580       Also issued in combined ed. with: NOAA weather charts. Chart
series A, Surface and upper air weather charts ; and: NOAA weather charts.
Chart series B, Initial analysis and forecast charts.
21 650  0    Precipitation (Meteorology) ǂx Observations ǂx Charts, diagrams,
etc. ǂx Databases.
22 650  0    Weather forecasting ǂx Charts, diagrams, etc. ǂx Databases.
23 710 2     National Climatic Data Center (U.S.)
24 787 1     ǂt NOAA weather charts. Chart series A, Surface and upper air
weather charts ǂw (DLC)sn 96028318 ǂw (OCoLC)35564548
25 787 1     ǂt NOAA weather charts. Chart series B, Initial analysis and
forecast charts ǂw (DLC)sn 96028319 ǂw (OCoLC)35564585
26 787 1     ǂt NOAA weather charts ǂw (DLC)sn 97032475 ǂw (OCoLC)35745348
```

Example 68. NOAA Weather Charts. Chart Series C, Tropical ...

Comments

General: No sooner had I cataloged the three separate titles (one of which is shown above; each came separately packaged) than the next shipment came with the three titles packaged together under the collective title. To make this more fun, some of the sets had earlier dates than the ones I had cataloged separately, and some had later dates. One of the joys of serial cataloging! They seem to be published both ways, but they seem to be shipped to us randomly in the depository shipments. I shifted our holdings to the collective title.

Examples 68 and 69 show the complexity of serial records for government publication computer files. My workload has increased greatly since GPO began publishing these things.

Cataloging: This example does show where the GMD goes when the title includes a part number and part title. Subfields "a," "n," and "p" together make up the title proper, and the GMD follows the title proper.

These examples are slightly edited from the way they appeared in OCLC, spring 1997.

Notice all the 246 fields, and all are needed.

Example 69. NOAA Weather Charts

Front of container

C 55.281/2-7: V 3/Nⁿ 4

NOAA WEATHER CHARTS

Produced by:

National Climatic Data Center
151 Patton Avenue
Asheville, North Carolina 28801-5001

Technical support:

(704) 271-4702

Back of container

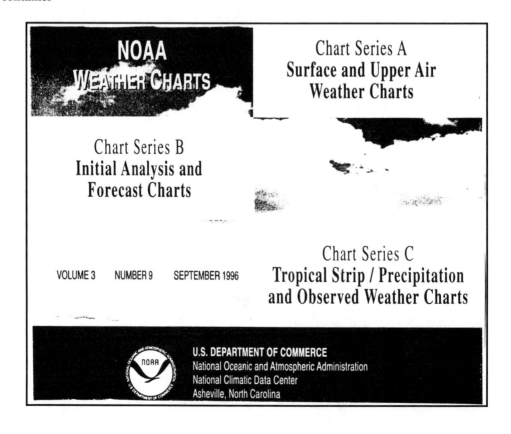

Example 69. NOAA Weather Charts

```
Type: m    ELvl: I    Srce: d    Audn: f    Ctrl:       Lang: eng
BLvl: s    File: m    GPub: f               MRec:       Ctry: ncu
Desc: a                          DtSt: c    Dates: 1994,9999
```

 1 040   XXX ǂc XXX
 2 006   [smr   f0 a0]
 3 007   c ǂb o ǂd a ǂe g ǂf u
 4 090   QC980 ǂb .N6
 5 049   XXXX
 6 245 00 NOAA weather charts ǂh [computer file].
 7 246 1   ǂi Container spine title: ǂa Chart series A/B/C
 8 246 1   ǂi At head of disc label title: ǂa NOAA chart series
 9 260   Asheville, N.C. : ǂb U.S. Dept. of Commerce, National Oceanic
and Atmospheric Administration, National Climatic Data Center,
10 300   computer optical discs ; ǂc 4 3/4 in.
11 310   Monthly
12 362 1   Began in Oct. 1994?
13 538   System requirements for IBM: IBM PC or compatible; MS-DOS
version 3.3 or higher and graphics software capable of reading PCX files;
printer capable of 300 DPI output; CD ROM drive.
14 538   System requirements for Macintosh: Macintosh; System 7.5 or
higher and graphics software capable of reading PCX files; printer capable of
300 DPI output; CD-ROM drive.
15 500   Vols. for <1996- > contain 3 discs, separately entitled: Chart
series A. Surface and upper air weather charts -- Chart series B. Initial
analysis and forecast charts -- Chart series C. Tropical strip/precipitation
and observed weather charts.
16 500   Description based on: Vol. 3, no. 2 (Feb. 1996); title from
container insert.
17 516   Written in ISO 9660 format.
18 580   Continuation of NCDC's microfilm archive.
19 580   Each chart series also published separately.
20 650 0 Atmosphere, Upper ǂx Observations ǂx Charts, diagrams, etc. ǂx
Databases.
21 650 0 Climatology ǂx Observations ǂx Charts, diagrams, etc. ǂx Databases.
22 650 0 Precipitation (Meteorology) ǂx Observations ǂx Charts, diagrams,
etc. ǂx Databases.
23 650 0 Weather forecasting ǂx Observations ǂx Charts, diagrams, etc. ǂx
Databases.
24 710 2   National Climatic Data Center (U.S.)
25 740 02 Surface and upper air weather charts.
26 740 02 Initial analysis and forecast charts.
27 740 02 Tropical strip/precipitation and observed weather charts.
28 787 1   ǂt NOAA weather charts. Chart series A, Surface and upper air
weather charts ǂw (DLC)sn 96028318 ǂw (OCoLC)35564548
29 787 1   ǂt NOAA weather charts. Chart series B, Initial analysis and
forecast charts ǂw (DLC)sn 96028319 ǂw (OCoLC)35564585
30 787 1   ǂt NOAA weather charts. Chart series C, Tropical strip/
precipitation and observed weather charts ǂw (DLC)sn 96028320 ǂw
(OCoLC)35564692

Example 70. LC Cataloging Newsline

List of issues available

LC Cataloging Newsline

Online Newsletter of the Cataloging Directorate

Library of Congress

ISSN 1066-8829

NOTE: Back issues through Volume 3 are available on the LC MARVEL gopher server at
gopher://marvel.loc.gov/11/services/cataloging/lccn

Volume 5
    Number 1 January 1997
Volume 4
    Number 1 January 1996
    Number 2 February 1996
    Number 3 March 1996
    Number 4 March 1996
    Number 5 April 1996
    Number 6 May 1996
    Number 7 May 1996
    Number 8 June 1996
    Number 9 June 1996
    Number 10 August 1996
    Number 11 September 1996
    Number 12 October 1996
    Number 13 November 1996
    Number 14 December 1996
    Number 15 December 1996
    Number 16 December 1996

Go to the Library of Congress Home Page

Library of Congress
Comments: lcweb@loc.gov (06/07/96)

Example 70. LC Cataloging Newsline

Contents of one issue

LC Cataloging Newsline

Online Newsletter of the Cataloging Directorate, Library of Congress

Volume 5, No. 01, ISSN 1066-8829, January 1997

Contents

Example 70. LC Cataloging Newsline

```
Type: m    ELvl:      Srce: d   Audn: f    Ctrl:      Lang: eng
BLvl: s    File: d    GPub: f              MRec:      Ctry: dcu
Desc: a                        DtSt: c    Dates: 1993,9999
 1 010      95-660725 ‡Z SN92-583
 2 040      NSD ‡c NSD ‡d DLC ‡d EYM ‡d OCL ‡d EYM
 3 006      [s x1p f0 a0]
 4 007      c ‡b r ‡d c ‡e n ‡f u
 5 012      ‡i 9505 ‡k 1 ‡l 1
 6 022 0    1066-8829
 7 037      ‡b Library of Congress, Cataloging Directorate, Washington, DC
20540 ‡c Free
 8 042      nsdp ‡a lc
 9 050 00   Z693.A15
10 082 10   025 ‡2 12
11 090      ‡b
12 049      XXXX
13 110 2    Library of Congress. ‡b Cataloging Directorate.
14 210 0    LC cat. newsline
15 222 0    LC cataloging newsline
16 245 00   LC cataloging newsline ‡h [computer file] : ‡b online newsletter
of the Cataloging Directorate, Library of Congress.
17 246 2    Library of Congress cataloging newsline
18 246 13   LCCN
19 260      [Washington, DC] : ‡b The Directorate, ‡c [1993-
20 310      Irregular
21 362 0    Vol. 1, no. 1 (Jan. 1993)-
22 538      Mode of access: Internet email, telnet, gopher, and World Wide
Web.
23 500      Description based on printout of online display; title from
title screen.
24 516 8    Electronic journal in ASCII text, and HTML format vol. 4-
25 650  0   Cataloging ‡x Periodicals.
26 850      DLC
27 856 0    loc.gov ‡f LCCN ‡h listproc ‡i subscribe ‡z Email subscription
28 856 2    marvel.loc.gov ‡l marvel ‡z Telnet connection to gopher server
29 856 7    ‡u gopher://marvel.loc.gov:2070/11/services/cataloging/lccn ‡2
gopher ‡3 vols. 1-3
30 856 7    ‡u gopher://marvel.loc.gov:70/11/services/cataloging/lccn ‡2
gopher ‡3 vols. 1-3
31 856 7    ‡u http://lcweb.loc.gov/catdir/lccn/ ‡2 http ‡3 vol. 4-
32 936      Vol. 4, no. 9 (June 1996) LIC
```

Comments

General: This record is for an electronic serial. I have edited it only slightly from the way it appeared in OCLC, spring 1997.

Cataloging: You will note this cataloging does not carry field 256 that is required by the cataloging rules. That field could say, based on the revisions to the ISBD(ER), "Computer journal".

Access: The five 856 fields provide access through the five methods named in field 538. Note the two gopher sites carry only the first three volumes. Beginning with volume 5, as indicated in field 516, it was available in HTML format through the Web.

Chapter 12

KITS

What is a kit?

Kit. 1. An item containing two or more categories of material, no one of which is identifiable as the predominant constituent of the item; also designated "multimedia item". 2. A single-medium package of textual material. (AACR 2, p. 619)

Kit. A collection of articles forming part of the equipment of a soldier, and carried in a valise or knapsack ... A number of things or persons viewed as a whole; a set, lot, collection. (*Oxford English Dictionary*, Oxford: Clarendon Press, 1933, v. 5, p. 716).

The definition of kit as used in the library field has changed over the years. Earlier school/library usage called any package containing more than one type of material a kit. Determination of predominant component was a later concept. There is still little agreement among catalogers as to what is, or is not, a kit. Some packages contain so many items that they clearly fall into the above definitions. Other packages are borderline.

A package containing a filmstrip with narrated sound on a sound cassette or disc and a guide or script is not a kit because the filmstrip is considered to be predominant with the other materials accompanying the filmstrip. A package containing a filmstrip and a sound recording that is not narration and is not used simultaneously with the filmstrip would be a kit, because the package contains more than one type of material and no one type is dominant. The *Reading Habit Custom Pack*, containing 211 discussion cards for children's favorite books, 24 creative activity cards, and two cut-apart card games, would be a kit.

The *OED* definition given above is helpful. "A number of things ... viewed as a whole" is a useful definition when examining materials such as the reading materials mentioned above.

A footnote about kits on page 20 of *AACR 2* was deleted in *Amendments 1993*.

Rule 1.10 in *AACR 2* is the only rule for the cataloging of kits. However, the word "kit" is never mentioned. The rule is confusing, because it begins by saying it applies "to items that are made up of two or more components, two or more of which belong to distinct material types (e.g., a sound recording and a printed text)" (p. 56). This has led some to believe that anything with two or more components is a kit.

The rule continues, "If an item has one predominant component, describe it in terms of that component and give details of the subsidiary component(s) as accompanying material following the physical description or in a note." At this point, rule 1.10 should refer the cataloger to the appropriate chapter for describing the predominant component, for example to chapter 8 for a filmstrip.

For rules and/or areas not discussed here, see chapter 2 of this book.

Chief Source of Information

The chief source of information for a kit is the whole item; information for cataloging may be taken from anywhere on the item. Usually there will be a container that will have information useful for cataloging.

Physical Description Area
MARC field 300

There are three methods given in 1.10C2 for physical description. We are told in the rules to apply whichever is appropriate.

1.10C2a. Give the extent of each part or group of parts belonging to each distinct class of material as the first element of the physical description (do this if no further physical description of each item is desired). *Optionally*, if the parts are in a container, name the container and give its dimensions.

```
300     8 filmstrips, 4 sound discs, 18 charts and
posters, 34 identical elementary booklets, 1 secondary
booklet, 1 teacher's guide ; ǂc in box 34 x 34 x 34 cm.
```

1.10C2b. Give a separate physical description for each part or group of parts belonging to each distinct class of material (do this if a further physical description of each item is desired). Give each physical description on a separate line....

```
300     8 filmstrips : ǂb col. ; ǂc 35 mm. + ǂe 4 sound
discs (analog, 33 1/3 rpm ; 12 in.)
300     8 charts : ǂb b&w ; ǂc 28 x 22 cm.
300     10 posters : ǂb col. ; ǂc 36 x 24 cm.
300     34 identical elementary booklets (32 p. each) :
ǂb ill. ; ǂc 28 cm.
300     1 teacher's guide (32 p.) : ǂb ill. ; ǂc 28 cm.
300     All in container 34 x 34 x 34 cm.
```

1.10C2c. For items with a large number of heterogeneous materials, give a general term as the extent. Give the number of such pieces unless it cannot be ascertained [easily]....

```
300     various pieces
300     28 various pieces ; ǂc in box 34 x 34 x 34 cm.
```

Notes Area
MARC fields 5XX

Types of notes:

1.7B1.   Nature, scope, or artistic form
1.7B2.   Language of the item and/or translation or adaptation
1.7B3.   Source of title proper
1.7B4.   Variations in title
1.7B5.   Parallel titles and other title information
1.7B6.   Statements of responsibility
1.7B7.   Edition and history
1.7B9.   Publication, distribution, etc.
1.7B10. Physical description
1.7B11. Accompanying material and supplements
1.7B12. Series
1.7B13. Dissertations
1.7B14. Audience
1.7B15. Reference to published descriptions
1.7B16. Other formats
1.7B17. Summary
1.7B18. Contents
1.7B19. Numbers borne by the item
1.7B20. Copy being described, library's holdings, and restrictions on use

1.7B21. "With" notes

1.7B22. Combined notes relating to the original

Explanation of notes

Each of the notes will be explained in the following section and examples of their use given.

1.7B1. Nature, scope, or artistic form (MARC field 500)

To be used to name or explain the form of the item as necessary.

```
500      A supplemental teaching unit.
```

1.7B2. Language of the item and/or translation or adaptation (MARC field 546)

To be used to name the language or languages of the item cataloged if not obvious from other information given.

```
546      Text in German.
546      Posters in German and Swedish.
```

1.7B3. Source of title proper (MARC field 500)

To be used if the title proper is taken from other than the chief source of information.

```
500      Title supplied by cataloger.
```

1.7B4. Variations in title (MARC fields 246, 500)

To be used to note any title appearing on the item that differs significantly from the title proper. It is coded as a 246 if the title applies to the whole item.

```
246 1    ‡i Title on cassette: ‡a Step by step 2
```
        (*Title proper:* Step by step two.)

1.7B5. Parallel titles and other title information (MARC field 500; field 246 if added entry is required)

To be used for parallel titles and important other title information not recorded in the title and statement of responsibility area.

```
500      Subtitle from guide: A supplemental teaching unit from
the records of the National Archives.
```

1.7B6. Statements of responsibility (MARC field 500)

To be used to record important information not recorded in the statement of responsibility area.

```
500      Project designer, John Victor ; programmers, Stephen
Chmielewski, Kathleen Fortmeier.
```

1.7B7. Edition and history (MARC field 500)

To be used for information about earlier editions or the history of the item being cataloged.

```
500      Continuation of: New step by step.
```

1.7B9. Publication, distribution, etc. (MARC field 500)

To be used for important information not recorded in the publication, distribution, etc., area.

1.7B10. Physical description (MARC field 500)

To be used for any important information not given in area 5, the physical description area.

```
500      HO scale.
```

1.7B11. Accompanying material and supplements (MARC field 500)

To be used for any important information not given in the accompanying material part of area 5.

```
500      Teacher's guide includes bibliography, exercises,
worksheets, glossary, time line.
```

1.7B12. Series (MARC field 500)

To be used for any important information not recorded in the series area.

```
500      Filmstrips previously issued as part of series:
Minnesota, its land and people.
```

1.7B13. Dissertations (MARC field 502)

To be used for the standard dissertation note when applicable.

```
502      Thesis (Ed. Sp.)--Mankato State University, 1980.
```

1.7B14. Audience (MARC field 521)

To be used to record the intended audience of a work; use this note only if the information is stated on the item. The note may be quoted. Do not attempt to judge the audience for an item. If no display constant is needed, use first indicator "8".

```
521 8    "For ages 8 years and up".
```

1.7B15. Reference to published descriptions (MARC fields 510, 524)

To be used to refer to published descriptions of the material.

1.7B16. Other formats (MARC field 530)

To be used to list other formats in which the work is available. The Library of Congress lists all formats commercially available in this note.

```
530      Issued also with intermediate-level guides.
```

1.7B17. Summary (MARC field 520)

To be used for a brief objective summary of the content of the item.

```
520      Introduces young people to the field of archaeology
through stories of discoveries made by children, stories of
youngsters who were influential in ancient times, and stories
recreating childhood experiences from other times and cultures.
```

1.7B18. Contents (MARC fields 505, 500)

To be used for a formal (MARC field 505) or informal (MARC field 500) listing of the contents of the item.

```
505 0    America moves toward war -- Women and the war effort --
Uncle Sam needs you -- Reactions to the call -- When Johnny comes
marching home.
```

1.7B19. Numbers borne by the item (MARC field 500)

To be used to list any important number appearing on the item other than those to be recorded in fields 020, 024, 028, or 037.

```
500      "Y 2259-2"
```

1.7B20. Copy being described, library's holdings, and restrictions on use (MARC fields 506, 590)

To be used for any notes applicable only to the particular copy of the item being described (MARC field 506). Also used for local library restrictions (MARC field 590) on the material being described or for information of use only to patrons of the local library.

```
590      Color fading on library copy.
```

1.7B21. "With" notes (MARC field 501)

To be used for "with" notes.

Kit Problems

Office practice sets and accounting practice sets may be considered kits. A package containing all the materials (workbooks, charts, quizzes, etc.) that would be used in a year of fifth-grade social studies could be a kit. These kits are designed to be used up by a class.

A set of material (transparencies, activity cards, models, games, etc.) purchased bound together in book form but designed to be taken apart for use could be cataloged as a kit. There should be a note on the bibliographic record for such an item indicating the item was purchased in book form.

How would you catalog this?

    This is a book of songs with printed music. There is a tiny electronc piano with numbered keys fastened inside the
back of the book; each page has a cutout so the keyboard can be used to play the song.
    This is a collection of Mother Goose songs, so don't forget to do something for Mother Goose.

Example 71. The Immigrant Experience

Some of the kit contents

Container

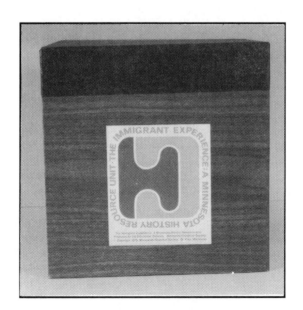

Example 71. The Immigrant Experience

From the container label

The Immigrant Experience: A Minnesota History Resource Unit
Produced by the Education Division, Minnesota Historical Society,
© Copyright 1979, Minnesota Historical Society. St. Paul, Minnesota

Container, showing 3 boxes, each with container label

Example 71. The Immigrant Experience

```
Type: o    ELvl: I    Srce: d    Audn: d    Ctrl:      Lang: eng
BLvl: m    TMat: b    GPub: s    AccM:      MRec:      Ctry: mnu
Desc: a    Time: nnn  Tech: n    DtSt: s    Dates: 1979,
 1 040       XXX ‡c XXX
 2 007       g ‡b o ‡d c ‡e j ‡f b ‡g d ‡h f
 3 043       n-us-mn
 4 045       w4x7
 5 090       F606 ‡b .I5 1979
 6 049       XXXX
 7 245 04    The immigrant experience ‡h [kit] : ‡b a Minnesota history resource
unit / ‡c produced by the Education Division, Minnesota Historical Society.
 8 260       St. Paul, Minn. : ‡b Minnesota Historical Society, ‡c c1979.
 9 300       8 filmstrips, 4 sound discs, 10 biography banners, 1 intermediate
booklet, 30 identical copies of secondary booklet, 1 set of resource
materials, 1 teacher's guide ; ‡c in box 34 x 34 x 34 cm.
10 500       Resource materials include reproductions of tickets, posters, ship
manifests, blueprint of Ellis Island, maps, census schedules, birth, death,
and marriage certificates, and time line; teacher's guide includes scripts of
sound filmstrips.
11 520       Designed to present intermediate and secondary students with an
historical account of the migration and immigration of people to Minnesota,
with particular emphasis on the nineteenth and twentieth centuries.
12 651   0   Minnesota ‡x Emigration and immigration.
13 651   0   Minnesota ‡x History ‡y 1858-
14 710 2     Minnesota Historical Society. ‡b Education Division.
```

Comments

General: A brief form of this bibliographic record is included in chapter 2 of this book as an example of level one cataloging.

This package has no dominant component, so is cataloged as a kit. It does contain narrated filmstrips, but it also contains a significant amount of other types of media including maps, posters, and other graphic materials, and facsimile documents.

Cataloging: In area 4, we could say "The Society" instead of "Minnesota Historical Society," but the fuller form supports searching by the name of publisher in field 260.

According to the rules, we cannot add descriptive information in parentheses to terms in area 5. To do so, we would have to use repeatable fields 300.

MARC coding/tagging: Field 007 is for the sound filmstrips.

Processing: Every item in this package would need a label.

Example 72. World War I: The Home Front

Kit cover and some contents

Information on box cover

> # NATIONAL ARCHIVES
> ## and
> ## SirS, Inc., Publishers
> ## P.O. Box 2507, Boca Raton, Florida 33432

Example 72. World War I: The Home Front

```
Type: o    ELvl: I   Srce: d   Audn: d   Ctrl:      Lang: eng
BLvl: m    TMat: b   GPub:     AccM:     MRec:      Ctry: flu
Desc: a    Time: nnn Tech: n   DtSt: s   Dates: 1982
 1 040      XXX ǂc XXX
 2 020      0897770153
 3 043      n-us---
 4 045      x1x1
 5 090      D570.A35 ǂb .W6 1982
 6 049      XXXX
 7 245 00   World War I ǂh [kit] : ǂb the home front.
 8 246 30   World War I, the home front
 9 246 30   Home front
10 260      Boca Raton, Fla. : ǂb National Archives and SirS, ǂc [1982?].
11 300      4 posters, 1 chart, 12 reproductions of photographs, 2 news
sheets, 28 reproductions of documents, 1 teacher's guide ; ǂc in container 37
x 23 x 2 cm.
12 500      "A supplemental teaching unit from the records of the National
Archives"--Teacher's guide.
13 500      Teacher's guide includes bibliography, exercises, worksheets,
glossary, time line.
14 520      Designed to be used by students for a better understanding of
history through the study of original source documents.
15 505 00 ǂt America moves toward war -- ǂt Women and the war effort -- ǂt
Uncle Sam needs you -- ǂt Reactions to the call -- ǂt When Johnny comes
marching home.
16 650  0   World War, 1914-1918 ǂz United States ǂx Sources.
17 650  0   World War, 1914-1918 ǂz United States ǂx Historiography.
18 651  0   United States ǂx History ǂy 1913-1921 ǂx Sources.
19 710  1   United States. ǂb National Archives and Records Service.
20 710  2   Social Issues Resources Series, inc.
```

Comments

General: This is a kit composed of all paper materials, but it includes several types of media (posters, charts, reproductions of photographs, and facsimile documents) with no one form dominant.

Cataloging: The publisher information is given in a different form in each location where it is used, but the form found on the container (the chief source) is used in area 4 of the bibliographic record. That form is reproduced as part of this example, so you can see why I transcribed it as I did.

Access: In line 20, the "inc." begins with a lower case letter because the old form is still the form in the LC authority file.

Example 73. Step by Step Two

Contents of kit

Information from title page of workbook

Project Designer:	*JOHN VICTOR*
Programmers:	*STEPHEN CHMIELEWSKI*
	KATHLEEN FORTMEIER
Editor:	*LYN DANDOW*
Graphic Design:	*HOWARD PETLACK*

Cassette label

Step By Step 2

VOICE CASSETTE 3
side A/lesson 4, part 1

PDi Program Design, Inc. 11 Idar Court Greenwich CT 06830
Copyright Ⓟ © 1983 by Program Design, Inc.

Example 73. Step by Step Two

```
Type: o    ELvl: I    Srce: d   Audn: f    Ctrl:      Lang: eng
BLvl: m    TMat: b    GPub:     AccM:      MRec:      Ctry: ctu
Desc: a    Time: nnn Tech: n    DtSt: s    Dates: 1983,
 1 040      XXX ‡c XXX
 2 007      s ‡b s ‡d l ‡e m ‡f n ‡g j ‡h l ‡i b
 3 007      c ‡b j ‡d a ‡e o
 4 090      QA76.73.B3 ‡b S7 1983
 5 049      XXXX
 6 245 00   Step by step two ‡h [kit] : ‡b an intermediate course in BASIC
programming.
 7 246 3    Step by step 2
 8 260      Greenwich, CT : ‡b Program Design, ‡c 1983.
 9 300      4 sound cassettes, 2 computer disks, 1 workbook ; ‡c in container
30 x 26 x 5 cm.
10 538      System requirements: Apple II computer; sound cassette player.
11 508      Project designer, John Victor ; programmers, Stephen Chmielewski,
Kathleen Fortmeier.
12 500      Second disk is backup.
13 650   0  BASIC (Computer program language) ‡x Study and teaching.
14 700 1    Victor, John.
15 700 1    Chmielewski, Stephen.
16 700 1    Fortmeier, Kathleen.
17 710 2    Program Design (Firm)
```

Comments

General: This is an older example, but one I kept because the sound cassettes are not narration or accompanying material; they lead the user through the lessons on the use of the computer. Neither sound cassettes nor computer files are dominant—they are used together and I considered them to be equally important, so this is cataloged as a kit.

This could have field 006 for computer files added as well, for those who search for it as a computer file accompanied by sound recordings.

Cataloging: Chief source of information for this kit is the container.

MARC coding/tagging: The first field 007 is for the sound recordings, the second field 007 is for the computer file.

Processing: This item needs some type of label if you use a magnetic security system — you do not want this being sensitized or desensitized.

Example 74. Speedy Andrews' Repair Shop

Kit box cover

```
TL        Speedy Andrews' repair shop [kit]. -- Moorestown,
153          N.J. : Tyco Industries, c1977 (West Germany :
.S6          Pola).
1977            76 pieces ; in box 17 x 32 x 4 cm. --
             (Tycokit)

                HO scale.
                "For ages 8 years and up."
                Summary: To be assembled into plastic model
             of automobile repair shop of the 1920's.

                1. Service stations.  I. Tyco Industries.
```

Example 74. Speedy Andrews' Repair Shop

```
Type: o    ELvl: I    Srce: d    Audn: f    Ctrl:       Lang: eng
BLvl: m    TMat: b    GPub:      AccM:      MRec:       Ctry: nju
Desc: a    Time: nnn  Tech: n    DtSt: s    Dates: 1977,
 1 040       XXX ǂc XXX
 2 090       TL153 ǂb .S6 1977
 3 049       XXXX
 4 245 00    Speedy Andrews' repair shop ǂh [kit].
 5 260       Moorestown, N.J. : ǂb Tyco Industries, ǂc c1977 ǂe (West Germany :
ǂf Pola).
 6 300       76 pieces : ǂb plastic, col. ; ǂc in box 17 x 32 x 4 cm.
 7 440 0     Tycokit
 8 500       HO scale.
 9 521 8     "For ages 8 years and up."
10 520       To be assembled into plastic model of automobile repair shop of
the 1920s.
11 650  0    Service stations.
12 710 2     Tyco Industries.
```

Comments

General: This is a traditional kit. For people of my generation, this is what we think of when we hear the word "kit." We bought these to make models.

For people in Great Britain, a "kit" was what they take when camping.

Cataloging: The scale note is important, because these were sold to be used with HO scale model railroads.

How would you catalog this package?

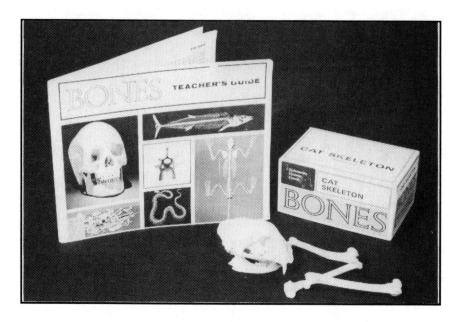

End of container

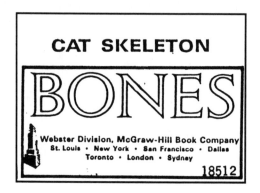

Top of container

Here we have a box of real (not plastic) bones with a text about skeletons. There were a series of these boxes —
also available were *Rabbit Skeleton, Mink Skeleton*, and *Mystery Bones.*

INDEX TO EXAMPLES BY TITLE

INDEX